ROUTLEDGE LIBRARY EDITIONS: COLONIALISM AND IMPERIALISM

Volume 27

FABIAN COLONIAL ESSAYS

FABIAN COLONIAL ESSAYS

Edited by
RITA HINDEN

With an Introduction by
A. CREECH JONES, M. P.

Taylor & Francis Group

LONDON AND NEW YORK

First published in 1945 by George Allen and Unwin Ltd

This edition first published in 2023
by Routledge
4 Park Square, Milton Park, Abingdon, Oxon OX14 4RN

and by Routledge
605 Third Avenue, New York, NY 10158

Routledge is an imprint of the Taylor & Francis Group, an informa business

© 1945 George Allen and Unwin Ltd

All rights reserved. No part of this book may be reprinted or reproduced or utilised in any form or by any electronic, mechanical, or other means, now known or hereafter invented, including photocopying and recording, or in any information storage or retrieval system, without permission in writing from the publishers.

Trademark notice: Product or corporate names may be trademarks or registered trademarks, and are used only for identification and explanation without intent to infringe.

British Library Cataloguing in Publication Data
A catalogue record for this book is available from the British Library

ISBN: 978-1-032-41054-8 (Set)
ISBN: 978-1-032-44637-0 (Volume 27) (hbk)
ISBN: 978-1-032-44638-7 (Volume 27) (pbk)
ISBN: 978-1-003-37313-1 (Volume 27) (ebk)

DOI: 10.4324/9781003373131

Publisher's Note
The publisher has gone to great lengths to ensure the quality of this reprint but points out that some imperfections in the original copies may be apparent.

Disclaimer
The publisher has made every effort to trace copyright holders and would welcome correspondence from those they have been unable to trace.

FABIAN COLONIAL ESSAYS

by

H. N. BRAILSFORD
M. FORTES
J. S. FURNIVALL
C. W. GREENIDGE
RITA HINDEN
J. F. HORRABIN

A. CREECH JONES
SIR DRUMMOND SHIELS
H. STANNARD
IDA WARD
LEONARD WOOLF
MARGARET WRONG

With an Introduction by
A. CREECH JONES, M.P.

Edited by
RITA HINDEN

London
GEORGE ALLEN AND UNWIN LTD

FIRST PUBLISHED IN 1945

THIS BOOK IS PRODUCED IN COMPLETE
CONFORMITY WITH THE AUTHORIZED
ECONOMY STANDARDS

ALL RIGHTS RESERVED
PRINTED IN GREAT BRITAIN
in 11-Point Fournier Type
BY UNWIN BROTHERS LIMITED
WOKING

Contents

	PAGE
FOREWORD	7
INTRODUCTION A. CREECH JONES, M.P.	9
SOCIALISTS AND THE EMPIRE H. N. BRAILSFORD	19
GEOGRAPHY AND THE BRITISH EMPIRE J. F. HORRABIN	36
THE CHALLENGE OF AFRICAN POVERTY RITA HINDEN	51
THE CONDITIONS OF SOCIAL POLICY AND ITS COST A. CREECH JONES, M.P.	67
THE POLITICAL ADVANCE OF BACKWARD PEOPLES LEONARD WOOLF	85
SELF-GOVERNMENT FOR ADVANCED COLONIES SIR DRUMMOND SHIELS	99
LANGUAGE AND THE AFRICAN IDA WARD	131
IS LITERACY NECESSARY IN AFRICA? MARGARET WRONG	145
SOME PROBLEMS OF TROPICAL ECONOMY J. S. FURNIVALL	161
LAND HUNGER IN THE COLONIES C. W. W. GREENIDGE	185
THE BRITISH WEST INDIES HAROLD STANNARD	202
AN ANTHROPOLOGIST'S POINT OF VIEW M. FORTES	215
COLONIES AND WORLD ORDER ANONYMOUS	235
HOW A POLITICAL SOCIETY FUNCTIONS RITA HINDEN	248

Foreword

This series of essays has been collected by the Fabian Colonial Bureau, the special department of the Fabian Society created in 1940 to study colonial affairs. Many of the contributors have been actively associated with the work of the Bureau since its inception; all are in broad sympathy with its viewpoint. But there has been no attempt to bring the contributors together in order to formulate an agreed approach, as was done with the famous *Fabian Essays in Socialism*, published in 1889. Nor does the Bureau accept responsibility for the views expressed. The essays are offered by the individual authors as a personal contribution to the general body of thought on colonial problems.

FABIAN COLONIAL BUREAU,
11 DARTMOUTH STREET,
LONDON, S.W.1

September, 1944.

The Contributors

H. N. BRAILSFORD. Formerly lecturer in Glasgow University. A journalist and writer of international reputation, he has travelled widely in Europe, India, U.S.S.R., and U.S.A. Published many books, notably *Property or Peace?*, *Subject India*, and *Our Settlement with Germany*. Degree of LL.D. recently conferred.

DR. M. FORTES. Born in South Africa. Field work in West Africa in 1934, 1937 and 1941. Subsequently taught anthropology at the London School of Economics and at Oxford. Now Sociologist to the West African Institute of Industries, Arts and Social Sciences.

J. S. FURNIVALL. Formerly India and Burma Civil Service, and Lecturer at Rangoon and Cambridge Universities on Burmese history and language. Many publications, of which the most recent is *Educational Problems in South-East Asia*, 1943.

J. F. HORRABIN. When M.P. for Peterborough, 1929–31, specialized on colonial problems. His maps illustrative of economic, political, international and colonial problems are well known. Many publications, including *Atlas of Empire*, 1937.

DR. RITA HINDEN. Born in South Africa. Secretary of the Fabian Colonial Bureau. Author of *Plan for Africa*, 1941, and *The Colonies and Us*, 1942.

C. W. W. GREENIDGE. Secretary of the Anti-Slavery and Aborigines Protection Society. Born in Barbados. Formerly a Judge of Barbados Court of Appeal, Chief Justice of British Honduras and Solicitor-General of Nigeria.

A. CREECH JONES. Labour M.P. for Shipley, Chairman of Fabian Colonial Bureau and Labour Party Imperial Advisory Committee. Member of the Colonial Office Advisory Committee on Education and of the Higher Education Commission to West Africa, 1943–44. Executive Member British Council and Royal Institute of International Affairs. Delegate Institute of Pacific Relations Conference of 1942, Vice-President W.E.A.; former National Secretary Transport and General Workers Union.

SIR DRUMMOND SHIELS. Labour M.P. for East Edinburgh, 1924–31, Parliamentary Under-Secretary for India, 1929, and for the

Colonies, 1929–31, Vice-President Royal Empire Society, Member of Council Royal African Society.

H. STANNARD. Has long been associated with *The Times*. Widely travelled. Recently spent twelve months in the West Indies as Adviser to the British Council. Former Member of Colonial Office Advisory Committee on Education.

DR. I. C. WARD. Since 1937 Head of the African Department at the School of Oriental and African Studies, London University. Has done field work in West Africa on linguistics, 1933, 1939 and 1943. Many publications on West African languages.

LEONARD WOOLF. Author, journalist and publisher. Editor *The Political Quarterly*; partner in The Hogarth Press; Chairman, Labour Party Advisory Committee on International Questions; Secretary, Labour Party Imperial Advisory Committee. Author of *Empire and Commerce in Africa, International Government*, etc.

MARGARET WRONG. Secretary, International Committee on Christian Literature for Africa. Has travelled widely throughout Africa south of the Sahara. Has prepared, with the International Institute of African Languages and Cultures, bibliographies on various subjects for use in Africa. Author, *Land and Life of Africa, Five Points for Africa*, etc.

Introduction

by A. CREECH JONES, M.P.

This book of essays is a contribution to the study of a few aspects of colonial policy and development. It is published in the year of the Fabian Jubilee and takes its humble stand alongside the famous collection of Fabian essays which long since has enjoyed a distinguished place in socialist literature.

The subjects dealt with are of immense practical moment in present-day discussion of colonial problems. Their treatment indicates the change which has taken place from the propaganda days of analysis and exposition to the more practical and responsible days when policies have to be implemented.

The Fabian Colonial Bureau thanks the authors of the essays for their generous contributions to this volume and believes that this collection will not only elucidate some of the current problems of overseas dependencies but also offer some contribution of permanent worth to an understanding of the socialist approach to imperialist issues. The Bureau does not necessarily associate itself with all or any of the views expressed. It puts this book into the expanding pool of constructive ideas as public opinion in Britain and abroad becomes more definite and pronounced that colonial peoples must move to responsibility and enjoy social well-being.

In the last few years a new phase of colonial discussion has begun in Britain. A wider and better informed public is interested in the affairs of the dependencies. The songs and dreams of an earlier imperialist faction no longer excite emotion or response. The sober prosaic work in colonial territories presents a less romantic adventure and colonial responsibility looks to be as much the black as the white man's burden. Yet it is well to remember that for a century or more the afflictions of weak and backward peoples have aroused interest and concern in British public life on frequent occasions. Philanthropists, religious bodies and radicals have stirred the conscience of the nation and at times won from governments pronouncements on policy couched in fair and noble terms. Whatever the practice in some of the dependencies, such declarations have soothed the British conscience and have, at least, set standards and given directives to those in high responsibility overseas.

Socialist criticism has deepened this stream of humane and liberal sentiment. It has stressed the nature of capitalist development both at home and overseas and has analysed economic imperialism. If it derives something of this from Marx, it owes much to the challenging work of J. A. Hobson, H. N. Brailsford, Sidney Olivier, E. D. Morel, Leonard Woolf, Charles Roden Buxton, MacGregor Ross, Norman Leys, Frank Horrabin, Leonard Barnes and many others. They, with workers in the mission and administrative fields, have créated the present public sense demanding constructive change and colonial advance.

Britain now enters a new phase of policy in colonial development. The conditions existing in the colonies before the war have vastly changed. The status of the dependencies as imperial possessions is, in content, changing also. A world emerges in which areas hitherto treated as "non-adult" must share in the general life of mankind. Our enlightened self-interest demands such adjustment as well. The incidence of power politics and the new alignments make it imperative. Colonial people who have been disturbed by education and other services, into whose lives new economic and cultural influences have penetrated and who have been touched by the moral and political forces fermenting in the modern world cannot be insulated and left alone. Nor will they, themselves, have it so. The backward areas menace the rest of the world if they remain undeveloped with low standards of living, with disease rampant and the people weak and ignorant. In that condition they would be a continuing cause of friction among the imperial powers. Their development is necessary for the larger security of the world; their products and resources are wanted in the outside world; their low standards depress our higher levels; their disease threatens our health; their poverty, prejudices our prosperity—in short, these distressed areas must be developed and integrated as progressing regions into the commonwealth of free nations. Already the outer world has shrunk as knowledge has expanded. The colonies to-morrow will be right in the midst of our normal life, and that fact must compel us to overhaul our methods of administration and the conventional assumptions of colonial policy so that rapid advances in welfare and development are secured and adjustments made to standards consistent with civilized living.

A few "progressives" in past days, in moments of aberration, have expressed virtue in imperial expansion and on the second prong of the dual-mandate have satisfied themselves of the justice of permanent tutelage and of the material exploitation of dependent areas. They have thought themselves tougher than the vast majority of socialists who, influenced by humane sentiment, have deplored the harsh conditions and misery of the colonial peoples and criticized the *laissez-faire* attitude of governments to economic activity and social organization. But the broad socialist attitude has been that colonial administration has been helped rather than weakened by those who have questioned the working of capitalism and financial exploitation overseas and who without displaying enthusiasm about the advantages alleged to accrue from these economic activities have challenged the motives of concessionaires and traders. It should be remembered that in the field of administration, it is not socialists who have traduced those of our race who without gain or much recognition have brought order and disinterested service into backward areas, and who have competently, as well as devotedly, tried to improve the quality of life and lay the lines. of progress for the colonial peoples. The main complaint has been that policy conceived in London, in spite of the generous phrases of government and the liberal sentiment of the British people, has left too much to "the-man-on-the-spot" without providing him with the tools to do his job, or the conditions in which it could be done, or with means of resisting the influences that must inevitably play on him. Too big a field in policy was left to private enterprise, to speculators, concession hunters, profit seekers and land-grabbers, who had too little sentiment in their hearts for the backward people who were so conveniently exploitable. The threatening shadow of racial discrimination hangs heavily across vast British African territories to-day as a result.

Political and economic domination by one people over another is preposterous to-day and contrary to all our professions. Infinite harm was often done to achieve it. A different relationship is necessary, for governments in most dependencies are "alien." British control is generally tolerant and easy going and the majority of the people are consequently acquiescent and embarrassingly loyal to Britain. But it would be folly to ignore the stir going on beneath the surface everywhere, just as it would be criminal to attempt to repress the emerging political activities which too many imperialist blimps have sought to stifle in other days. It ought no longer to be the function of colonial governments to hold the ring for alien interests to exploit and develop what natural wealth there may be; to see the surplus wealth drained overseas for the enjoyment of anyone outside the people who produce it or whose natural resources it is; to remain indifferent to the claims of health and education and social advance; to concede little to the people in the way of consultation and collaboration or of political representation and responsibility. The time has come when Britain must renounce an imperialistic relationship with the colonial peoples and government be inspired by new conceptions of purpose.

Socialists have no right to be apathetic to the working out of this approach to "empire." A new positive and constructive attitude has been built up as a result of their criticism but it must be added that that attitude also owes much to men who have carried great imperial responsibility, to publicists and research workers, to teachers in the universities and critics in the British Parliament. Even imperialists and big interests also protest that beyond the economic development and exploitation they desire, the colonies must enjoy more welfare and a better standard of living. Socialists cannot, of course, be satisfied with this, the incidental good which may come to people by a more energetic prosecution of economic activities by private interests. At the same time because of their dislike of imperialism and control of one people by another, they cannot stop their ears to the claims of the colonial peoples and renounce responsibility towards British territories because of some sentimental inclination to "liberation" or international administration. To throw off the colonial empire in this way, would be to betray the peoples and our trust. Colonial regions cannot remain uninfluenced by and protected from the penetration of the predatory and callous influences which socialists deplore, any more than trade and economic development in backward areas can be denied. Soviet Russia, we are told, has profoundly transformed her backward regions. If Britain in Africa cannot act for a variety of sound reasons as Soviet Russia did to develop her own regions, at least Britain must co-operate generously, energetically, and speedily with her colonial peoples for their freedom and good social and economic well-being.

Colonies must therefore be the avowed concern of socialists. It matters little to-day how they were acquired, the predatory and possessive character of imperialism in the past, or indeed, the ugly episodes and exploitations many of them experienced in the past. Our concern must be the discharging of this legacy of responsibility, i.e. a legacy of service and contribution. That responsibility carries the socialist well beyond the sentiments expressed by others professing sympathy with the colonial people. How are we to cut the roots of imperial domination and the economic exploitation that remain? How destroy colour discrimination and create genuine democracy? How organize the economic resources and activities for the social good? How bring the colonial environment under control and direct the harsh forces of nature to the will of man? How integrate the small colonial units into the political and economic life of the world? These problems were obvious before this war—they have a fierce urgency now which we neglect only to our own peril.

Their solution can be found, in my judgment, only along the lines of socialist thought.

It is important to emphasize this because the dividing line between socialists and others is often blurred in the constructive work being done on colonial policy to-day. All political parties tell us they want welfare and economic development, the speeding up of education, health and other services, political progress and freedom from fear and want, the removal of blatant abuses and gifts for social advance and grants of capital for development. Socialists may think that the plaudits from their political opponents are hollow when they protest against the practice of colour bars, race superiority, segregation, and the establishment of exclusive white colonies in black men's countries; it is commonplace to hear Conservative approval of the colonial co-operatives, trade unions, of civil liberty, communal ownership of land and control of big business. The truth is, of course, that people of all shades of political colour can walk together some distance in their quest for things which they are all agreed are important to the colonial people. But the genuine progress of the colonial people is achieved by policies which must include the elements of socialist economic principles.

Fabian socialists fit their views of change into a socialist pattern. In the first place, what is the job, the need, the work to be done? It is not a question as between reformism and revolution. We seek immediate practical solutions because such are permanent steps to the greater freedom we are anxious men should enjoy. Social reforms in themselves are often slow and laborious and invariably less spectacular than the quick and exciting slogans and destructive criticism which some socialists made in earlier days. Vague and general terms are out of place when policies have to take shape and obstacles to be overcome. Practical achievements depend on knowledge, technical skill and hard thinking; escapism into the philosophy of Lenin or socialist monasticism will not bring better nutrition or the rearing of cattle in the tsetse forest belt. The working class of Britain can go forward in their struggle for power to-day because of the numerous reforms achieved in the past century. Likewise, the changes Fabian socialists demand in the colonies, the reforms they urge, the opinion they create, the research they do, all contribute as essential elements to the progress of the peoples. Advance is made possible because of the reforms and changes that are secured now.

It is necessary therefore to guarantee to the dependencies the institutions and liberty, the social health and material prosperity on which their struggle depends. Fabians are therefore concerned with constructive reform and with the detailed items involved in social and economic policy. Civil liberty, local government, preventive medicine, nutrition, mass education, literacy, free association, co-operative organization, trade unionism, political representation—these things have been or are being won. The pace of advance will depend on the confidence Britain wins, the degree of consultation and co-operation she inspires, the funds available for the work, the trained personnel for the tasks, her courage in devolving responsibility and the imaginative quality of her social planning. At bottom must be the idea of "freedom." Britain to-day hesitates to try the responsibility of the colonial people enough. Their land is still Britain's; their products and wealth are our possessions; and most of their governors are superior and belong to a different tradition. But the Socialist also feels that a genuine partnership in the creation of "nationhood" cannot emerge without the application of socialist ideas in the economic life of these dependencies.

Some control of the economy of the colonies has developed during the present war. There is a better balance between subsistence and export crops and governments have gone in for the bulk purchase of colonial products and minerals at fixed prices and for marketing and grading and storing. Imports and exports have been regulated to demands in the light of the shipping space available. Almost everywhere the governments in the colonies have been required to create the frame-work on which the social and economic life of the community depends. In Africa until now it is usually the Government which has had to cut roads, make railways, create ports, supply water, develop power, stop soil erosion, conserve forests, establish communications and pursue preventive measure against disease. Indeed, the essential key services, whether social or economic, depend almost entirely on public enterprise. It is the government technical services which undertake the improvement of soil, irrigation, surveys, agricultural development, clearance of bush and swamps, and encourage co-operative practice in production, credit, marketing, etc. In the African colonies the land, apart from white settlement, is crown land or communally owned though production is individual. Into some areas has come wage employment on plantations, but the future progress of agriculture would also seem to lie in the development of co-operation and in many areas of large-scale farming and production on collectivist lines.

As yet there are few industries and commerce and trade are proportionately small because of the poverty of the people. It is important that many of the processing industries should be run in state factories as public concerns. Private enterprise can only operate where it is profitable, but then its motive is its profit and not the well-being of the colonial people. The problem in most colonial areas is the building up of higher standards of living by increasing the taxable capacity of the people, improving prices and wages and preventing the creation of useless operations between producer and consumer. All these are matters for a socialist economy.

Industrialism has not yet gone far though wage earning employment has steadily increased. The public control of industrial development and the regulation of employment are essential factors in any planned economy. In Africa, much mineral wealth has been discovered and exploited to the profit of external interests. All mineral resources should be owned by the territory in which they exist and their exploitation should be controlled by the Government and the operations should be publicly conducted. No surplus can accrue in Africa for the production of other wealth if all rewards of work are at poverty levels and the value of the products is enjoyed overseas. It is in all these respects that we see the touchstones of socialist policy in the colonies and what differentiates socialist from those who want little more than reform in social standards and material prosperity.

The days are passing when policies can be made independent of the colonial peoples. If there are grave responsibilities on us, there are responsibilities no less burdensome on the peoples concerned. Most of us can press the importance of hard and disciplined work, of moral integrity and social service, of tolerance and initiative, and we can stress that foundations in the colonies must be built in education, nutrition, preventive medicine and health. New values have also to be established, new traditions built up and the conventions and habits encumbering new ways broken down. But people must not wait on governments to act. Through their own free and voluntary movements they should initiate their own enterprise and work out their own way of life. It is not easy to conceive of public service, to develop sound judgment, to look dispassionately and objectively at issues which have moved men for generations, to approach problems in the scientific spirit, to break with custom and act independently or to carry responsibility of an exacting kind. These things are learnt from experience and it is important that the people through their own free organizations should learn and themselves work and plan for change. Just as the British workers through trade unionism, and co-operation, adult education, political responsibility in local government have moved forward, so should the colonial peoples create their societies and institutions and learn responsibility in their own way and on their own initiative go forward to the society they themselves seek.

This book is therefore offered less for propagandist purposes but more for acquainting ourselves as to the nature of some of the colonial problems to be solved. There are serious difficulties to be grappled with, however clear we see the destination we want to reach. The brittle foundations of imperial power begin to crack. Acquiescent people begin to stir in revolt and to disturb our peace. Power politics in the world shift and take on new patterns. The world contracts and science makes playthings of the ambitions and temporal achievements of earlier imperialists. Our friends and allies question our conduct and prerogatives. The war jolts us from our complacency. Our policies perforce must be less paternal and more generous, less self-seeking and exploitory, and more courageous and imaginative. To that end this collection of essays is contributed.

A. CREECH JONES

LONDON,
August, 1944.

Socialists and the Empire
by H. N. BRAILSFORD

Amid the mortal anxieties of the second world-wide war we have found the leisure of mind to do something and plan more for the progress of our dependent empire. We have set apart a fund for its development, inaugurated a series of social and political reforms in the West Indies and turned our attention in earnest to the study of education, with the idea of creating a university for Africans. It is normal that war should stir our social conscience in this way. It reveals the shortcomings of our civilization and stimulates our will to make good what was amiss.

Turning over these generous projects in my mind, I went back to one of the world's seminal books which first explored this question of the duty of civilized men towards the backward races. It was written in 1793 by a leader and victim of the French Revolution, who was perhaps the noblest character, as he was the most fruitful social thinker of his day. Condorcet was an outlaw awaiting the guillotine when he wrote his *Sketch for an Historical Picture of the Human Mind*. With perfect serenity, aware of the end that awaited him, he penned the most hopeful outline ever drawn of human progress. After analysing the past centuries, he confidently predicted the happy changes that would follow the triumph of liberty and equality. Some of the good things he foretold for Africa have come to pass. Slavery and the slave trade were ended. Its tropical produce, as he foresaw, is cultivated on a great scale. Europeans no longer scourge its tribes with their "brigandage"; they have become, as he expected, settled and industrious colonists. In a sense they have carried with them, as he hoped they would, the light of science and their stores of useful knowledge; nor was he wholly mistaken in expecting that trade would be freed from the fetters of monopoly. But it is difficult to read the rest of his forecast without bitterness. He based his hopes for human equality chiefly on two reforms which were for him fundamental—the spread of free and universal education and the adoption of social insurance. A century and a half has passed and Africa is still the illiterate continent. Who among us is bold enough, even in the more advanced of its colonies, to propose a Beveridge plan? And have we yet left behind us what Condorcet called "our bloodstained contempt for men of another colour and another creed"? Do Africans even now find in many of the Europeans they encounter "brothers," whose "friends and pupils" they are eager to become?

It may be salutary to recall such a forecast as this. Condorcet was no naïve enthusiast; his was a lucid, analytical mind, trained in mathematics and the physical sciences. Why is his prediction, in some points shrewd and far-sighted, so dismally remote from the contemporary facts? To answer that question adequately would require a study of the entire history of the intervening generations. This brief essay can attempt only a few summary and superficial suggestions, which may conceivably help us to see our problem in perspective. Condorcet went astray, first of all, because the revolution, as he conceived it, had not triumphed and has not triumphed yet, even in France where he believed it was supreme, or in North Africa. The passion for liberty and equality, which he and a few idealists and thinkers like him were capable of feeling with equal warmth for all the races and classes of mankind, retained its universal sweep only in the first years of enthusiasm. In the splendid dawn of their Revolution, the French did honestly mean to free the negroes of their West Indian possessions: they ended by driving their former slaves under Toussaint l'Ouverture into revolt. For an instant they carried their doctrines to India and Tippoo Sahib at their prompting planted a Tree of Liberty. But as the years went on, the universal passion for liberty and equality shrank into something smaller and meaner and disclosed its real significance in the march of history. What was effective in it was the demand of the new middle class for equality with the old feudal class, if not for predominance. It made an end of slavery in the colonies, as it abolished serfdom in Europe. But in the modern society which gradually took shape, such vestiges of its original philosophy as found their way into its legal codes did little to bestow the reality of equality on men even of its own colour and creed, to say nothing of Africans. Condorcet and the liberals of his generation pitched their hopes too high, partly because they over-estimated the driving power of their ideas, but chiefly because they failed to recognize the influence of economic trends in shaping history. What, in fact, took charge of the destinies of Africa and the colonial peoples was economic imperialism, evolving through successive phases, as capitalism itself evolved.

Socialists when they aspired to take the torch from the hands of the exhausted liberals, found it far from easy to define their attitude to the dependent empire. What we have to frame is a positive policy. Because we reached, earlier than any other political group, a full and happy consciousness of international unity, we should also be the pioneers in showing how the primitive and colonial peoples can be integrated within the organized life of mankind. Our duty is to find for these backward races a function which fits them and yet assures them a prospect of reaching equality with liberty. But long before the time was ripe for facing these positive tasks, socialists were involved, rightly and inevitably, in a root and branch hostility towards imperialism. Their attitude towards the colonial empire, when they tried to analyse its origin, was necessarily negative. They traced it in its modern form to causes deeply rooted in the system which they are bent on superseding. It came into being as a by-product of the exploitation of the white proletariat at home. Each in his own way, in successive generations, Marx, John A. Hobson and Lenin gave us his analysis of the fatal flaw within the capitalist system which explains the outward thrust in its structure. This restless tendency to expand in search of colonial markets and fields of investment is a consequence of the wrong distribution of the product of industry. Always characteristic of our unequal society is over-saving by the few and under-consumption by the many. The ability to consume cannot keep pace with the increasing capacity to produce with which science and organization endow us. Because in one degree or another capitalist industry must starve its internal market, mainly composed of its wage-earners, it is driven to seek markets abroad. The danger of this process increased in the last quarter of the last century when the leading capitalist Powers, no longer content to sell consumers' goods in foreign markets, began to export capital goods, notably railway equipment, in steadily increasing volume to backward and unstable countries. This kind of trade, like international usury, calls on the State to protect and promote its investments. So we enter an era of monopoly and power-politics, in which spheres of interest become the chief stakes of diplomacy and a race in armaments sets in, with these places in the sun as its prizes.

The technique of modern imperialism has varied significantly from decade to decade, but always the outward thrust has its explanation in under-consumption at home. Why did the Nazis organize the entire mental and material life of Germany for the conquest of an empire, with Eastern Europe as their colony and the Slavs as their subject race? Obvious psychological explanations lie ready to our hands: these played their part. More than most of us, the Nazis were the victims of the lust for power. But the ultimate explanation may depend on the fact that the purchasing power of the German wage-earners was in 1933 stereotyped at the abysmally low figure to which it fell during the World Slump. Whereas in Great Britain the ratio of wages to the value of industrial output stood in 1938 at the relatively high figure of 48 per cent, in Germany this ratio fell during the slump to 31 per cent, and at that level it remained throughout the Nazi regime. Because the wage-earning masses could buy back less than a third of the value they produced, German industry, but more especially heavy industry, had to be expansionist and aggressive. The steel which could not be used to serve the well-being of the German population had fatally to go into cannon and tanks.

These were some of the associations that clustered for socialists round the idea of empire. It began in social and economic inequality at home and ended in the starvation wages and fabulous dividends of the Calcutta jute mills, in the rural slums of Jamaica, or else in the marvels of racial privilege on which society in Kenya is built. Year after year, socialist parties were absorbed in rearguard actions against the graver abuses of imperialism. The Belgian party under Vandervelde was mainly responsible for ending King Leopold's private slave empire on the Congo. The German Social-Democrats exposed the horrors of the Herrero war, while in their own fields the French and the Dutch were active. Our own Labour Party used its opportunities in Parliament steadily to combat various forms of forced labour, to check the filching by white settlers of native land, to further the interests of native workers in African mines and to check abuses in taxation. It was seldom, however, in this thankless but necessary work of criticism and opposition that the chance came to socialists to state their own positive ideas, still less to apply them.

Yet another difficulty stood in the way. Long before socialists won representation in Parliament, Liberals treading in the footsteps of the old Abolitionists, were bringing their own principles to bear on the administration of the dependent empire. They stressed the political and underestimated the economic problems. They did good work in combating relics of slavery and they stood for the civil rights of the natives. Above all, they tried to hasten the evolution towards self-government. This was useful work and socialists were well-advised to support it. But it ignored our economic approach to the problems of empire. The day can be foreseen—be it near or far ahead—when Africans will be the responsible rulers of the West Coast colonies. It is indispensable that they should be educated for this responsibility, both by the improvement of our colleges and schools and by their admission, meanwhile, to a steadily growing share in the work of administration.

In order to foster their intellectual self-confidence as a race, it is important that they should be helped to enter the learned professions in large numbers. But is that all? Are we content that the colony they will one day inherit and shape as they think fit, shall be built meanwhile on a capitalistic pattern? Must they cope with the problem of socializing this railway or that mine, or should we try to do it now? Could we promote the growth of co-operation in agriculture, or must this also wait for full self-government? Should we, in short, try in so far as we can to develop the colonies in a socialist sense, while their peoples are still our wards?

The answer to this question will vary in different parts of the empire. It is too late, for example, even to state it in regard to India. There our duty is plainly to hasten the grant of unqualified self-government, which means, if Indians insist upon it, independence. If socialism is to come to this awakened land, only Indians can engineer its coming. The answer may be much the same in the case of Burma, Ceylon and Malta. As for Cyprus and Hongkong, our plain duty is to fulfil the will of their inhabitants by handing them over to Greece and China. How boldly in the case of Jamaica we should try to shape its economic pattern in accordance with our own views, is a question that calls for tact and leadership; we should not in such a case try to go far, until we had with us a considerable volume of local support. In the case of an African colony everything makes for a bold initiative. Its economic structure was imposed from above and from outside; we need not scruple to re-shape it. But here also it is obvious that we should prepare the ground for innovation by spreading our ideas before we attempt administrative action. We should not wait until a fortunate general election has sent a socialist to the Colonial office. We should make up our minds in good time where we mean to begin. Shall it be a railway, an electric power station, a plantation or a mine that we socialize? We should then familiarize both African and British opinion with our scheme. It is a disturbing reflection that we have done no organized missionary work to spread our socialist ideas, either in India or in the Colonies. Have we ever as a party sent even one lecturer or organizer thither, at our own charge? If our ideas have reached these lands, they have travelled on their own wings.

What does reach the workers of the colonies more promptly than our social theory is our technique of organization. Everywhere, in the interval between the two wars, trade unions have begun to spring up. There are now over three hundred of them in the Dependent Empire, and some of them have proved their solid organization in difficult but victorious strikes. There are also Co-operative Societies, which in some colonies are notably successful, more especially in organizing peasant producers for the marketing of their crops. Among some African tribes there has been a spontaneous growth of organizations concerned with education, notably in Kenya. To help these movements, without trenching on their independence, should rank among the proudest and most important of our duties.

This is, however, a naïve and old-fashioned way of stating our problem. Where do we mean to begin? The Great Powers of the modern world are daily setting their problem for us and hurling their challenge. Here the colossus that bestrides a continent or steps from island to island is a privately-owned air-transport company. Elsewhere it is an oil monopoly enthroned as the emperor of the desert. On the African coasts the King of Kings is the combine that deals in vegetable oils. When we dare to propose to socialize one of these dinosaurs, we shall have joined battle in earnest as socialists with the real enemy, and not till then. One of the central aims of socialism, perhaps the central aim, is to win economic power for the community.

Is the next of these central aims to achieve equality, social, cultural, and economic, as far as may be, and as promptly as may be, among all the citizens of our society? If it be so, I think we may give it in its bearing on the dependent empire a definite contemporary meaning. I believe it would help our thinking to look at the social question of the empire as part of a much wider problem. The inequality that vexes us when we compare the standard of life of the African who hoes mealies or raises coffee with that of the Englishman who makes some component of a motor-car beside a conveyor belt, is not determined primarily by his colour or even by the flag under which he is policed and taxed. This inequality is, with interesting variations, universal: always the primary producers are less fortunate than the industrial workers. The Africans may be in the worst case of all: the agricultural populations of India and China stand only a little higher in the scale: the white skin of the peasantry of Poland, and the Balkans does not save it from the same ill-fortune. In America it is hard to believe that the half-starved, disease-stricken, nearly illiterate share-cropper (i.e. small tenant farmer) of the Southern States, who lives in a shanty and is never out of debt, is a fellow countryman and a cousin of the sturdy, prosperous, industrial worker of the North, with his full life, his comfortable home, his car and his relatively wide mental horizon. The contrast between the English agricultural worker and his brother in an engineering shop may be a little less crude but it is marked enough. Of the two the countryman is often, indeed usually, much the more skilled and versatile craftsman, and he works longer hours in all weathers with more muscular strain. His money wage may be about half the townsman's income: his real wage perhaps 60 per cent of it—for this is said to be the average ratio in Europe generally.

We should do well, I think, to take it as socialists, as one of our primary objectives to raise the level of life of the primary producers up to that of the industrial populations. The worst flaw in our civilization is the existence of these countless millions of submerged rural workers, who are leading sub-human lives in the villages of the backward agricultural lands that range from Poland to China and from Spain to Rhodesia. It may be doubted whether any single cause on earth compares with this in retarding human progress—hardly even war itself. Unknown and invisible, these peasants, who can never satisfy their elementary wants, none the less govern the economic lives of the most advanced communities in the West. If they were able to make on industry even the minimum demand for tools, shelter and clothing, which average health and efficiency require, our cities would realize with ease an economy of plenty on a scale that would baffle the most daring dreams.

What, in outline, would this aim—the equalization of our standards of life—imply in the first stages, let us say, for Africa? It might mean, first of all, a determined attempt to adjust world-prices for the benefit of the primary producer. It is probable that in comparison with steel, oil, chemicals, basic industrial commodities subject to price regulation by trusts which aim at a slight scarcity, such typical African commodities as maize, coffee, cocoa and palm oil are relatively too cheap, since their producers cannot combine in a policy of restriction. The result is that the labour embodied in these agricultural products can never be rewarded at a rate comparable with the wages of the workers who produce the industrial goods. The aim should be, of course, to lower the prices of the industrial goods and play for plenty. To raise the agricultural prices by methods familiarized by the New Deal would be a less satisfactory but still defensible expedient. It is doubtful whether any economic authority that fell short of world-wide jurisdiction could fully succeed in either of these operations.

Even more hopeful than the adjustment of prices is the adoption of a policy of industrialization. The argument that agricultural populations are commonly under-employed and wastefully employed is familiar to all of us in its application to India and the Balkans. In both cases we realize that the first remedy is to acclimatize here, preferably in the villages, suitable industries which will employ the surplus labour now squandered in uneconomic methods of cultivation. Fewer hands in India must raise more wheat; those released from useless toil in the fields must build houses and weave cloth. This argument is equally applicable to Africa. The first enterprises to encourage are obviously processing industries based on the local crops, spinning and weaving of cotton and the making of pottery and furniture. This development obviously depends on the availability of cheap hydro-electric power and on transport facilities.

So far there is general agreement among all progressive

thinkers. Americans of Henry Wallace's school are bent on assisting the industrialization more especially of India, China and Latin America. The bolder of them wish to control overseas investment and to canalize it into such channels as this. They would create a long-term international investment board on which borrowing as well as lending States would be represented. This would offer some guarantee that investment should not be used in weak countries as an instrument of political pressure or penetration.

Socialists may be able to carry this idea further. If loan capital at fixed interest rates and possibly with a State guarantee can be provided in this way, could it be used to finance socialized or disinterested undertakings in the dependent empire? These might include the generation of electric power, the types of light and processing industry already mentioned, mines and finally trading corporations. These latter, collecting and exporting the agricultural produce of the peasants and importing manufactured wares in return, might be of immense benefit by delivering the natives from exploitation by dealers and middlemen, and assuring to them the advantages of large-scale organization. It should be provided that these corporations should enlist and train Africans, who would be eligible for the highest posts. An advisory board should represent the interests of the populations affected. Any profits made by these concerns should be spent in the colonies on projects of development or on health and education. The same provisions should apply to any mines or industries that may be socialized or run as public utilities. Several forms of organization are conceivable; only the old-world bureaucratic pattern need be ruled out.

Socialists will take a generous view of the terms that should govern the supply of machines and equipment to these colonies. It is a paramount aim of our policy to level up their standards towards our own. Our own existence will be the richer and our prosperity the greater, when they are well-equipped, healthy and well-educated. It is reasonable, therefore, that we should use our revenues for these purposes without reckoning on repayment and still less on profit. In due time, albeit indirectly, we shall reap a rich reward for this expenditure. That is the object of the Welfare Fund, of which the only criticism that need be made is that it is much too small.

Furthermore, it would be wise to promote the export of machinery on easy terms to the colonies as a means of warding off a trade depression. A slump always strikes the industries making capital goods with early and disproportionate severity. It will be better to employ them in equipping the backward peoples than in making armaments—the customary expedient. The cost to our pockets will be not the whole value of this machinery, but merely the difference between the wages and the unemployment allowances of the workers who make it. How much should be given free, how much exported on Lend-Lease terms (i.e. interest free), how much against reduced and deferred payments, need not be considered here. The principle is that we should treat these colonies as we should treat a depressed area at home.

Emphatically it is our duty to make handsome grants in aid to foster the educational and health services of the colonies. Our fathers were ashamed that the slave trade should linger on under the British flag, and spent considerable sums, year after year, through several generations to suppress it. That malaria, hookworm and illiteracy still flourish under our flag is hardly less shameful. We owe it to our self-respect to blot these curses out. Among the free gifts we should hasten to bestow on the African villager wireless sets and broadcasting stations rank high. Nothing would contribute more rapidly to his education or teach him more quickly how to apply the lessons of science to his daily problems at home and in his fields.

There is much more that should be done in pursuit of the ideal of equality. Should not the I.L.O. attempt to define what in the varying climatic conditions of Africa and Asia a minimum living wage should amount to? The question to which we want an authoritative answer is: What sum would suffice, in a dozen typical places, to maintain health and efficiency, assuming that a good use is made of the commodities there available? The standard should be the physiological needs of an average family—food, clothing, and shelter—to which a percentage should be added to cover savings and cultural needs and pleasures. The answer would probably name a figure far in advance of what is usual or even possible: it could not at once be enforced, but it would serve as a norm which Trade Unions and legislators would try to reach. Research should be carried on to discover hygienic and pleasant designs for native housing. Pioneering work of this kind has been done by architects in India, Palestine and the Italian colonies. There is equal need, as the work of the League of Nations has shown, for research into diet. In its turn, the subject of diet and food supply raises the largest question that dominates colonial economy. Should colonial production aim firstly and chiefly at the raising of crops for export, or at varied and balanced farming, designed to satisfy the elementary needs of the inhabitants?

This question is fundamental. The economy which subordinates everything to the raising of "cash" crops for export is colonial in the worst sense of the word. It uses the inhabitants and their natural resources as means to serve the ends of the ruling race in the distant metropolis. The cash crop—the sugar cane, let us say, of Jamaica—is a tribute in kind. Grown in the past by slaves, it is now raised by workers who are under-nourished, scandalously housed, scourged with preventible diseases and strangers to all the graces and decencies of life. "At this price," as Voltaire put it, "we eat sugar in Europe." There was little improvement when bananas and pineapples were added to the sugar cane. So extreme in Jamaica is the specialization, that fresh vegetables are almost unknown: only canned goods are obtainable in the shops of this island whose climate and soil make it the ideal garden of its hemisphere. This is imperialism: the island was regarded as a mere appendage to the life of Great Britain. The practice of the early slave-owners was hardly rendered more respectable when it was justified by the Liberal doctrine of the division of labour. This principle of specialization has been so applied that all the more profitable functions, from money-lending to industry, were retained by the armed imperial Power for its own people: the subject races grew cash crops and enjoyed the standard of life appropriate to primary producers.

Socialists call, therefore, for a review of the traditional economy that descended from the colonial age, whether in Africa or the West Indies. We must cease to think of these countries as colonies: their economy must be planned with the good of the inhabitants as its guiding principle. The first charge on the soil is that it shall provide for them the most healthy and varied diet which science can suggest and the climate produce. To that purpose, before all else, a sufficient part of its area must be assigned. Cash crops mean one of two things. They can be exchanged for imported goods which raise the local standard of life. They also represent the rent, profits and interest of the white master-race, which it enjoys for the most part, like an absentee landlord, overseas. The aim of socialist policy is first to reduce and, as soon as possible, to end this tribute.

"Tribute?" Is the word just? It is not the imperial government which receives this tribute. It goes for the most part to the owning class at home, which has invested in shipping, mines, or plantations, or in one or another of the pioneering companies which "opened up" the colonies. What happens is that a physical transfer of real wealth takes place from the colony to the metropolis. The gold or the copper is literally dug out of the soil and transported. Our argument assumes that this wealth so transported is not in the long run balanced by the wealth shipped in the opposite direction—the machinery, the cotton cloth, and what not.

"Well," the reader may say, "it represents the mine-owners' profit; possibly excessive. But is it any worse than the coal-owners' profit in South Wales?"

It differs substantially from such a profit; in its economic effects. The Welsh owner spends his gains in Wales or at any rate in England. They circulate here and call forth goods and services from Welsh or English workers. The miner certainly has been sweated but some of the profits wrung from the sweat of his brow go back to his daughter, who is housemaid in the owner's mansion, and some go to his son, who helped to make the magnate's car. That sort of thing does not happen in the case of the gold mine. None of the profits go back to the West African village: they are spent in Kensington or on the Riviera. If any workers are benefited, they have white skins. This is the nature of empire. It means conquest and exploitation by an absentee overlord.

This steady drain of wealth, year in, year out, from the colonies means something else: they never can accumulate capital for their own development. It has all gone to England and year by year it has equipped our well-endowed island with all that Africa lacks—cotton mills, electric generators, roads and cars, with hospitals and schools as well. It may be of interest to glance at some typical cases. The Ashanti Goldfields Corporation, for example, paid during the last eight years of peace dividends that ranged from 70 per cent to 100 per cent and during four of these years it paid large bonuses as well.[1] The average wages for natives were 1s. 5d. a day, or £26 10s. a year. All told, the mines of the Gold Coast in the last year of peace sent to London in net profits over £2½ millions. They spent in wages to natives less than a million sterling (£993,000), and paid in taxes and royalties some £400,000. It is possible, including the salaries of European employees, that at the outside £2 millions remained in the country. Those fabulous dividends, had they been at the disposal of an enterprising and intelligent local government, might have transformed the face of the colony in a decade, by building roads and schools, equipping factories, and combating pests.

This is no isolated case. In the last three years of peace the annual profits of the copper mines of Northern Rhodesia varied from £5 to over £10 millions.[2] All this wealth went to London.

[1] For details see Dr. Rita Hinden's valuable *Plan for Africa*, pp. 135-9. [2] See Hinden, *op. cit.*, p. 52.

The share that remained behind as the wages of the native workers was in 1936 only £235,000. To measure the significance of this annual drain of wealth one need only state that the entire budget of this colony is only a little more than a million sterling. A sum that varies from five times to ten times the entire revenue of the dependency is carried off as a tribute to London.

If socialists could have their way, we might in face of facts like these hesitate for a moment between two possible courses. Should we tax these profits to vanishing point? Or should we socialize the mines? Painful though it would be to pay compensation, socialization would be the proper course, since the mines could then be run in a way that would add much to the prosperity, happiness, and self-respect of the native workers. But short of this, one reform is easy and should be non-contentious. Like so many colonial companies these mines are registered in Great Britain and consequently pay income-tax to our Exchequer. Part of the proceeds, but never more than half, is now returned to the colony. The whole amount should go back; but on the clear understanding that it shall be spent on native welfare and development.

Is that all? I realize as I reach the last pages of this essay that I have discussed many details of a socialist policy for the Empire and left out the only things that matter. My stage is empty. I have brought on to it neither the Africans nor ourselves. I have assumed that we socialists, if we get the chance, will carry out these rather difficult measures and persist in them, while our opponents, the best of them sincerely, the worst of them from interested motives, mobilize against us all the forces of tradition. Why should we do that? Because we believe that sound economics point this way? Because we think that in the long run our own interests will be served by these measures? Never. Men who have no hotter fire than that in their bellies will stammer and wilt and yield, as soon as the battle looks doubtful. We shall do all this for the simple peoples of the Empire and do it at some cost to ourselves, only if our motive is brotherly love. Whether we think of them as our fellow-workers, or as our fellowmen, it must be a warm impulse of fraternity that drives us to defend them and to aid them. If we have in us the faith and the love this great adventure demands, we shall succeed. If we lack this principle of action then our plans are a dreary intellectual exercise and nothing more.

But what of the Africans? I have left them out also. I have written as though it lay with us to plan for them and build without their leave the house we think would be good for them. It must not happen like that. We, more clearly than they, may see the full measure of the wrongs done to them in the past. We, better than they, may know how to deal with their exploiters, our countrymen. But at every step of the way into the future, we must consult with them, and hurry on the development of the institutions that will enable them to mould their own future.

It is quite certain that these Africans possess their own tradition of a true and fraternal society, which in its own simple way may be as genuine as ours and more instinctive. Tribes differ greatly from one another over this vast continent and some have already half adopted our Western commercial outlook with our money economy. But where this has not yet happened, there survive, embodied in the institutions of daily life, social instincts that might, if they had their chance, preserve the kindliness of the primitive village, while adapting its way of life to our highroads and machines.

I am thinking of such a tribe as the Lovedu of the Northern Transvaal, whose collective personality has been described in an unusually instructive book.[1] Their queen can make rain with surer magic than any other priest or king. They live very close to their ancestors, whose ghosts visit them at their solemn dances and rites. Their economic life is governed by the principle of mutual aid. They think it shameful to buy labour-power or to sell it. When a peasant faces a task beyond his own power, he calls on his friends and neighbours, who work for him and with him without pay. Custom, however, expects of him that he shall provide beer for the volunteer labourers to drink.

[1] See *The Realm of a Rain-Queen*, by E. J. and J. D. Krige.

In this way toil is turned into a love-feast. The law courts of these villages are equally interesting. The ideas of crime and punishment in our sense of the words are unknown to them. What they are concerned with is disputes—breaches in the harmony that should unite all the families of the village. The sole business of the court is to reconcile those who have quarrelled or injured one another. We are told that this tribunal of neighbours relies solely on its moral authority, never uses force and never fails to bring about a reconciliation. It is painful, though it is not surprising, that this gentle and happy society views the invading white man with suspicion and dread, finds his code of behaviour deeply immoral, dismisses his profit motive as shameful and turns away from his churches because they also are built on a cash nexus.

It may be that such a society as this has no future. It will be crushed and superseded as much by what is evil in our world as by what we take to be good. But I believe that instincts capable of creating a group-life as admirable as this will live on and may yet have a creative part to play. When African tribes become familiar with agricultural co-operation, as in some regions they already are, will they be content to take it over from Europeans unmodified? They may transform it, and as time goes on they may in other directions also translate the socialist idea to suit their habits of thought. In short, let us cease to think of socialism as a white man's invention. What is it but a technique for realizing liberty, equality and fraternity? Because it is alive, it will adapt itself to every climate that receives it.

Geography and the British Empire
by J. F. HORRABIN

The late-Victorian theory that the British Empire was brought into being "in a fit of absence of mind" is not particularly apparent from the point of view of the historical geographer or the geo-politician. To them, its growth and development would rather seem to be the result of a well-laid plan, or series of plans, embodying a quite clear-cut purpose; the consolidation of British supremacy, in the continents outside Europe, as a maritime trading power. True, the plans were seldom initiated, and usually only partially carried out, by British governments. They were the work in the main of well organized, licensed groups of British traders or capitalists; fore-runners of those great industrial combines which to-day are clearly the most dangerous threat to the effective working—and the further progress—of political democracy. Such capitalist monopoly groups laid, well and truly, the foundations of British imperial power in the modern world.

It is important, for at least two reasons, that Socialists should have in their minds a clear outline of the actual course of the Empire's growth; first, in order to realize what far-reaching and indeed revolutionary changes will need to be made within the Empire if Britain is in truth to stand as the advocate and protagonist of a "civilizing mission"; and second, so that they may see the Empire as the rest of the world sees it—as the outcome of a particular social system and of a series of certain historical conditions and events, and not as a divinely ordained institution resulting from very special relations between the Almighty and the British people. At every stage of its growth geographical facts and factors have played a part in shaping and influencing its development. It is the purpose of this essay to suggest that, to-day, the facts of geography are again dictating a particular line of advance.

. . . . .

GEOGRAPHY AND THE BRITISH EMPIRE

From the earliest beginnings of organized trade in these islands overseas connections—and, consequently, merchant shipping—were basic factors. The first English trade relations were with Flanders, the nearest corner of the European mainland, where industrial and mercantile activity was much further developed than in Britain; and, through the Hanseatic League, with wider areas of northern Europe. Until Tudor times, indeed, as Sir Halford Mackinder pointed out, London and southern England were much more closely linked, economically, with Flanders and the cities of the Hansa than with Wales, Scotland, or Ireland, or even the northern half of England itself. Early in the fifteenth century—three-quarters of a century before the first of the Tudors mounted the throne—the Company of Merchant Adventurers was formed in London to contest the Hansa's monopoly in the trade of the North Sea and Baltic areas; and before the end of the century English merchants and merchandise had attained to a dominant position in both those zones. Increasingly the Crown came to depend on the funds which this and succeeding merchant companies could supply. Increasingly, therefore, the English State became identified with the activities of the "enterprisers."

The great opportunity for the English mercantile class came, of course, when, at the close of the century, Genoese and Portuguese sailors opened up the two great world ocean routes; the way by the Cape of Good Hope to Asia, and the way westward across the Atlantic to a hitherto unknown continent. Thenceforth the oceans were the world's great highways; and the states on Europe's western coastline, fronting the open ocean, had—at last—an advantageous geographical situation. For the greater part of two centuries, after English traders and colonizers had begun the process of establishing bases on the farther side of the oceans, England was to be engaged in a series of wars with the other coastal states—Spain, Portugal, Holland France—with the clear purpose of securing for her dominan class the fullest fruits of that position.

English merchants had, indeed, before Vasco da Gama sailed

as far south as the Cape, planned a trading expedition to West Africa, on the heels of the Portuguese explorers. And within four years of Columbus' first voyage—while men still thought of the islands of the West Indies as outlying parts of Asia—Cabot sailed westward from Bristol under licence from Henry VII "to discover unknown lands under the King's banner" (His Majesty to take a one-fifth share of any profits). It was about a century later that Newfoundland was formally annexed to Britain; but in the intervening period it had become, with certain areas on the West coast of Africa, an integral part of the English overseas trade system. England, that is, was already established, though not yet politically, on either side of the Atlantic. The two Tudor Henrys, moreover, had laid it down that all commodities imported into England from abroad must be carried in English ships; so changing State policy, in Bacon's words, "from consideration of *plenty* to consideration of *power*." And their policy was, of course, carried further, later, by the Navigation Acts of Cromwell and Charles II.

There was at first no necessity for a policy of actual annexation. The various companies of English merchants, chartered by the Crown, found the new trade routes open to all comers, and national monopolies were not yet securely established. When the Pope's delimitation of the whole world outside of Europe as the sole possession of Spain and Portugal inaugurated such monopolies, the English challenge to Spain led to a struggle in which plunder and piracy were for a time even more profitable than ordinary trade. The Spanish *conquistadores* preyed on the American natives, and the English adventurers preyed on the *conquistadores*. Yet even while the war with Spain proceeded English merchant ships were sailing through the Mediterranean to the Levant, and through stormy northern waters by the North Cape to Muscovy. In the Atlantic itself John Hawkins was laying the foundation of the slave trade between Africa and Central America, in a ship lent him by Queen Elizabeth, herself the grand-daughter of a Merchant Adventurer.

While England's Atlantic bases were thus in process of consolidation, English sailors dared greatly in attempts to find a north-west or north-east "passage" from the northern Atlantic to Asia—a route which would be safe from interruption by Spain or any southern power. But the conquest of the Arctic was not yet; and English merchants decided that the risks of the southern route were worth taking. At the turn of the century, in the year 1600, the greatest—and longest lasting—of all the Chartered Companies, the East India Company, began its two and a half centuries' of highly prosperous history; and so inaugurated that imperial connection between Britain and Asia whose problems are among the most urgent and difficult of those we are facing to-day. Africa, Asia, America; within a century and a half of the discovery of the world ocean routes English merchants had gained a footing at favourable points in all three continents. Those footholds, with the sea-ways between, formed the 'skeleton' of the British Empire. Surveying the breathless activities of those earlier years one is scarcely conscious of any noticeable "absence of mind."[1]

This "skeleton" of empire was based, as we have seen, on the two great trade routes; the one which crossed the Atlantic to North America, and the other which went round Africa into the Indian Ocean. The necessity of safeguarding England's western coasts and ports for the Atlantic trade led, under Elizabeth and again under Cromwell, to the systematic and ruthless completion of the conquest of Ireland (the process called "pacification" by more recent imperialists). Britain's advantageous situation would have vanished if any hostile power had held the island covering her western approaches. The Atlantic route, too, lent special importance to the islands of the West Indies, both as ports of call on the voyage to the North American

---

[1] Nor was realization of a purpose confined to the Crown and the merchants. "In 1617 a joint-stock subscription (for overseas ventures) of over a million and a half sterling was put up by a thousand persons, including fifteen peers and thirteen peeresses, eighty-two knights, eighteen widows and spinsters, twenty-six clergy and physicians, besides merchants and tradesmen" (Waters, *Economic History of England*).

mainland and as sea-bases invaluable in case of any renewed aggressiveness on the part of Spain. Barbados, the Bahamas, Antigua and Jamaica became British. Recognition of the strategic value of the islands was quickly followed by realization of their economic value. And this led in turn to the rapid development of Britain's share in the African slave trade—which made the consolidation of British bases in West Africa essential. Forts were accordingly established at the mouth of the Gambia and on the Gold Coast. So the slave trade came to form the basis of that triangular connection between Britain, West Africa, and the West Indies which was so prominent a feature of British overseas commerce in the eighteenth century.

These West African forts were of value also as safeguards of the second great trade route, to the Indies. For all along this route, as well as at its goal, rivals were already established. The Portuguese, who had discovered it, had not only made themselves supreme over most of the Indian Ocean, but had also seized large portions of the African coastline. The Dutch, a little later, were established at various points along the route. Not until the middle of the 17th century did the British acquire the mid-Atlantic island of St. Helena, a useful port of call on the return voyage from the East.

Forestalled by the Dutch in the "Spice Islands" of the East Indies—chief goal of all the earlier trading voyages—the British turned to the great mainland peninsula of India itself. There is no need to retrace here the history of the seventeenth and eighteenth centuries—the wars with Portugal, with the Dutch, and finally with the French—which led at last to the establishment of the British East India Company as the dominant political power in the Indian Ocean (and which also, on the other side of the world, made Britain supreme—for a short while—on the continent of North America). But since we are especially concerned with the geographical factors in the story it is perhaps worth noting that the three Presidencies—Bombay, Bengal, and Madras—into which India was later divided under the Company's rule had their origins in the trading stations first acquired

GEOGRAPHY AND THE BRITISH EMPIRE

by the Company from the Mogul emperors or from other Indian rulers: Surat (later Bombay itself) on the west coast; Fort William (Calcutta) on the Hoogli; and Masulipatam and Madras on the east coast of the peninsula. It may be added, though it has nothing to do with geography, that the close connection between Crown and Company was still maintained. The charter was granted by the monarch himself, and not by Parliament. Charles II confirmed and extended the Company's monopoly in the trade of the whole of the East Indies; and as Mr. Maurice Collis recalls in his *Siamese White* (the life story of a poacher on the Company's preserves) "For the bestowal of his grace the King had substantial consideration. It has been calculated that the total value of loans and presents of cash received by Charles from the Company between 1660 and 1684 was £324,150, which represents a million and a half of our money at the least." British forts and factories—as Siamese White's exploits remind us—were not confined to India, but were established at various points in the Indian Ocean—in the Persian Gulf, in Burma, and in Siam.[1]

We leap forward to the end of the eighteenth century. The geography of Britain's empire is still based on the same two great trade routes. But as a result of the long wars with rivals, particularly with France, the skeleton has to some extent been filled in by territorial acquisitions in Asia and America. Large areas of India are now held and ruled by John Company. But in North America, the revolt of the colonies, following quickly on the successful conclusion of the war with France, has reduced British possessions to the lands around the St. Lawrence Gulf, the southern shores of Hudson Bay, and the island of Newfound-

[1] Two of the arguments used at this same period by those critics who attacked the East India Company's monopoly, have a peculiar interest at the present day. One was "that it took away capital which would be better employed on the internal development of Britain (e.g. on roads and the draining of marshes." The other objected "that its close monopoly and joint-stock enterprises put power into the hands of a few men, who could and did fix prices to suit themselves without any consideration for the general public" (Waters, *op. cit.*).

land. Far away again, in the south-western Pacific, a coastal area of the newly-discovered island of Australia has been annexed for Britain. "The British empire of the mid-eighteenth century," says Professor Knaplund,[1] "had virtually fulfilled the requirements of a self-sufficient economic unit. It was based on the theory that if the economic interests of any part of it clashed with those of England, the former must be sacrificed." This, of course, was the conception which led directly to the American Revolution. And the loss of the American colonies was by no means counterbalanced either by the acquisition of Australia or by the extension of the settled area of Canada.

The new century began with a renewal of the war with France —revolutionary France, led by the "upstart Corsican." Napoleon aimed at the restoration of the overseas empire which France had lost to Britain during the preceding century. One of his dearest dreams was to destroy the British power in India, source of the wealth which made the nation of shopkeepers across the Channel so formidable a rival. When he was finally defeated, by British sea-power as well as by British gold, Britain's industrial organization had been enormously accelerated while that of France was set back, and the skeleton of the British Empire was filled in a little more. Three important acquisitions strengthened Britain's hold on the route to the East—the Cape of Good Hope, Mauritius, and Ceylon. In the Mediterranean, not yet itself a main trade route but nevertheless impossible to leave to domination by France, Malta was added to Gibraltar (taken from Spain a century before). In the West Indies, Trinidad and Tobago, and on the South American mainland, British Guiana, were taken by the British.

.   .   .   .   .

We enter upon the more modern phase of the Empire's growth; the phase which sees an enormous increase in the extent of Britain's territorial possessions overseas, as well as in the tempo of their commercial development. "Between 1800 and

[1] *The British Empire*, 1915–39.

1850 the area of the Empire was trebled; between 1850 and 1919 it trebled again." Two great factors lay behind this phenomenal growth: the rapid development of the forces of production in Britain, resulting from the Industrial Revolution; and the application of the new means of power to sea transport. The advent of the steamship both shortened distances, measured in time, between every part of the world, and changed the old sea routes by doing away with the need to sail a course dictated by prevailing winds. "India was now nearer to Britain than Italy had been. The result was a complete re-organization of the British trading system. Capital turned over and earned its profits many times to the former once, all the earth was opening up as a source of raw material, all the nations had become markets."

Even before the Industrial Revolution (and, as the Hammonds have pointed out, an important contributory cause of it) a commercial revolution had occurred in European-Asiatic trade. That trade was now primarily concerned with commodities used or consumed by the mass of ordinary people; and not, as in earlier days, with luxuries for the few. The new machine-production accentuated this; and the great populations of Asia offered the most immediately profitable markets. The first half of the century accordingly saw British penetration carried further east in Asia, to China; and from the Indian Ocean far out into the Pacific. More key-points were added to the skeleton framework—Singapore, Aden, the Falklands, New Zealand, Hong-Kong.

Africa, especially now that the growth of humanitarian feeling had resulted in the abolition of the slave trade, fell out of the picture; to come back again later in the century, when capitalist-industrial development had reached a point where the exploitation of new sources of raw material was at least as important as the acquisition of markets. Only at the southern extremity of the continent where, in the Cape Colony, the area of white settlement was steadily pushed north and north-eastward at the expense of the native Bantu peoples, was there any extension of British territorial possessions before the great Scramble began in the eighties.

That Scramble, in which all the European powers took part, marked the end of the period of Britain's unchallenged supremacy in world trade. Germany and the United States were rivalling her production in the heavy industries. France, although behind those countries in large-scale industrial organization, had surplus capital available for export. Outside Russia the European countries now possessed fairly complete and efficient railway systems, and the industries which had constructed these were ready for new worlds to conquer. Henceforth the new industrial powers challenged Britain overseas; and modern Economic Imperialism—the deliberate acquisition of territory, particularly "undeveloped" territory, in order to win monopoly control of valuable raw materials and build railways to make them more accessible—came into being.

In the Scramble for Africa Britain held her own—or indeed increased it—against her rivals. J. A. Hobson estimated that during the years 1884–1900, chiefly in Africa, Britain acquired some 3 million square miles of territory, with 57 million inhabitants; France, $3\frac{1}{2}$ million square miles with 36 million inhabitants; Belgium, something less than a million square miles, with 30 million inhabitants; Germany, a million square miles and 14 million people; Portugal (by claiming the hinterlands of her old coastal colonies) three-quarters of a million square miles and 9 million Africans. The British gains included suzerainty over Egypt, doubly important now that the cutting of the Suez Canal had made the Mediterranean-Red Sea route the main sea road to the East; the whole Upper Nile area, Uganda, and what is now Kenya, in East Africa; the Rhodesias and Bechuanaland in the south; and very considerable enlargements of her West Coast possessions, the Gold Coast and Nigeria.

This expansion was largely carried through by means of a revival of the original form of British colonial enterprise—the chartered company. Between 1881 and 1889 charters (now statutory, and not granted by the Crown alone) were given to four companies—the East Africa, the Royal Niger, the South Africa, and the Imperial Borneo. This reappearance of the chartered company was due to the inevitable time-lag between the actual facts of economic progress and the ideas of politicians. Only Disraeli, among Victorian statesmen, thought or planned in terms of imperial expansion. The handing over of power and responsibility to a capitalist company was a convenient way out for politicians who preferred to evade the risks and difficulties of opening-up "backward" territories. Moreover, as Professor Knaplund points out, the chartered company was "not the only device for disguising political control" employed during this period. There were in addition the various types of protectorate, condominiums, and spheres of interest. Joseph Chamberlain, at the turn of the century, voiced the needs of the newer capitalism, which wanted annexations, monopoly control, and empire development. In South Africa Cecil Rhodes carried that policy into effect. And, as H. N. Brailsford observes, "the methods by which economic opportunity, in the shape of concessions, was obtained within recent recollection were, on occasion, as predatory as any that our fathers used in the early days of the East India Company."

The final stage of British colonial expansion came at the close of the war of 1914-18, when Germany's first challenge to the established industrial empires ended in her defeat, and her colonial possessions were shared out, as "mandated territories," between the victors. Britain's acceptance of the mandate for German East Africa (now Tanganyika Territory) filled in the only remaining gap in the great belt of British possessions stretching from the Nile to the Cape. The Empire thus emerged from the First World War greater and more powerful than ever, at least in extent of territory and the number of its subject peoples. If British power still fell something short of Hitler's reputed aim of world domination, at any rate British dominance extended to areas in every continent. Newly discovered raw materials —copper in Rhodesia, tin in Malaya—were moreover giving a new importance to relatively "backward" areas.

But British rule, as regards certain of these areas, was much less centralized than it had once been. The revolt of the colonists of North America against their colonial status had been followed, at various times during the nineteenth and twentieth centuries, by the grant of dominion status (i.e. of self-government) to all the chief areas of white settlement in the empire—Canada, Newfoundland, Australia, New Zealand, and South Africa. The dominions now formed, with the "mother" country, the British Commonwealth of Nations; in which people of European stock exercised political and economic power, and inhabitants of native blood (as in South Africa) were legally assigned to an inferior status. The rest of the empire—India, Africa, the West Indian and Pacific Islands, peopled by non-white races—has not so far been considered "ripe" for self-government. The British government has taken over the administration (as distinct from the economic development) of most of the territories lately held by the new chartered companies. Political control from Whitehall, working through various forms of local colonial government, now operates throughout the colonial empire. But the colonial policy of Whitehall, however enlightened in this or that aspect at one time (or one place) or another, is always subordinated to the primary aim of benefiting British investors; that great aim which found its highest expression in the decisions of the Ottawa Conference. So, to quote Mr. Brailsford again, the "fundamental bond of Empire" came more and more to be the "relationship of creditor and debtor—the relationship that produces a tribute for Property." "Mr. Chamberlain used to say that 'the Empire is Commerce.' It would be more accurate to say that the Empire is Debt."

.   .   .   .   .

These words are being written as we approach the conclusion of a Second World War; a war after which it now appears certain that Britain, largely by virtue of her empire, will rank as one of the Four Great Powers of the victorious United Nations. But one obvious difference between the British Empire and its allies

GEOGRAPHY AND THE BRITISH EMPIRE 47

at once strikes the geographer. The United States of America, the Union of Socialist Soviet Republics, and the Republic of China, are each of them geographical entities; coterminus territories which, though like the U.S.S.R. they may stretch across the width of two continents, are undivided by any intervening alien sovereignties. Not so with the empire of Britain; scattered around the seven seas and ranging from poles to equator. The British Empire is a geographical dis-unity, linked only by those long sea ways which are also high roads for the traffic of the rest of the world.

Can it, without defying the plain facts of the twentieth century world, remain for much longer a political or economic unit? It is, as the barest sketch of its history shows, the concrete expression of two things; the first, European domination of other continents; the second, European monopoly of industrial activity and development. And both these things belong to the past. For four centuries, from the time of the discovery of the ocean routes by European voyagers down to the end of the nineteenth century, the European states, primarily on account of their superior technique, claimed and assumed superior rights over the peoples of the rest of the world. That domination has now been challenged, not only by the migration of people of European stock to other continents, and the founding of centres of European civilization outside Europe itself; not only by the renaissance, with a basis of European industrial technique of the older Asiatic civilizations—India, China, Japan—and their claim to equality with Europe; but also by the first steps towards civilization made by hitherto backward races, in Africa and elsewhere, and their demand both for better access to civilized living and for full human rights. Any empire based on the idea of racial superiority—and despite all rhetorical declarations to the contrary the British Empire has been and still is so based—cannot survive unless it is prepared to maintain itself by the Hitler method of brute force; and brute force becomes less and less practicable now that Europeans no longer possess a monopoly either in the use or the manufacture of death-dealing instruments. The Empire may transform itself, by the free and equal will and co-operation of all its peoples, into a federation or commonwealth of free nations. In that case, however, it would not be specifically "British"; for the majority of its present inhabitants are not of that race; nor would it be an empire.

But would the maintenance of such a federation or commonwealth, separated politically from the rest of the world, be justifiable from the point of view of general world welfare? Why should the facts of geography be defied, and certain varied territories in Africa or the Pacific be isolated from their neighbours and linked with an island off the north-west coast of Europe, and with other specially separated areas in other parts of the world? If such a grouping be designed, exclusively or predominantly, for the benefit of some one country among them —let alone of one class within that country—then the arrangement is plainly indefensible by any civilized twentieth-century standard. Even were its aim the common welfare of all the peoples within the group, both ethics and economics suggest that a more worthwhile aim would be one directed at securing the maximum welfare of the world's people, without regard to particular political groupings.

There remains only one cogent reason for the continuance, for a period at all events, of the British Empire as it has been developed in four centuries of British capitalist enterprise: the fact that it exists, that to a considerable extent it "works," and that even if it worked less well than it actually does it would still be better than no sort of organization at all. There is a strong, probably a decisive, case for that argument. Nevertheless it is plainly essential, if Britain is to stand before the world as a disinterested champion of a new and better World Order, that the reasons for and against continued British administration of what have hitherto been British "possessions" should be fully and openly discussed. It is also clear that such administration, if it continued, will have to be modified by co-operation with other states and peoples, and by the re-drawing, if not the total abolition, of many of those frontiers which at present demarcate those possessions in various parts of the world. This war has already emphasized such forgotten facts of geography as, for instance, that there is a natural unity between all the lands bordering on the Indian Ocean, and that full economic efficiency can only be gained by increasing their interdependence. The further industrialization of India, or of any other Asiatic country, will inevitably lead to still closer links with neighbouring territories, and a relatively looser connection with Europe. And the east coast lands of Africa, too, it should be noted, border the Indian Ocean, not the Atlantic. Regional planning and regional administration would seem to be indicated by economics and geography alike.

This war has also made it grimly plain that the problem of Empire defence can only be successfully solved if the hitherto subject peoples are given grounds for believing that their own future welfare is guaranteed by the maintenance of the British connection; in short, that they are permitted to win, and exercise, their freedom.

Again, if Britain's connection with her colonial territories in Africa, the Caribbean, or the Pacific is to continue, the eighteenth century conception which regarded colonies as sources of raw material serving the needs of the "mother" country will have to give place, in their case as assuredly as in the case of the countries where white men have settled, to a recognition of equality; and, until such time as Africans or Polynesians are fully capable of controlling and running the machinery of twentieth century civilization for themselves, to the acceptance of responsibility by Britain for ensuring the development of their territories primarily in the immediate interest, and for the immediate benefit, of their inhabitants.

Now, if anything is crystal clear it is that such development cannot be carried through if the profit motive which, as we have seen, has been the basic factor in the growth of Britain's empire is still to dominate Britain's relations with the colonial countries. To prevent that, "administration" must take on a far wider meaning than it has hitherto possessed. To "keep the ring" between powerful capitalist combines and ignorant, defenceless Africans is not enough. Britain's colonial heritage will remain what Mr. Lloyd George has said much of it actually is, a "slum empire," unless colonial governments are henceforth not only really masters in their own territories, but are empowered, endowed and equipped to carry through those changes without which the people for whom they are responsible cannot take their place in the world march to a sane civilization, nor the resources of their territories function properly and efficiently as parts of the world economic order on which that civilization will be based. Every area must, in Dr. Julian Huxley's words, "have its roads, railways, harbours, storage and marketing facilities, power; its rivers must be tamed, its forests properly exploited, its soil conserved and drained and fertilized, its dangerous diseases brought under control; its people must be equipped with a reasonable standard of health and security and education." There must, that is to say, be "a positive policy of development."

Whether any such policy is likely to come into being unless and until the same kind of political and economic programme becomes the main objective of British governments here in Britain itself may be open to question. But no Socialist will wish to deny that such a policy would alone justify the continuance of the Empire; nor could any economic-geographer challenge its urgent necessity. And if the British accomplish the tasks ahead of them they will, in the words of a recent writer, "have made a contribution to human history by comparison with which all their Empire-building hitherto will seem no more than a primitive overture, rather analogous to the period of the Anglo-Saxon kingdoms in the history of Great Britain herself."

The Challenge of African Poverty
by RITA HINDEN

The poverty of Africa is a challenge. Here is an immense continent brought by modern communications to the very doorstep of Europe and in it live about 150,000,000 people,[1] most of them at the lowest level of human subsistence. Scores of reports—official and otherwise—have described African economic conditions; the wretched diets and universal evidence of malnutrition; the deplorable housing conditions; the lack of essential clothing—the lack even of a minimum of footwear to protect against the hookworm; the primitive, often harmful agricultural methods; the mere pittance which is paid in wages; the inadequacy of social services, education and health provisions. This degrading poverty is a challenge to us, for Britain is the greatest colonial power in Africa, and we have appended our signature to the Atlantic Charter, proclaiming as our aim "that all men in all lands may live out their lives in freedom from fear and want." Nor do we seek to deny the wretchedness of African conditions or our responsibility for improving them. When we disagree among ourselves, it is only as to how far European penetration must bear the blame for African poverty and—more important—what exactly can be done about it?

To think constructively about these questions, we must not picture the Africans as an inchoate mass of poor, ignorant and "exploited" people. Africans vary considerably in calling and education, and can be divided into certain categories according to their occupation. We will not get far without making the classification, tracing the problems with which each category is confronted to-day, and analysing how our advent in Africa has contributed to these varying problems—or could alleviate them.

The subsistence peasants are the first broad category—the

[1] In the British African colonies, with which we are concerned, there are about 42,000,000 people.

farmer who does little more than produce his own food, and has only the weakest links with the market and the outside world. In almost all British territories these peasants constitute the majority of the population. They are still bound, for the most part, to the old shifting method of agriculture. The peasant burns the bush, cultivates the burnt patch for a few years till its fertility dwindles; then moves on to a new habitation while the bush springs up again behind him. Modern ideas of crop rotation, the use of fertilizers, proper irrigation, machinery—all these are unknown. As long as the land is sufficient to allow him to move on, and to allow the bush time to regenerate behind him, he can continue to eke enough from the soil to keep body and soul together.

Secondly, there are the peasants producing crops for export—cocoa, palm products, cotton, groundnuts. These farmers have an entirely different orientation from the subsistence peasant. The home market is negligible and they look outwards to the world market, to the prices they may hope to get for their crops, and the prices they have to pay for the imports they purchase in exchange. But they, too, remain bound by primitive methods. The productivity of their farming is very low, and if they can compete on world markets, it is natural advantages alone which makes it possible. They exploit the soil ruthlessly in order to satisfy the demands of overseas consumers, and when diseases spread and the natural strength of their forests and soils is sapped, they do not understand how to combat the menace, nor do they have the power to enforce preventative measures. They are pitifully dependent on the fluctuations of world prices over which they have no control. They have no organization to protect them against the vagaries of the market, or the machinations of traders.

The next big category is the wage-earners, though relatively to the whole African population they are few in number. They are drawn into wage labour in the towns, on the farms (perhaps of Europeans, as in East Africa) and in the mines. They are usually not a permanent labour force, but leave their own villages and "reserves" for a few years' work after which they may return to their traditional lives. Their migrations are induced either by a prod from behind, in the shape of the need for cash to pay taxes; or by the pull of the attraction of money and all that money can buy, and the equally strong pull of adventure and the excitement of a new way of life and contact with Europeans. These workers are ignorant, easily exploitable, poor in the weapons of self-defence. The wages they are paid throughout Africa, except perhaps in the more sophisticated towns on the West Coast and on a few of the better-managed mines, are miserably inadequate. Nor do they have the training or opportunity to do much more than menial jobs.

Finally, as a thin veneer on the surface of African life, are the traders, professionals, clerks, officials and craftsmen. In some parts of Africa this veneer does not yet exist. In other parts it is expanding and deepening yearly, though it is rare for any real wealth to be made by even the most educated of Africans. It is among this class that political consciousness is developing, partly because the educated African rarely has the same pay or opportunities as a European of similar qualifications. And here, too, there is a sharpening recognition of the limitations which poverty and ignorance impose on African advance, and a growing resentment against any one or anything that stands in the way of that advance.

Here, in broad outline, is the economic picture presented by the people of British Africa. It is an unhappy picture. How far are we to blame that African economic opportunity is so hopelessly confined? It would be foolish on our part to blame ourselves entirely, and to suggest that all Africans were happy and prosperous before we came. From what we know of their earlier history they have, with a few minor exceptions, lived for centuries on a low and backward level; we may have brought some diseases, but there were many others to reduce their strength and vitality long before our advent; superstition and ignorance can scarcely be more now than they were; and there is little in the meagre population estimates that we have to suggest that at any time the population was much larger or wealthier than it is at the moment. It can indeed be convincingly argued that in many respects the African standard of living has benefited from the arrival of Europeans. If there are few schools and hospitals now, there were still fewer before. Even if the worker or peasant is underpaid, his income is nevertheless higher than what it was, and, scant as clothes and household goods are, they are more abundant than they were two generations ago. Opportunities for advancement may be cramped, but more and more of the young people are beginning to find their way overseas to study in British and American universities. Impressive leaps in the totals of trade revenue and expenditure can be shown in every British Colony, and everywhere increases in road and rail mileage, public works of all sorts can be pointed to.

We may have done all this and much more, but it has brought no real happiness and satisfaction. Why? Because, reducing the answer to the simplest terms, our coming has upset whatever balance there was in African life. We have brought new ideas, new standards of living, new wants and new visions. Yet we have prevented the Africans from taking their full share of all these new desirable things which we have held before them. We have upset the old while withholding the new—or at least any but the most shoddy fraction of the new.

Sociologists would trace the malaise we have brought yet deeper. It is not the changes we have induced that have caused the trouble, but the *unevenness* of the change. If productivity and incomes are stepped up without corresponding changes in the means of political expression or in education, social and personal frictions are erected. The African is accused of not knowing how to use his new wealth, of becoming lazy and shiftless, of indulging in unconstructive political agitation— all of which may be true, because one part of his life is now out of tune with the other. Or if one part of a country, say a mining area, is intensively developed along modern lines, while the surrounding countryside is left to stagnate, a conflict is set up within the minds of the men who spend part of their lives in the mines and part in the village, and this conflict is carried over into every aspect of family and tribal life. A stable social advance involves advancing simultaneously in all aspects of life, which must be geared one to the other. It is in this that we have so markedly failed.

But, to keep to economics only, how, in regard to each of the four economic categories of Africans, has our coming overthrown the old equilibrium while failing to establish a new one? Take the subsistence peasant. We have described how he can manage to scrape along on his primitive methods of agriculture, if the land is sufficient. That "if" is the crux of the matter. Owing to our coming, in large parts of Africa the land is no longer sufficient. The wretched story of conflict over land in East Africa must be a heavy burden on our consciences. It is not that the actual area of land which has been alienated to Europeans in Kenya or Tanganyika or the Rhodesias is in itself so large, but it usually represents a heavy part of what good land there is in any of these territories. Population maps show an extraordinary concentration of Africans in certain limited areas. It is dishonest, when discussing the availability of land in the "settler" countries, to talk in terms of the total square mileage. There are enormous arid, barren wastes in all these territories. The good land is divided up with preposterous inequity between a few hundreds or a few thousands of European settlers on the one hand, and millions of African peasants on the other. The results have been inevitable and obvious. Crowded into the reserves, their cattle increasing (mainly, it is true, because of the new veterinary knowledge, brought by Europeans—another example of "unevenness of change"), but still uneducated in better methods of agriculture and the preservation of the soil, still unprovided with irrigation facilities, the Africans are rapidly sucking dry the fertility of even what land they have. With new methods of agriculture it is possible that their land may be adequate. But the puny size of the Government agricultural staff can barely touch the fringe of the problem. So fertility dwindles, and soil erosion is to-day pointed to, with growing alarm, as one of the major problems of Africa.

Not only has the African peasant been shorn of the minimum of land on which he can carry on, but his villages have been denuded of the better part of their manpower. The drain on workers to the towns and farms and mines has had the most unhappy effects on African village life in many areas. There are villages where it is a normal thing for over half the able-bodied men to be away at work—perhaps many hundreds of miles away from home. The work is left to the already overburdened women and old men. There is no energy for maintaining even the old efficiency; still less for tackling anything new or presenting an open mind to the instruction of transient Government officials. The impoverishment of African village life proceeds year by year. Its tragedy is not to be expressed in economic terms alone, but in the break-up of families with the consequent moral deterioration and the frightening spread of venereal disease.

The peasant producing for export has different problems. It is not a question of pressure on land, drainage of man-power and break-up of old ties. His problem is his helpless dependence on an outside market—a market in which there is no stability and over which he has no control. The crops he produces are bought by powerful trading firms and the price they offer him may seem to the producer to bear no relation whatsoever to his own costs or efforts or needs—more a dispensation of God than of man. In the violent fluctuations of the world market in the inter-war period, colonial producers suffered profoundly. It is true that they had their prosperous times and on the whole the cash wealth which accrued to the Colonies and showed itself in trade and revenue figures was greater than before. Nevertheless, the individual felt himself a prey to unknown forces against which he had no defence.

As he began to understand more, he saw, too, that only a fraction of the value of his product was left to him. Not only did the weakness of his own marketing arrangements compel him to take a low price and watch the trading profits go into the hands of a chain of middlemen, but his failure to accomplish efficiently even the preliminary stages of processing his product, or to tackle the easier forms of manufacture based on his own raw materials, meant that the wealth created through secondary industries was denied him as well. Further, in exporting, for example, the whole of the oil-seed overseas instead of extracting the oil and using the husks for cattle food or returning them to the soil, he was actually exporting the soil fertility of his own country. And as he cut down the protecting forest and ruthlessly exploited the soil, crop diseases spread and there was no power to combat them. What did he receive in return for his exports? The goods produced by Europeans with their high trade union rates of wages and the profits of monopoly importers tacked on. Expensive goods of inferior quality were exchanged for the cheap produce of the tropics.

The problem shifts again when we come to the wage-earners. These are the men drawn from the villages, leaving their families behind, more or less at the mercy of new masters. Sometimes the masters would be benevolent and far-sighted, sometimes not. Usually the desire was for a temporary labour force only, which would be housed in "compounds" or locations, carefully docketed and ticketed and registered, and subjected to curfews and pass laws and a host of restrictions and humiliations. The argument was that it was better to have men drawn from the villages who, if employment failed, would have a home to go back to. The silent argument underlying this was that it would be possible to pay the men less if they had no dependants with them, and it was known that their dependants were supporting themselves in their own villages. In other words, the village and reserve would subsidize wage-earning employment. Penal sanctions were at one time common to give the employers powers under contracts of employment to invoke the criminal law against defaulting workers. But, largely owing to the work of the I.L.O., penal sanctions are now abolished in almost all of British Africa. Like the peasants producing for the export market, the wage-earners have little defensive organization—the beginnings of trade unionism are of the most recent date and have only nibbled at the edge of the problem. And through lack of education, failure to provide any opportunities for acquiring technical skill, and, in some territories, through the operation of an industrial colour bar, the African worker is kept to the most poorly paid unskilled grades of work.

The fact that the remaining class of African—the thin veneer of traders and professionals—is so small, is mainly because of the lack of education which would enable Africans to perform the more complicated economic functions; because of the colour bar operating in some areas which makes it impossible for Africans to assume more responsible work even if they could acquire the necessary skills; and finally, because so much of the wealth of Africa which ought to be processed, worked up and retained for economic advancement inside the country, is drawn off overseas. If it were not, the problem of lack of education and absence of skills could so much more easily be tackled. The numbers of educated Africans and their opportunities would increase, and the frustrations and resentments, now becoming so common in parts of Africa, would find their legitimate solutions.

It is a serious charge to make—that the wealth of Africa is drained away—and too often it is made without a practical content being given to the allegation. What, in concrete terms, is meant? Minerals are one of Africa's most precious assets, yet the mines are almost always operated by European capitalist companies, which pay dividends to their overseas shareholders, heavy remuneration to their directors, as likely as not the lion's share of their taxes to the British Exchequer, royalties to venerable but functionless companies, and enormous wages to local European employees. What remains for the African workers and for the African exchequers are the crumbs from the rich man's table. It is no argument to point out that millions of pounds have been lost by European investors in Africa; that, taken over a period of years, the return on mine capital may be only a very few per cent; that, without investors to take risks, the mines may never have been opened up at all. All this may be true, and is a sad reflection on the inefficiencies of the way in which we allow these things to be done. But it does not get over the fact that to-day the mines *are* being operated, and that whatever wealth they produce is taken—certainly the greater part of it —out of the country. That is a basic, inescapable fact—one of which the Africans are increasingly aware, and which world public opinion is decreasingly able to stomach.

The position is the same in kind, if not in degree, as regards the other primary materials. We have already explained how little of the final price which his product fetches, after shipping, processing, refining and manufacture, actually goes into the pocket of the African. The price of a pound of manufactured chocolate paid by the British consumer is a heavy multiple of the price which the cocoa producer gets for a pound of his cocoa powder. Must this inevitably be so? Why should not the African engage in at least some of the preliminary processes of cocoa and chocolate manufacture? Could he not so organize himself as to retain a goodly share of the trading profits? Could he not, if he combined, organize his own shipments? In other words, instead of confining himself to the low rewards which accrue to those who engage in primary production alone, could he not aspire to the rewards of secondary production and even of the "tertiary" services of marketing and shipping?

Must he, in addition, continue to have even the limited wealth which he possesses drained away in payment for expensive imports? Could he not produce from his own local raw materials many more of the essentials of life, perhaps of a more satisfactory quality for his needs, and certainly at cheaper prices? The need for developing local secondary industries is now beginning to be widely recognized—as a precaution against the unruly world market; as a means for retaining wealth in the country, instead of frittering it away on what are often unsatisfactory imports; and as an outlet for the decaying craftsmanship and creative ability of the African. There is no suggestion here that African Colonies, or indeed any territories, should aim at complete economic self-sufficiency. There are certain goods which are the natural subjects for international trade, and which could only be produced locally at great cost to efficiency and ultimate wealth. But there remain nevertheless a whole series of simple products based on the local raw materials, which could be processed and manufactured by Africans for Africans.

Thus, the sum of our misdemeanours in Africa adds up. We are upsetting the old equilibrium of the subsistence peasant by taking away some of the best of his land, and drawing the able-bodied men into outside employment. We are confining the "export peasant" to the production of the crude raw materials which we want, allowing him little control over their marketing and processing. We have drawn wage labour from the villages to work in the towns, farms and mines, grievously disturbing the family and economic life of the countryside and offering employment opportunities at puny wages, in only the lowest grades of work and often under humiliating conditions. And we have given Africans scant opportunity to rise to any avocation other than that of primary producers and wage-earners, because we have kept the real wealth of the country (the mines, control of trade, etc.) and also—let it not be forgotten—a big share of the taxes, in our own hands.

And now—what are we to do? It is sometimes argued that, within the limitations of the present British, indeed the world, economic framework, little that we can do will be effective. But are we then to put a stopper on colonial advance until the millennium of a hypothetical "revolution"? At least, recognizing the limitations of our effectiveness, we can pave the way.

There are alternative methods, even within our existing framework, by which the challenge of African poverty may be met. There is the policy of "development and welfare," in which we now engage—a philanthropy-cum-public-works policy, whereby Britain grants free gifts of money to the Colonies to meet certain compelling needs. A swamp is drained here, an educational establishment is built there, certain new industries are encouraged, welfare projects of all sorts are put in hand; dents are prodded into the hard surface of colonial apathy and poverty and in a sporadic way a great deal of good is done. But this is no frontal attack on the major problems; it is neither democratic *laisser-faire*, nor is it state-planning; it neither springs from the people, nor is it the bold product of a planning agency; it is no more than a casualty clearing station on the way to more drastic treatment elsewhere.

Another method, peculiarly attractive in these days of totalitarianism, is "planning from above." By the formulation of a rigorous plan, by compulsion on the people on the spot to carry it out, by the granting of power to determined agencies whose duty is to secure a certain rise in productivity, a certain quota of public works, a certain improvement in the standard of living within a fixed period, it would be perfectly possible to open up territories, provide them with their capital equipment, train the populations and introduce a modern prosperous economy. Such methods, though in a less stringent and far-reaching shape, have been frequently discussed, even in Britain, in recent years. There has been pressure by certain groups to establish Colonial Development Boards, or other developmental agencies which would be free from the ordinary trammels of government and administration, financed perhaps by capital levies on the British public, or out of ordinary British taxes, or by international loans (the method is not very important as it is estimated that a profit will accrue) and armed with all the authority to undertake a rapid programme of development in British territories. These proposals have, perhaps unfairly, been dubbed "development without welfare." It is true that they put economic development, as such, in the centre of their programmes, without linking it to political, educational or social problems, and without connecting it in any way with the aspirations of an expanding democracy. "Thou shalt be developed," is the new commandment, "and we will show you how."

There remains the "democratic" method. This is in opposition to development schemes, however efficient, imposed from above, which may have no roots in the lives and needs of the people and, through ignoring all the processes of social change other than the economic, may make no real contribution to their ultimate happiness or self-respect. There is also the danger that such schemes, even while increasing prosperity, may concentrate power in the hands of the few bureaucrats at the top who will manipulate the economy of the country in their own interest. The democratic approach is, rather, to suggest that changes must come from the people themselves. Outside help and direction is needed, in the circumstances of the closely-knit world of to-day, but there are limits to this guidance.

In brief, what is required is not a sort of fascist regimentation on the one hand, nor an endless philanthropy on the other. As democrats we must inevitably view regimentation and control from above for the sake of "economic development" with suspicion. At the same time, benevolence is not desired by—or even perhaps desirable for—the Africans (or any people) in any long-term sense. "We do not want your charity," is a common enough African complaint. "What we want is to control our own destinies."

If, then, Africans are to develop in the way they want, we must appreciate the limits to what we can and should do. There are three types of action which should be Britain's contribution in the opening phase of the new relationship—"partnership"—which is before us. In the first place, we must make it possible for Africans to help themselves. We must enable them to create both the means of self-defence and the constructive organizations which are the basis of their own future prosperity. In the second place, we must cease to draw away the wealth of Africa so that there will be the straw from which they can make bricks. And thirdly, we must provide some of the essential capital equipment and the skilled technical assistance which they themselves are as yet unable to supply for themselves.

What do these three important duties entail? What is meant by the statement that we must help the Africans to the means of self-defence and of constructive organization? Does this

THE CHALLENGE OF AFRICAN POVERTY

lie in our hands? As long as Britain continues to be responsible for the administration of the Colonies these things *do* lie, directly and intimately, in our hands. It depends on us whether African workers can combine to defend themselves in trade unions, whether African peasants can band together to control their markets through co-operative organizations, and whether the African people, as a whole, can exercise political responsibility and control in their own councils of government. These are the weapons of democracy, and it rests with us, in the first place, to put them in the hands of the colonial peoples. It is our duty to see that political and industrial organization is protected by law in every Colony, and is allowed to function without victimization; what is more—that the colonial peoples are encouraged and educated in the knowledge of these weapons. Once this is done, they themselves must use them and perhaps adapt them to their own conditions. But we, as the senior partners, with generations of experience behind us, and with, still, the power in our hands, must strive to secure for the colonial peoples the means which have been so important in the advance of our own people.

There is still an enormous amount to be done in Africa in this regard. It is true that in the last few years trade union laws have been brought up-to-date, and certain encouragement given to the formation of trade unions. But this is only at the veriest beginning—and in East Africa it has barely begun at all. Political representation of Africans in the central organs of Government is also still in an embryonic form, and in no British colony do the Africans feel that they are able effectively to participate in the control of their own country. Co-operatives, which have a vital role to play in the future of Africa are, with a few honourable exceptions, all but unknown. There are only a couple of African territories where even the necessary legal framework for their development can be said to exist. In other peasant territories, the State itself has stepped in and done work of the first importance in encouraging co-operative organizations among the people. But in the whole of British Africa there is only one government co-operative department—in Nigeria.[1]

The second duty that falls on our shoulders is to put an end to the extraction of wealth from Africa in the European interest. Some solution must be found to the problem of the distribution of the wealth of the mines. It may not be simple or possible immediately to nationalize the existing mining operations; this cannot be done without the administrative framework required. But the mineral rights could certainly everywhere be taken over by governments; no new concessions need be granted to private companies, but efficient Mining Departments established to operate new mines; the leases of existing mining companies could be subjected to rigorous supervision; the taxation system could be overhauled so that local revenues drew the whole of the benefit; and employment opportunities for Africans in the mines could be equalized with those offered to Europeans. Similarly, a policy for the retention of a far greater part of the value of raw materials could be worked out. This would involve the development of secondary and processing industries and the organization of the producers, so that they could control their own markets and be fully represented in any world marketing organization. When it comes to land, our duty is clear. There should be no further alienation, even of Crown land, to Europeans, at least until African agricultural methods have been so revolutionized as to make a reasonable standard of living possible on the existing land areas. A strong case could be made out for the handing over of large tracts of unused land, already in the hands of Europeans, for African occupation. But it is essential to look at this subject from a constructive point of view, for there is justice in the claims of some of the European settlers, that if more land is transferred to Africans, it will only be ruined as well. The matter is not one of a fixed number of acres, but how these acres are treated, and, as more land is handed over, it must coincide with the education of the

[1] It has just been decided to establish a Co-operative Department in the Gold Coast as well.

African in how to use it. Even that is not enough. The means to improved agriculture, to putting lessons into practice, must be made available as well. The peasant must be afforded the facilities for purchasing improved seed, fertilizer, the minimum of machinery, the necessities for improving his flocks and herds. This may again be a case where co-operative organization can solve the difficulties.

Another aspect of the withdrawal of wealth arises in the vexed problem of "jobs." There is a two-fold problem here—Are Europeans to continue to have the plums of employment in the Colonies, spending a good part of their salaries and pensions overseas, even though paid for by colonial taxpayers? And are they to receive higher salaries than Africans, even though for similar work? This is the most hardly-felt and pressing grievance among the African educated class. There are difficulties enough in solving it. In certain grades of work, European skill is still essential, but the type of European needed for this work could not be induced to go to Africa at much less than his present rate of pay. Yet if African salaries were raised to this high level, the local revenues would be quite unable to support the number of officials required. Remedies have, of course, been proposed —such as granting a basic rate of pay for every official of the same status and qualifications, but adding special expatriation allowances for the Europeans, paid for by the British Treasury. For Britain to pay the whole of European salaries would mean taking the control of these officials more than ever out of the hands of the local population. At least Africans should feel that every job in their own country is open to them, depending only on their own skill and merit, and that no one is being specially favoured by privileged rates of pay drawn from the taxpayers of the Colony.

We come, lastly, to the provision of capital for colonial development. There are those who would put this first, even in the democratic approach. But I feel that, unless it is accompanied from the start by the necessary democratic safeguards, the pouring in of capital will result in a barren and soulless "development," which may not be even in the economic interests of the many, let alone the social. I would even put the provision of capital lower on the list than our duty to cease extracting the existing wealth of Africa, because the wealth of mine and plantation and land is something which is the African's own, to which he has a right, without being beholden to anyone; whereas the provision of capital from outside carries in it always the dangerous seeds of outside economic domination. Nevertheless, a supply of capital equipment and skill from the richer countries to the poorer will continue for a time to be as necessary in Africa as it has been inside the U.S.S.R. How the wealth and knowledge and skill from the richer industrial areas at the centre were spread to the poorer periphery of the Soviet Union, thus knitting Russia together in an enthusiastic "commonwealth," is one of the great lessons which we in the British Empire have still to learn. It more than brings its own reward in the increased prosperity of the whole. But this has to be done without economic domination, without "philanthropy," and without the pauperization of the people it is designed to benefit. It will only ultimately be possible if the people have been allowed to develop their own political and economic strength, and are associated fully with the development of their territories.[1]

It is, therefore, a full and heavy task which Britain has before her, but what, in concrete terms, can the partnership of which we talk mean, if not this? If we plan and organize and develop everything according to our own wishes, we are not partners; and if we content ourselves with palliatives, or merely with holding the ring, we are not partners in any active sense either. But there is room and need for a real partnership, where Britain will give of her knowledge and democratic experience and superior skill and wealth; and where Africans will utilize the new opportunities opened to them, and so organize themselves as to develop their own lands in their own ways.

[1] The capital should be made available in the form of large public loans, at low rates of interest, and be administered through strengthened government departments or public utility agencies.

Some Considerations of Social Policy and its Cost
by A. CREECH JONES

The need of an accelerated policy of social reconstruction in the colonial empire to-day is recognized in all quarters and few reactionaries would challenge its importance. Squalid dependencies damage our prestige, assault our intelligence, deny our liberal sentiment, and menace our enlightened self-interest. Our self-esteem suffered when we were confronted with the grave reports from the West Indies and elsewhere in the years immediately before the war. The allegations against British policy and administration when Singapore fell troubled the national conscience. Recent American criticism, usually uninstructed, has been useful insofar as it has caused us to review the policies being pursued in the dependencies. Parliament has also shown impatience with the slow rate of change and has voted money for assisting schemes of welfare and development which are too costly for local colonial revenues to bear. Constructive trusteeship has become official and public opinion in Britain to-day.

It is hardly necessary to indicate how this change has come about. It is due to a number of influences, not the least of which is socialist analysis and advocacy. It should be remembered also that one important influence derives from officials in the field. The frustration of administrative and technical officers and others has caused not a few of them courageously to insist in confidential and public reports how hopeless were the tasks they were often expected to perform while the principles of colonial policy remained what they were. Grants-in-aid and the working of the Colonial Development Act of 1929 proved utterly inadequate for backward regions whose economic development had been slow, unprofitable and irrational, or whose economy was unbalanced and without regard to social wellbeing. The important Act of 1940 was an indication that a new approach and method were imperative if progress in the dependencies was to be made possible. So to-day, in most quarters, a plea is heard that economic and social development under conditions guaranteed by the Government should go forward more energetically. Development, however, must start from the standpoint that the primary consideration must be the social and economic welfare and happiness of the colonial peoples, and with that, the general interest of mankind.

There are difficulties in the way of building up social standards and achieving the economic progress which is universally recognized to-day as proper for the colonial peoples. The cost of such development is very considerable and that is a factor of some importance in any consideration given to the prospects of early achievements. What is the nature of the colonial problem? No formula adequately expresses it. Colonies obviously offer a complexity of problems which are seldom the same in any two territories, and which differ from colony to colony according to climate, natural resources, social development, alien penetration and contact, and other numerous physical, psychological, and cultural factors. What, however, is essential to attain in all colonial areas is responsibility and freedom, the eradication of ignorance and disease, the control of environment and the direction of natural and human forces to secure the basic conditions of good living.

Declarations of liberal and generous policy in the colonial field do not necessarily result in colonial progress. It should also be noted that ability to apply good policies is not always merely a matter of motive and will. Colonial affairs are more obstinate than that. It is important, therefore, to note that in the new conditions of the colonial scene, influences are at work awakening men's minds to demand of themselves new purposes and for themselves new conditions of living. Where that process has begun it is unlikely that communities will look back. By small beginnings in education and health we have contributed to it. The somewhat vague but potent influences working on men's minds everywhere to-day are unsettling and upsetting to colonial people and administrators alike. They produce hope and frustration, achievement and discouragement. Policy must now be conceived in terms of the new life and thought stirring in the world, and at the same time it must be both sympathetic and generous. But it must also be shaped in sternly practical terms and based on genuine knowledge.

The social conditions in many British colonies are a reflection on our past policy. We cannot escape the charge of neglect and indifference. But it is fair that our shortcomings should be considered in their historic setting, in relation to the growth of social ideas and economic change. Britain has, of course, some disreputable episodes in her colonial record. As an imperial power she could have done more in creating the conditions of material progress for the colonial peoples. That indifference has aggravated colonial problems to-day. Too much was left in the dependencies to the colonial executive, limited in its actions by political considerations and by inadequate local resources. When Britain assumed administrative responsibility in dependent areas, Governors were expected to hold the ring while trade penetrated and unregulated economic interests exploited natural wealth and labour. The result was often seen in the breaking down of indigenous societies and systems of living. Luckily, in some cases, enlightened men "on the spot" prevented the worst from happening.

It is relevant in this connection to remind ourselves that even when, in the colonies, the worst features of alien rule, of external financial and commercial domination, and of the uncontrolled exploitation of human labour and natural resources have been eradicated, great colonial regions may still remain poor, squalid, disease-ridden and ignorant, and, maybe, the prey to their own internal forces, and with no prospect of broad social development. The corollary of the liquidation of imperialism is therefore a sound policy of economic reconstruction and social welfare.

Another fact is often forgotten. The weakness and ignorance of many colonial people often explain their mishaps and condition: advantage was taken of them. But whatever the explanation and excuses offered for their condition, no practical effort to-day can afford to ignore the character and quality of the people whose advancement is wanted. Few persons dare venture to assess the quality and potentialities of any people in whatever stage of social development, but considerations of the character of a people are relevant in any estimate of the pace that can be made in accelerating their practice of direct responsibility in social and political affairs in the modern world. And while it is important and desirable that change should be made with goodwill and agreement, frequently progress is impeded as a result of consultation and collaboration with people who are ignorant and steeped in reactionary tradition.

But there are other considerations which should be weighed when social improvements are being sought. When services of social benefit are being created, how far can they be made to depend on the people's own effort and their co-operation? Should all necessary services in a community be sustained from a dependency's own resources, or how far should such services extend if economic resources cannot provide them? Is it practicable to call on British assistance and personnel without weakening colonial self-respect? These considerations will be answered variously in different places, but they are of some significance when social advance is being planned, and when, on the spot, the situation has to be sized and a line of action determined.

It is important that in the unfolding of colonial policy the self-respect of the people concerned should be preserved. Too much dependence on outside sources of income may not only sap integrity and responsibility, and possibly prejudice the growth of self-responsibility in government, but it may tend to weaken the moral fibre of a people, create a dependence which lessens self-respect and make people feel as "poor relations" inside the larger group. In the realities of the colonial scene, such matters are often difficult to handle. One thing, however, is certain. In the light of experience in many modern countries and the growth of modern scientific knowledge, much development can be quickened and telescoped, and considerable welfare secured at a rapid pace. Such change need not necessarily involve the muddle and waste which certain European countries suffered in their growth. Whether some of the waste, misery and ugliness which often accompany progress will occur in British colonial areas will depend in no small part on the degree of disinterested planning which Britain is prepared to commit herself to. British colonial success will undoubtedly be measured in terms of the co-operation that can be evoked from the colonial people concerned, and the manner in which these people are prepared to struggle for and contribute to the progress they want. It will depend in part on the equipment which can be supplied and which can be used by the people because of their appreciation of its value and significance to themselves. It will also depend on the provision made for health, education, and local autonomy, and how far natural and economic resources are capable of being developed in order to sustain improved standards of living and social life. Not least, success will depend on British ability to inspire in the people a great measure of social responsibility and moral integrity, and on British courage and restraint in helping the emergence of new leadership among the people. It cannot be emphasized enough that progress will not be attained by excess of admirable sentiment and sympathy or condoning the shortcomings of the colonial people; the respected leaders in the colonies to-day know that their people have a responsibility for change not less than that of Britain herself, and that it can only be discharged by their service, sacrifice, and integrity.

All the foregoing, are then, considerations concerned with the achievement of social progress. But what is the help which must be forthcoming from Britain if, in most colonies, any big and important forward steps are to be effectively taken? The assistance necessary is not only a matter of personnel, technical knowledge, research, and advice and guidance, but also of capital and grants. The idea has been abandoned that no direct financial assistance should be given from the British exchequer, except on occasion to make good unavoidable deficiencies in the revenue. Some Colonial Governments still seem reluctant to resort to London for the balancing of their budgets, and the ideal seems still to be to them that an equilibrium should be maintained between local revenue and expenditure. But, while it is desirable that a colony should exercise financial prudence and not live by grants-in-aid and loans from outside, further substantial development is hardly possible without external help. Nigeria has, for practical purposes, stagnated in social and economic development for many years because it could not afford to buy the reconstruction and economic changes her Government knew to be necessary. Under the Colonial Development Act of 1929 she was only able to receive, in spite of her pressing needs and great population, less than a quarter of a million pounds. Writing in 1939, Sir Alan Pim pointed out that comparative financial stability had been secured to British African tropical territories only by a total expenditure by Britain in grants-in-aid of approximately £12,174,000 to which should be added £2,654,000 received through the 1929 Act. This latter is a small sum for development for which the territories were unable to borrow, but it reveals how difficult dependencies found it to carry on at all, let alone advance. It should be added that in 1940 some of the debts which had accumulated in the past, and were beyond the capacity of the poorest colonies to meet, were taken over by the Imperial Government.

The 1929 Act contributed £8,875,000 to British dependencies —£3,203,000 by way of loan and £5,672,000 by way of grant. The estimated expenditure on the schemes assisted was £19,285,000, which had to be found by the Governments concerned out of their own revenues or by loans. The Act, however, proved of least value to dependencies where the finances were weakest and the need for assistance greatest. It was primarily concerned with economic development and not social services. Undoubtedly, it assisted a limited amount of material development: for 30 per cent of the gifts and loans was granted to assist internal transport and communications, 10 per cent water supplies and water power, 16 per cent public health, £600,000 (7 per cent) scientific research, £770,000 (9 per cent) developing mineral resources, £534,000 (6 per cent) agriculture development, £991,000 (11 per cent) harbours, fisheries, forestry and surveys; £444,000 (5 per cent) land reclamation and drainage, and £164,000 (2 per cent) electricity.

But the terms of the 1929 Act were such that the £1,000,000 annually available in the Development Fund each year could not be absorbed. The restrictions imposed on schemes involving long term recurrent expenditure were too onerous. A distinction was drawn between expenditure on development and that of an ordinary administrative kind, or of a recurrent nature which should normally be met from the ordinary resources of a colony. How could colonies entertain schemes when there appeared no reasonable ground for anticipating that they would be in a position to meet from their own resources the subsequent necessary cost of maintenance and upkeep? Obviously, if they could not find these costs, the initial capital expenditure would be wasted. The Act, however, had this merit: it attached importance to substantial participation by the Colonial Governments in the financial obligations involved in any scheme assisted from imperial funds. It thereby secured their interest in its effective and economical carrying out.

To-day, under the 1940 Act, it is not suggested that Britain should open her coffers and without restraint give great sums for creating and sustaining vast new services, and for welfare and economic development generally. The colonial people do not feel that way, and the most enlightened amongst them recognize that they should not be spoonfed, and that they should make contributions to costs within their capacity, and carry what burden they can in respect to any development and service they know to be necessary. Nevertheless, we should be generous. Western civilization needs sometimes to be reminded that it has a debt to meet in respect of some of the backward areas. Colonies have often been exploited as "possessions" for their wealth and resources; and both colonial wealth and the colonial people have contributed in a material way to Western progress. For many years there has also been a contribution from the profits of colonial enterprise to the national revenue of Britain. Dependencies also have their uses in any system of world security.

The fact is, of course, that the condition of vast colonial areas is utterly bad; the equipment is so poor, the ignorance and poverty are so great that without aid from outside no start can be made. The pump cannot be primed or any substantial advance achieved. In many colonies, the foundations of social policy are hardly as yet, laid. It is therefore more than a sentimental gesture of the nation when it asserts that colonial policy in the social and economic fields should be made more positive and constructive. It is a mood that will cost a great deal of money.

Nevertheless, investment in good health and education and economic development is, on a long view, profitable not only in the human, but also in the material sense. By building up the quality and standard of living, new consumption is stimulated, new markets are opened, there are demands for products which cannot be made in the colony, and employment in Britain and the colonies is expanded.

The commitment of Britain to guide and help financially in the rebuilding of colonial life was appraised in 1940 at about £5,500,000 a year. But it has often been acknowledged that this is only part of our liability. The Royal Commission to the West Indies reported in 1940, and formulated plans for which £1,000,000 a year may be required. In this welfare and development work the cost to the dependencies themselves will be considerable, apart from British grants, even if only a proportion of the "urgencies" are provided over a longish time schedule. Some changes cannot of course be hurried, but some of the first in any list of priorities are in cost well beyond the present capacity of most colonies to bear. And it may prove in the long run wise and politic that development should not extravagantly

SOCIAL POLICY AND ITS COST

overreach the economic capacity of a colony to sustain it, should external revenue be no longer obtainable.

Some colonial revenues could, of course, be increased to some extent. In a number of colonies, only a start in direct taxation has as yet been made, and there are untapped sources of revenue and classes of both alien and native people who should be required to pay more for their privileges and security. Nevertheless, it is broadly true that most colonies are very poor, and cannot do much for themselves. With their present limited resources, the unpalatable fact may have to be faced that, because of the limitations on British financial contributions and capacities, some of the colonial peoples will have to be content for a time with comparatively poor standards of living and remuneration in order to sustain and develop the services they require. They will have to tolerate for a time, many fundamental services that are inferior and less adequate than those enjoyed in many parts of Western Europe.

British aid and capital in any case are essential. Some local Colonial Governments have done what they could in making a beginning with the framework of public works and services necessary for better social living. Others would have done better. The social services everywhere are inadequate and patchy, though much excellent work is being done. In some respects British enterprise in the colonies looks less bold and imaginative than the enterprise of some other colonial powers. Capital from Britain has flowed only in a narrow stream compared with the flow necessary to provide the public works and economic and social developments essential. Also grants for social development to improve standards and get reforms working have been slender. The colonies are consequently confronted in the emerging conditions of the modern world with the need of desperately urgent services involving enormous expenditure.

I do not propose to indicate these vast needs. Copious evidence exists in published reports and governmental statements. It is not only a matter of immediate expenditure on the varied and overwhelming needs, but also a question of the inadequacy of trained staffs and professional personnel, most of whom cannot now be quickly and easily supplied. The present educational basis in the colonies is too narrow. There are also too few laboratories and insufficient research in all fields of social and economic life. In medicine, for instance, medical training is inadequate, specialization too restricted, hospitals and dispensaries are insufficient, and preventive work is hopelessly inadequate. Organized campaigns against insects and water-borne and infectious diseases are urgently necessary. Health, too, is linked with housing, sanitation, water supply, diet, labour conditions, and, particularly in tropical climates, with agriculture, forestry, and veterinary measures. All these things involve heavy capital expenditure.

The technical and administrative officers of the colonial services have been asked, particularly in recent years, to make bricks without straw, to achieve results without staffs and technical assistance, to expand without capital and funds and to carry on in many cases where populations are illiterate and ignorant, and in areas with very slight administrative structure and apparatus. They work to-day often with indifferently trained people, in climates that sap vitality and create ill-health, in conditions which constantly frustrate. They can only touch the fringe of the vast problems compelling attention. There are still great colonial areas where life is lived in the most primitive conditions, where people are profoundly ignorant, living in the hovels of the bush, with no water supplies within many miles, with a margin of existence incredibly low, with no possessions except a few pots and primitive tools, with their soil impoverished and infertile, and they themselves suffering from disease and malnutrition. Every need is interlocked, and every reform urgently calls to be done at one and the same time —preventive and curative medicine, improved agriculture and water supplies, better housing and nutrition, more communications and markets, education and community services, and an infinite number of other things.

As we have noted, the colonies have not been able to provide the capital themselves. Too much wealth is taken from them that they have little surpluses for internal development. So far, private capital has been invested in little more than mining or in wealth that was accessible and readily exploitable. In the predominantly agricultural colonies money invested is mainly public capital, though private investment has been made in colonies where plantations or wage employment (usually at low levels) was possible. Conditions in colonies with few roads, poor transport, few ports, no sanitation, bad health, do not attract private capital—without these public works by public investment, private enterprise, except in unusual cases, is cautious and not easily tempted. Public investment in the past has been mainly concerned with establishing a framework of communications and necessary public works and an administrative organization. On the other hand, in earlier years, private capital was seldom able to carry the cost of administering and developing the territories for which it had responsibility. Its object was not the organizing of constructive activities but profitable and quick returns.

The 1940 Act makes provision for some of the capital required for development. What also is needed is more direct help to guarantee loans, and loans free of interest charge. Such facilities must be conceded cautiously so as to avoid any weakening of colonial financial responsibility. Already the Crown Agents provide facilities for the colonies for right management and repayment of colonial loans; and such loans become trustee securities under the Colonial Stock Acts.

We have seen that the colonies have not been able to provide the revenue for the services they require because their income has been dependent on countries that are undeveloped and poorly equipped. The prevailing standards of production are often primitive, economic activities are uncontrolled, and industries hardly existent. Moreover the steady drain of wealth year in and year out from the colonies means that capital cannot accumulate for savings and economic development. It also means that too little wealth can be distributed to build up better standards, and that in turn means loss in markets, miserable social services, small industrial development, and no capital equipment.

Development has depended on the ability of an area to attract investment for profitable rates. Consequently, great regions need roads and bridges, rural housing and village communities, irrigation and water supplies, transport and sanitary services, health services, and an infinite list of utilities involving enormous expenditure. And fundamental to them all is health and education. Even in education, the liquidation of mass illiteracy and the founding of modest educational systems for the children of school age involve incredibly large sums which the immediate resources of few colonies in their existing condition can command. Estimates of some such reforms and developments have been made by many Colonial Governments, and their totals are formidably high.

It is well that such tough facts as these should be looked in the face. Colonial economy ought not to be built up on the simple assumption that loans and grants will always be forthcoming from Britain. The local resources must be developed as well. If proper social services are to be provided, a review of the existing economic arrangements in most colonial areas seems called for. Colonial economics have received too little study in the past, and insufficient thought has been given as to how standards can be raised and economic activities contributing to colonial wellbeing stimulated. In fact, economic activities in colonial regions have until comparatively recently seldom been primarily concerned with the welfare of the colonial people themselves. Their economic problems have been approached from the wrong end. Consequently the economy of colonial areas has often become lopsided, while interests have been created and conserved which have distorted the life and severely reacted on the economic growth and social advance of the peoples concerned.

A résumé of some of the adjustments which might be brought

SOCIAL POLICY AND ITS COST

about to aid colonies in finding the means for meeting their social services can only be briefly sketched. It is the case that often too big a proportion of the revenue of a colony is used to meet charges which are paid outside its frontiers, such as high rates of interest on past loans (which have been borrowed not always in the interests of the indigenous people, and at best only to their indirect advantage). Sometimes, charges are in respect of services which could with advantage be borne by the metropolitan country, such as official overseas allowances, passages and pensions. Of the revenue of Nigeria, for instance, a third went out of the country each year. Similarly in the Gold Coast a proportion as high was also transferred each year. Nigeria pays each year a considerable sum to British officials, a substantial proportion of which is spent out of the country in the way of provisions, leave, equipment, and families overseas. The Nigerian budget in 1937–38 showed that £1,876,336 was paid to European officials (in the way of salaries, personal allowances, gratuities and pensions); £1,067,050 was paid in the U.K. in pensions, family allotments, and leave pay; and £100,000 to a shipping company for passages of officials and wives.

At the same time, direct taxation contributed too little to revenue. It is obviously desirable that all companies operating in colonies should be registered in the colony and/or London, in order that all should bear tax at a rate not less onerous than that imposed on the companies that are registered in London. Also, that part of British income tax on the profits of colonial enterprise registered in London, and retained in Britain, should be transferred to the colony. As the technique of direct taxation is mastered, and untapped resources made known, direct taxation in respect of all economic enterprise should be developed more and more in the colonies.

In colonial areas it often is the case that no substantial proportion of the value of the wealth exploited accrues to the advantage of the area. That happens frequently, with minerals; in respect, for instance, of royalty payments and the profits of enterprise, e.g., copper in Northern Rhodesia, and tin in Nigeria. Up to 1938–39 £1,700,000 was paid in royalties to the Royal Niger Company in addition to £865,000 paid by way of compensation in 1899. The Nigerian Government has thus paid twice as much as the U.K. Government has paid, and yet there are still between fifty and sixty years of future royalties to be paid. Other instances can be quoted. Again, as Native authorities increase and control their treasuries, royalties and mineral income received by them should be safeguarded for public use.

Another source of income might be by means of levies on the value of suitable export products, as, for instance, cocoa in the Gold Coast. The cotton cess imposed in Uganda is a graded charge levied on the price of cotton down to a certain figure, and this income has been of general benefit to the Protectorate. Fiscal taxes should be imposed only with care, or the balance of economy may be upset in favour of particular imports and exports at the expense of living standards. Exports encouraged by the import of tawdry goods when serviceable goods could be equally well manufactured in the colony and local materials used, militates against the internal development of a colony and its greater internal stability.

Fundamental, also, is the question of the price paid to small farmers and the primary producers and the protection of their markets. The periodic crash of world prices and markets can be averted by international action, through commodity schemes controlled or permitted by Governments. The effects of failure of crops can be counteracted by exercising foresight, building up reserves of stocks, and equalizing arrangements over periods as between good and bad years. Again, by the guarantee of steady prices, and with Government buying, and the development of co-operative enterprise, middlemen and useless agents can be eliminated and some improvement in the conditions of peasant producers be secured. Agricultural development with ancillary co-operative practice is of vast importance in eradicating debt, extending credit and the use of machinery, in buying seeds, in grading and marketing. The better provision of water,

SOCIAL POLICY AND ITS COST

the development of collectivist farming in certain areas, the extension of mixed farming and control of animal and vegetable diseases are all calculated to increase the wealth of the country and the taxable potentiality of its people. The world now appreciates that in addition to national action in respect of commodities there must be international action for the regulation of prices, quotas and markets, and provision made for international storage and distribution.

Commercial and mining enterprises, many of which are reaping much profit, should be brought under greater public control. They should pay more respect to public needs and services, and show a greater sense of public responsibility in respect of their enterprise. Some of these big interests exercise, by the methods of their operations, a banal effect on the economic life of important areas. Many concerns could increase their efficiency and the wealth of a colony by better production methods and by improved welfare arrangements. Better housing and medical provision ought also to be arranged, and some regard shown for disturbance to people and families brought about by their operations. Many mining firms have, of course, done much in these directions, but some, making considerable profits, are insensible to social needs, and only responsive to the creation of profits for shareholders.

The introduction of a money economy, the effects of taxation, and the increase of industrial and mining enterprise and plantation labour have created in many colonial areas large numbers of persons in employment and dependent on wages, either all the year through, or for part of each year. The wages paid are usually very low and inadequate for the elementary and increasing necessities of life. A higher standard of remuneration in most wage-earning employment is imperative, if better living standards are to be reached. Such improvements in income would increase both production and efficiency, and add to the demand for goods. An effort is being made to-day for the establishment of small industries for supplying local needs, personal household wants and everyday things. Processing industries connected with primary products are also being considered. The need for more balanced economies against excessive export production is imperative, and there is scope in most colonies for new enterprise. Such a policy calls, of course, for careful economic planning.

There is reason to believe that with planned economies, including effective control of disease of plant, animal and man, and control of irrational and wasteful exploitation of natural resources, with the provision of water, health, education, and cheap communications, with proper surveys and controlled concessions in mining, with direct taxation and reliefs on loans and other Government charges, and with a wide extension of mutual aid and co-operation in agriculture, the establishment of small industries for the supply and distribution of household needs and stores, more wealth could be created in the colonies and higher living standards and taxable capacity be secured. In the long run the revenue for the necessary services of a colony might be found in the colony's own resources. Such is a longish and difficult policy, but it can be hastened by the deliberate application of scientific knowledge and by Britain "priming the pump." The co-operation of the colonial peoples must, however, be secured. Their effort, contribution and understanding are necessary for these changes to be brought about.

It is important to keep in mind that social and economic development is the necessary condition of freedom and independence. The mere declaration of freedom is of no avail if the people of a territory are too weak, too poor, and too inexperienced to stand on their own feet. In this insecure world of power politics, small peoples are, of themselves, likely to be unable to maintain independence and meet the needs of defence and economic stability. Yet, they must be helped to pay their way and sustain the fabric of civilized life. They must know how to work political institutions and engage in administration. But these things depend on the development of the resources of a territory, and the growth of economic organization and sound social conditions. It means that there must be achieved a wide advance in education and the conditions for preserving important social services and standards of living. The alternative to absolute independence is their integration in some wider regional grouping or imperial organization in which something of their individual sovereignty is surrendered to achieve wider collaboration and effective authority, and to attain the assistance which comes from the stronger and wealthier parts of the organization. Unconditional subsidies sap, in the long run, integrity and self-reliance, but on these qualities, freedom and real independence depend.

The importance in some areas of international collaboration and regional planning in assisting colonial development and economies in services has not been discussed in this essay. Its possibilities and difficulties are discussed in a Fabian pamphlet.[1] Many services in the administrative, economic and scientific spheres can be organized more efficiently and cheaply on a wider basis than the limitations of separated colonies make possible. Problems of health and labour, agricultural disease and pests, communications, soil conservation and irrigation, are usually not problems of a single territory, but are relevant over big areas. Inside the colonial empire, the very smallness and poverty of many territories make it difficult for them to tackle their own services effectively, even with aid from outside. Indeed, without adjusted frontiers and closer financial association and, in certain cases, some kind of federation, financial sufficiency is hardly possible.

The problems of colonial development and welfare are hardly measured as yet. Their solution calls for much time, patience, faith, energy and money. The immediate and ultimate effects of the impact of war are as yet only dimly perceived. European disaster in the Far East, the association in the theatres of war of white and black in common danger, the modification of colour conventions to meet new production and military needs, the wide participation by colonial peoples in defence and civic

[1] "International Action and the Colonies." Report to the Fabian Colonial Bureau (1s.).

responsibility necessitated by war, the enlistment of coloured troops for campaigning a long way from their own country with the provision of good food, clothing, health and welfare, not to speak of educational facilities—all these and many such factors must have an incalculable effect on the future of the dependencies. The new life stirring in the colonies and the liberal sentiment abroad in the world, should overcome the interests and obstacles which block the way to the realization of that partnership which has been described so eloquently in the pressure of war and in the noble declarations of many British statesmen.

The Political Advance of Backward Peoples

By LEONARD WOOLF

The backward peoples of the Colonial Empire are to be found mainly in Africa, though there are also some in the Pacific islands. This essay will therefore be mainly concerned with the fourteen African colonies which contain a population of nearly 50,000,000 Africans. The vast majority belong to the category of primitive or backward peoples; they live in primitive and often tribal societies; they are uneducated and illiterate, terribly poor, and ravaged by the major tropical diseases. They are incapable in their present condition of dealing intelligently and efficiently with the political and economic problems which the impact of European civilization, and particularly the economic system of Europe, is imposing upon them. Ever since the partition of Africa in the last century and their incorporation within the British Empire, they have been subject to British rule and administration, and except in purely local or tribal matters, they have had no say in the determination or management of their own affairs.[1]

This essay deals with a single question: what is to be the political future of these peoples? Is it our intention to keep them permanently in a state of complete political tutelage or eventually to give them self-government? And if our goal is the government of Africans by Africans, what are the stages and training which we envisage for the transition from political subjection to political responsibility?

Most of these colonies were acquired and were incorporated in the Empire during the second half of the nineteenth century, and it was during the same period that the main structure of

[1] As regards the recent developments of "indirect rule" in Nigeria, this statement will be considered by many people to need qualification. The subject will be dealt with below.

government and administration to be applied to such colonies was determined. In Britain it was an era in which liberal ideas, which ever since the French Revolution had been regarded by the governing classes generally with fear and disgust, at last acquired the social respectability which is a highly efficient instrument invented by governing classes for sterilizing dangerous ideas. Liberal doctrine required that people should be free and that peoples should enjoy self-government or responsible government. If they were uncivilized and therefore incapable of self-government they could and should providentially be ruled by Englishmen until such time as they became civilized and capable of managing their own affairs. These were the ideas which moulded the theory and practice of colonial government in its early days, and they were reinforced by historical memory and events connected with those British colonies inhabited not by primitive coloured peoples, but by white emigrants from the Mother Country. No people have a longer or profounder historical memory than we have and we have never forgotten how and why we lost our American colonies. Our treatment of what are now the Dominions was largely determined by the lessons which we learnt from George III, Lord North, and Edmund Burke. Canada, Australia, and New Zealand passed inevitably, so it seemed, from tutelage to freedom, from the government of Downing Street through self-government to responsible government. So it had been ordained by Providence who in the nineteenth century had clearly become a Liberal, if not a member of the Liberal Party.

The Crown Colony type of government, which is prevalent in our African territories, is the direct result of these historical events and political ideas. The day to day administration is carried on by a British Civil Servant. Above him are the Governor and central government, to whom he is responsible and whose orders and ordinances he has to carry out. Below him are the Africans whom he rules paternally through a native staff, emirs, chiefs, courts, and native councils or tribal organization, as the case may be. The central government has as its head a Governor,

THE POLITICAL ADVANCE OF BACKWARD PEOPLES 87

who is responsible to the Secretary of State, who in his turn is responsible to Parliament. Normally there are attached to the Governor two Councils, one Executive and the other Legislative. It is in these Councils that are to be found the peculiar features of Crown Colony government and the effects of history and political psychology referred to in the preceding paragraph. Everywhere else in the structure and machinery of colonial government the system is a paternal despotism; the Executive and Legislative Councils are definitely intended to be embryos of a parliamentary system and of self-government. The theory has always been that by changes in the constitution of the Legislative Council and so of the central government the passage from a paternal despotism to full responsible government could be made in stages. The first stage is a Council consisting entirely of official and nominated members; the second is a Council consisting of both official and nominated and elected members, the elected members being in a minority; the third is a Council consisting of official, nominated, and elected members, the elected members being in a majority, but certain subjects being reserved; the fourth and final stage is a Council consisting of elected members to whom Ministers forming a Cabinet or Government are responsible for the entire administration without reservation, the Governor being reduced to the position of the King in the British or the Governor-General in the Dominion system and the Civil Service being responsible to the Ministers.

Throughout the nineteenth century and well into the twentieth few, if any, people who were concerned with the practice or problems of imperial government would have denied that in theory the goal in every British Crown Colony, no matter how primitive, was complete self-government and that it was to be attained by modifications in the central government in stages, as described in the previous paragraph. In recent years there has been a distinct change in communal psychology in regard to these questions. The nineteenth century Liberal assumed that the goal in African colonies was self-government, and therefore admitted theoretically that the African would ultimately be as capable as the European of managing his own affairs and of enjoying the blessings of freedom and democracy. It is true that this theory had practically no effect upon practice. The lesser breeds were obviously at present incapable of managing their own affairs, and as little or nothing was done, as we shall see, to make them more capable, they remained under the paternal tutelage of Britons and would presumably be content indefinitely to continue under it. But during the last twenty-five or thirty years events in India, Ceylon, and even on the African west coast have shown that the subject peoples of the British Empire, whether Asiatic or African, are not prepared to wait indefinitely for freedom and democracy. The day when the African in colonial territory would, like the Indian, demand complete self-government, might be distant, but the question of his future political status could no longer be completely ignored. Moreover, consciously or unconsciously, events in a British Dominion, the Union of South Africa, complicated the problem and profoundly influenced opinion. The political status of the African in the Union was one of the major problems in South African politics, and South African opinion was overwhelmingly in favour of ensuring that the African should permanently have a status, political and social, which was inferior to that of the white man. In actual practice this has resulted in a policy of partial segregation and of denying to the South African native the democratic right to political or economic equality with the white man. This development in the Union's theory and practice has had a profound effect in colonial territories where there is a white minority, e.g., in Kenya and the Rhodesias, but indirectly it has had a considerable influence also upon the general postulates and the ideals of British colonial policy.

There are now many people who, either explicitly or implicitly, no longer accept the liberal assumption that African and other primitive peoples are capable of developing into "civilized" communities on an equality with those of white men, of learning the art of democracy, and of being gradually trained in the technique of self-government. The view finds expression in different forms. Some people, particularly white settlers in such colonies as Kenya, openly follow the South African example and demand that a few thousand settlers shall be given full responsible government, while the inferiority and political incapacity of the Africans shall be recognized by denying them any political rights and segregating them in Reserves from which they are only allowed to emerge if the white men require them to labour for wages. Other people, who do not openly take this extreme view and would, in some cases, probably repudiate it, in effect unconsciously make certain assumptions which would lead in practice to much the same results, namely the permanent imposition of an inferior social status, both political and economic, upon Africans and a permanent denial to them of democratic rights and self-government. The fundamental assumption is that Africans are "different" from white men, and by different they mean psychologically different and inferior, so that they are constitutionally incapable of acquiring the knowledge and understanding necessary for the political administration and the economic organization of every country in the complicated and integrated society of the modern world.

In some of its forms this assumption that the African is naturally inferior, uncivilized, and incapable of enjoying the democracy and freedom of western civilization is peculiarly insidious in its effect upon colonial policy because it is concealed in views about education and government which are extremely "advanced" and "up-to-date" and which, in the modern fashion, claim to be scientific because they are mixed up with one of the sciences, in this case anthropology. Thus it has become fashionable to maintain that our whole colonial and imperial policy has hitherto—thanks largely to Macaulay—been mistaken in trying to turn Asiatics and Africans into Europeans; what we should aim at is to do everything in our power to preserve the native culture and way of life, encouraging "progress" only so far as it is compatible with the social customs and institutions of the tribe, people or race for whose good and government we are responsible. In order to know what exactly the native culture, social customs, and institutions are which are to form the framework of his administration, the administrator must go to the anthropologist, and thus having behind them the authority of a science, policy and administration can now claim to be scientific and therefore, to all intents and purposes, infallible. This scientific, Africanizing attitude affects policy in various ways. In its extreme form it leads to an effort on the part of the administrator to preserve each native or tribal unit, with all their variations of customs and institutions, intact like a museum piece, insulated as far as possible from any of the disturbing and disintegrating influences of western or European civilization. It is extremely doubtful whether such an attempt to isolate and mummify African society in the closely integrated and explosive world of the twentieth century can possibly be successful; it might have been possible to keep savage Africa virgin and savage—if that be a reasonable object of government —if the governments had not let in the copper mining companies, the soap makers, the gold diggers, the cocoa buyers, and the white planters, but those who think that in an Africa which has already been moulded for half a century by these apostles of western civilization the Africans can be forced or cajoled into leading the life of noble savages—in the eighteenth century sense—are making the same mistake as those well-meaning mediaevalist enthusiasts who think that by exhorting English villagers to use spinning wheels and do poker work an oasis of arts and crafts can be preserved in the desert of the machine age.

Another aspect of this Africanizing attitude is to be found in the sphere of educational policy. The policy of developing the African on his own, and not on European, lines has led many of its adherents to maintain that education on western lines is unsuitable for Africans. In its extreme form this view is concisely expressed in a sentence quoted in Lord Hailey's *An African Survey* from the South African *Report of the Interdepartmental Committee on Native Education:* "The education of the white child prepares him for life in a dominant society, and the education of the black child for a subordinate society." If the native is subordinate and is to remain subordinate, all he requires is a certain amount of elementary education in a vernacular and such vocational education as is suitable to his inferior economic status. This, as I said, is the extreme view held by the white men in South Africa, Kenya, and Rhodesia who regard white men as a Herrenvolk and whose policy is directed to maintaining the political and economic ascendancy of the Herrenvolk. But in less crude forms the view has in fact determined the policy of many who favour vernacular rather than English as the language of education for Africans, who would limit them as far as possible to elementary and "vocational" education, and who would reduce to a minimum their opportunities of higher education.

Lastly we come to the vexed problem of "indirect rule." In recent years indirect rule has become the fashionable policy in British colonial Africa. The system consists in using or creating native institutions as the organs of government, so that the European official does not rule the Africans directly, but indirectly through native authorities. It is usually maintained that the system was invented by Lord Lugard in Nigeria. It is true that, thanks to Lord Lugard, Nigeria has provided the most highly developed and deliberate experiment in indirect rule and that it has had a considerable influence upon our policy in other African territories. But in the broadest sense the system is not a modern invention. Politically, the British are incorrigibly opportunist, and the Crown Colony type of government, though fundamentally paternal and authoritarian, has always at the same time had a tendency to rule "indirectly" by preserving, creating, and using native institutions. Forty years ago, when I was a district officer in Ceylon, my rule was no doubt to a large extent "direct," but in the villages it was also to a large extent indirect, for I ruled indirectly through the native authorities, the headmen and the Gansabhawa or native court. The same was true in nearly all British Crown colonies, including the African. The difference between such opportunist use of native institutions and the modern system of indirect rule in Africa is, however, considerable. For the modern system is not only a method, but a theory of government. Its adherents are committed to the policy of deliberately preserving or even creating purely native institutions and "authorities" and of "ruling" through them. The effect upon the African and his society will depend upon how we intend to use and develop this kind of administration. But it is clear that it can very easily become a powerful instrument of policy for those who hold that the African is incapable of democratic self-government of the western type and must be content indefinitely with an inferior political and economic status. Whether indirect rule is to be used as an instrument of "progress" or social fossilization and mummification will depend upon such questions as these: Who are the native authorities? Are they authoritarian or are they subject to control by the people? What in practice is the relation between the white administrator and the native authority? How is the native authority, which is an organ of local government, integrated with the central government, the Governor and his Executive and Legislative Councils?

These are some of the strands of political thought which are having an important influence upon the evolution of our colonial policy in Africa. No reasonable person will deny that in each of them there is considerable sound sense and truth. The services which the science of anthropology might render to the African administrator are immense, That the administrator should seek to know and understand the social structure upon which he has to work and that he should build for the future upon African society and institutions, as they exist to-day, is an admirable programme. It can also be agreed that our object in Africa should be to produce good Africans, not tenth rate imitations of fifth-rate Europeans. And we shall not achieve that by giving to a small minority of the population a smattering of English education. All this may he admitted. But the fundamental question remains: Is our main object to be the training of our African subjects in democracy and self-government so that eventually they may be able to manage their own affairs in their own way? If that is our aim, we do in fact hold that the African is not constitutionally or racially inferior to the white man and that he is perfectly capable, if he is given the opportunity, the education, and the necessary economic conditions, of taking his place as a free man in a free African community in the modern world. If on the other hand we take the South African view that the African is and should remain socially, politically, economically, and intellectually the white man's inferior, then we should say what we mean and face the consequences; we mean that we have abandoned the policy of democratic self-government for Africans, and our educational policy, anthropology, indirect rule are simply methods of providing a permanent social structure and form of government for people who will never grow up and who will always remain "backward," the wards and subjects of civilized Europeans.

I have not the space in this essay to discuss the question whether the African is so inferior psychologically that he cannot learn the technique of western civilization and form a self-governing community or the further question whether democratic freedom is desirable—to do so would require a book or two books. I can therefore only state my own opinion on these two questions in order to make it quite clear upon what assumptions the remainder of this essay is based. I believe, as Pericles, Montaigne, and Voltaire believed, that freedom is an essential part of civilization. A free man is better than a slave, no matter under what euphemism the latter conceals his lack of freedom, and a community of free men is better than a community of slaves or subjects. This fact is not altered by the colour of men's skins, hair, or eyes. Freedom is no less desirable in Africa than it is in Britain, and the lack or destruction of it is as ugly in Kenya as it is in Berlin. Without political freedom a community of free men is impossible and so far in its four thousand years of history the human race has found no road to freedom except by some form of democratic government. It follows that the ultimate aim of our colonial government in Africa should be, as our fathers thought, democratic self-government of Africa and Africans by Africans. There is only one fact which could invalidate that conclusion, namely, if it were true that Africans belong to a race so inferior morally and intellectually that they are incapable of acquiring the knowledge, experience, and moral qualities necessary for self-government in the modern world. There is in my opinion absolutely no evidence of any such racial incapacity.

If these premises be accepted, it follows that a primary duty of the Colonial Office and of British administrations in Africa should be to train the native inhabitants in each colony in democratic self-government so that they may at the earliest possible moment take over the administration of their own countries, and at every stage in this process to give to Africans the maximum amount of self-government of which they are capable. No real attempt has ever been made by us to perform this duty. That this is so is evident, as soon as one considers, as I now propose to do, the steps which would be necessary for fulfilling our obligations.

The vast majority of Africans are illiterate and uneducated. Their lives are to a considerable extent determined by the social and economic forces of European civilization, which is no longer European, but oecumenical. The Africans, like every one else in the world, are no longer capable of dealing with these forces and so of regulating their own lives and the life of their community, unless they understand the forces themselves and the world order from which they derive. They are totally incapable in their present condition of doing any such thing and we have done nothing in our African colonies to make them capable of doing it. One fact alone will show the position. We have governed Kenya for nearly half a century and in Kenya there are three million Africans. There is also a Legislative Council and on that Council are members nominated by the Governor to represent the interests of the Africans. But he nominates not Africans, but Europeans. And the reason given for this extraordinary position is still more extraordinary, namely, that after fifty years of British rule out of three million Africans there is not one single man sufficiently intelligent and educated to speak for them in the Council. And the reason why there is no such African is that the Kenya Government has never attempted to give Africans the opportunity of acquiring the knowledge and education necessary for a member of a Legislative Council.

If we accept the obligation to introduce democratic self-government at the earliest possible moment in our African colonies, our colonial policy will require radical reform in two directions, in the nature and extent of education and in the structure of administration and government. First with regard to education. In the whole world there is to-day no country, no town, no village which can isolate itself and live its life as a self-contained social unit; each is closely integrated in a complicated political and economic world system. The government of these villages, towns, and countries cannot be efficiently carried on unless those who direct or influence policy have some understanding of the world system of which they form a part and of the political and economic forces whose impact must continually be felt in the ordinary lives of ordinary people. When in the League Covenant it was stated that such "backward peoples" as inhabit African colonies are "not yet able to stand by themselves under the strenuous conditions of the modern world," the framers of the Covenant were drawing attention to this fundamental fact, namely that these backward peoples are not yet able to stand by themselves, are incapable of self-government, because they do not possess the knowledge or understanding necessary for self-government in the modern world. In the seventeenth and even eighteenth centuries the inhabitants of most villages in the world could manage their own affairs in their own way quite efficiently if their knowledge of the world was limited to an understanding of how the village pump worked; to-day, those responsible for the administration of a remote village in an African jungle will find that they cannot perform their task efficiently unless they possess some knowledge of, say, the working of the complicated economic machine in Wall Street or Lombard Street. That means that an illiterate and uneducated people are totally incapable of self-government under modern conditions.

It follows that a colonial government which really makes democratic self-government its goal must educate the Africans. Universal elementary education is a *sine qua non* of modern democracy. But elementary education is only the beginning, it is not the end of education. If Africans are to manage their own affairs, they must be given the knowledge of western civilization without which such management is impossible. That means the existence of a substantial minority with higher education on western lines. It means, too, an enormous increase of opportunity for Africans to train themselves as skilled workers, technicians, scientists, doctors, engineers, civil servants. Unless we are able to introduce in our African colonies an immediate, large-scale educational programme of this kind, our professions that the goal of our policy is self-government are dishonest, for we shall not have taken the first step necessary for making self-government possible.

But a programme of education is in itself not enough. It will take more than one generation to produce by education a sufficient number of educated Africans to make self-government possible. But that is no reason for postponing the practical training of the people in self-government until you have a population with the standard of education necessary for full self-government. In the last resort, the only way to learn to do anything is to do it, and this applies as much to government as to surgery or tight-rope walking. The training of the African in democracy and self-government must be gradual, but it should be deliberate and should begin at once. It should begin in the sphere of local government. Here we come back once more to the question of indirect rule. The system of indirect rule can be used as a highly efficient instrument for training Africans in

THE POLITICAL ADVANCE OF BACKWARD PEOPLES 97

local self-government, but only on one condition. It is not enough to use, develop, or create tribal or native institutions and authorities and then hand over to them power or the simulacrum of power. A native authority which in fact consists of an autocratic tribal chief or emir, discreetly impelled by a District Officer to establish a police force and drains, is not an emblem of democratic self-government. There is everything to be said for developing and creating native authorities as the organs of local government, but if they are to be instruments of training Africans in the art of self-government, they must be fundamentally democratic in the western sense. That means that the organs of indirect rule, the native "Authorities," must themselves be directly responsible to the native peoples; they must be democratized. Such democratic responsibility in local government is not foreign to the African mind or political institutions, as is shown by many features of tribal organization. In developing local government and co-operative institutions on these lines and in using them as a social and political training ground there is an immense field for immediate work open to our colonial administrations.

Finally we come to the question of the central government. Our nineteenth century ancestors showed sound political judgment in their conviction that the ultimate test of self-government will be found in the centre. The experience of India teaches the same lesson, for the question whether Indians are to govern themselves is finally determined, not by control of the provincial Government, but of the Government of India. For it is the central government, and therefore in African colonies the Governor in Executive and Legislative Councils, which decides what the social, political, and economic framework of the people's lives shall be, and therefore their position in the political and economic world order. In the Crown Colony type of administration, self-government will always depend upon the control and therefore the constitution of the Executive and Legislative Councils and Africans will never enjoy full self-government or responsible government until the Legislative

Council is elected by and is responsible to them. No amount of indirect rule or local government can alter this fundamental fact. It is only by following and accelerating the stages from a nominated and official to an elected council that the African can travel the road from subjection to political freedom.

Two conclusions follow. The existing system which attempts to separate the institutions of indirect rule or local government from central government is unsound, for it results inevitably in pseudo-self-government. The native authority and the organs of local government must be closely integrated with the central government, and the training of the African in controlling every part of the integrated structure of government must be continually and deliberately pursued. Secondly the process of democratizing the central government should be accelerated. On the west coast a larger measure of self-government could everywhere be introduced through the Legislative Council. In Kenya and other "backward" east coast colonies the number of members nominated to represent African interests should be greatly increased, and these posts should be filled as far as possible by Africans who have come to the fore in local government. These men will, no doubt, make mistakes, but, like ourselves and every other free people, by making mistakes they may eventually acquire the difficult art of governing themselves.

Self-Government for Advanced Colonies
Problems and Methods of Constitutional Progress

by SIR DRUMMOND SHIELS, M.C., M.B.

(*formerly Under-Secretary of State for India and for the Colonies*)

There is general expectation that the future of colonial territories will be prominent among post-war world questions. Various suggestions for changes in the control of colonies have been made. These include internationalization, which would involve the taking over and the administering of colonies by an international body. Another is that there should be supervision of the administration of all colonies (except those approaching self-government) by a new International Commission, on the lines of the former Mandates Commission, which would, similarly, receive periodical reports on the various territories, but which would also have some facilities for visiting them.

It does not seem likely that international administration will be favoured, as—apart from other important considerations—the practical difficulties would be too great. Some form of international collaboration in respect of the lesser-developed colonies, however, appears to be envisaged, the actual administration remaining in the hands of the Metropolitan countries. There will probably also be international agreement—as was the case in respect of the former Mandated territories—that one of the main responsibilities of the Metropolitan country will be the protection of those peoples who are backward, and the taking of progressive steps, in all cases, towards the largest possible measure of self-government, as being the ultimate objective and the justification of the relationship of the colonies to the Metropolitan country.

Whatever may be the decision on these and other matters in connection with the future of colonies, the problem will still remain, for the actual responsible authority, of the necessary or desirable steps towards self-government.

A previous essay in this series has dealt with the political and constitutional advance of backward peoples. The general principles covering progress towards ultimate self-government of backward and more advanced colonial units are the same. As communities and peoples become more articulate, however, new problems arise, and circumstances have to be taken into account which do not apply in the case of less developed colonies.

Backward peoples

In the case of backward peoples, the most important considerations for political progress are the wide-spread increase of ordinary education by the provision of elementary and secondary schools, of teachers, and—in due course—of educational institutions approaching University standard. Adult education, in which the cinema and radio should be widely used, is essential to develop, in reasonable time, the ability to work democratic institutions, and also to prevent the progress of the younger generation being checked by the lack of knowledge and of co-operative capacity in the older generation.

Along with this, there has to be political education by the setting up and development of local government bodies of various kinds, including Native Councils. As the author of the previous essay has pointed out, care has to be taken to see that indirect rule—which has much to be said in its favour—does not lead to the stabilizing of undemocratic forms of government, and the postponement of the adoption of the elective principle.

Co-operatives—concerned with health, agriculture, savings, etc.—on the lines pioneered by Mr. C. F. Strickland, are also of great value; the aim—in this sphere, as in that of Local Government—being to encourage the people to organize things for themselves, to become accustomed to working some kind of representative system, and to discover those members of the community qualified by ability and by the spirit of public service to work higher representative institutions with efficiency and integrity.

Towards Full Self-Government

Self-government, however, in its full content, means the ability of a particular community or body of people in some recognized geographical area to manage all its own affairs, and to establish and maintain normal relations with other similar communities or peoples. Only in some of our larger Colonies, for reasons which will be indicated later, can self-government, as thus defined, be achieved. Certain limitations are inevitable in the case of the smaller units. Progress towards a considerable measure of self-government is, however, possible for all. In the case of colonies already advanced to some degree in this direction, difficulties are experienced which do not arise in the case of peoples not yet ready for self-government, where law and administration, as well as relations with the outer world, are still under the control of a Metropolitan country.

Criticisms of British Colonial Policy

Charges have frequently been made against British Colonial Authorities that they have been slow to take the later steps towards self-government in the case of a number of our more advanced colonies. The basis of this criticism, so far as it is justified, had two main factors. The first was the lack of knowledge of and consequent lack of interest in the colonies by the British electorate. Our school-children were not told enough about the colonies, still less was it impressed upon them that the welfare of colonial peoples was a direct responsibility of the British Parliament, and, therefore, of the ordinary British elector. As these children grew up to be voters and became concerned with their own environmental conditions, the colonies to them became increasingly remote, and there was no realization of any personal responsibility in the matter.

As Members of Parliament tend to interest themselves in the things which interest their own electorates, only a relatively few Members of Parliament gave themselves to the study of colonial questions, and the colonies were consequently largely run by the officials of the government departments concerned.

These did their work conscientiously, according to the outlook of their times (and often—in Whitehall—with little or no personal knowledge of the territories they administered), but the pace of constitutional advance—as well as that of economic and social progress—lacked the attention and the drive which Parliaments more acutely conscious of their responsibilities in this connection would have given.

The position to-day

That is not the position to-day. There is still much need for Empire education, but many Members of Parliament are now actively interested, and large numbers of the electorate, for the first time, have come to realize that we are trustees for these colonial peoples. We have, indeed, rapidly passed into using the word "partnership" rather than "trusteeship" and there has been vigorous expression of the view that we must, as soon as possible, implement the pledges which have been given from time to time to the effect that the fullest possible measure of self-government for every unit in the Empire is the ultimate goal of British administration.

For, in spite of all our hesitations, Britain is outstanding as a Colonial Power which has categorically proclaimed this as its ultimate goal. Indeed, part of the criticism of our colonial policy we have brought upon ourselves because of the high standard we have set and the ideals we have proclaimed, when these have been compared with actual performance. This disparity has not been due to insincerity, as unkind critics have sometimes suggested, but to a certain characteristic national time-lag between intention and action. There has been a tendency to be satisfied with our high declarations and the knowledge of our good faith and to be rather annoyed and irritated with those who were always wanting us to be doing things. We have run great risks as a nation in other connections owing to this national characteristic, though it does give a kind of reserve of energy and power when the need for action arises.

Nevertheless, in the case of our colonies, substantial progress towards the implementing of our promises has already been made, and in the last ten or twenty years the need for more effective action has been increasingly realized, with a view to the general process of material and political progress being considerably hastened and extended. The Colonial Development and Welfare Act of 1940 not only marks the beginning of a new era of economic and social development, as well as in that of health and education, but promises also to make easier new advances in constitutional progress, which require for their success the co-operation of a healthy, educated and reasonably-contented people. The machinery of the Colonial Office has been modernized, and many forms of colonial development are being initiated or stimulated.

Need of a graduated programme

The second main reason for slowness in the later stages of self-government has been the absence of a clear and sensibly-graduated programme of political advance. There has been no philosophy of constitutional progress, and the method of going forward has been largely empirical. This is said to be the British way, but it has its drawbacks.

What system there was took the form of a retreat in good order from complete Imperial control, and depended very largely on the pressure exerted in the colonies themselves. It was seldom, if ever, that a new step in self-government was taken except as a result of local agitation. The impression was, therefore, created that the concession made was grudgingly given, and there was, consequently, no gratitude shown for it. It came to be believed that only by continuing the agitation could the next stage be achieved. The local politicians, usually enthusiastically supported by the local Press, naturally, in these circumstances, often demanded much more than the circumstances warranted, in the hope that some modicum of their claims would thereby be granted.

The first Legislatures were composed solely of officials.

Some Nominated Members were afterwards admitted. Elected Members followed, still leaving a majority of government representatives. The next stage was a majority of Elected Members, which was hailed on both sides as a great advance, even though the control of all government departments remained in official hands, and no responsibility was allotted to the elected majority. This led to a most unfortunate state of affairs, because the unofficial majority inevitably became an irresponsible Opposition, and frequently sought in such ways as were possible to it to obstruct and make things difficult for the Government, and for the Governor, whose reserved powers to veto legislation were always a focus of attack. And general criticism was frequently mingled with personal attacks on particular Government officials, to which they could not reply.

The unwisdom of this latter stage in the tactics of retreat was fully set out in the Report of the Donoughmore Commission on the Ceylon Constitution, presented to Parliament in July, 1928, which laid emphasis on the necessity for giving responsibility *pari passu* with any increase of power. (Something will be said, later, about other features of this Report.)

It has taken some time for this principle to be recognized by our Colonial Office, and there is no clear evidence that it is now accepted as the proper method of progress. A fairly recent new Constitution for British Guiana has an unofficial majority on the old traditional lines, though a more recent one proposed for Jamaica is more hopeful and suggests that some philosophy of constitutional advance is being worked out. It is desirable that this should be done if we are not to have haphazard and purely opportunist treatment of local situations.

A third reason

A third reason for apparent slowness in constitutional advance, for which neither the Colonial Office nor the British Parliament and electorate can be held responsible, is the presence of certain conditions in the colonies themselves.

Can general principles be applied?

It is sometimes suggested that, owing to the wide variety of conditions in our colonies, and the many different cultures and outlook of the numerous peoples represented, no general principles can be applied at all. Community aspirations, however, in the political field, and the desire for equal prestige and status, have similar aspects all the world over. It is true that the nature of these aspirations is conditioned by education and by the values to which different peoples have become accustomed. British colonial peoples have before them the democratic way of life and their ideals are shaped accordingly. As these British colonial communities become politically educated, therefore, with, perhaps, some experience in local government, and attain a certain responsibility for national government, the nature of their demands has a great similarity and their aim is the same.

Local conditions differ, and the rate of progress cannot be the same for all. It should be possible, however, to establish general principles in the advance to self-government, which could be applied with any necessary local modifications, and which would aim at anticipating local demands, thus earning appreciation and goodwill, rather than to incur the appearance of each advance having been wrung with difficulty from the British Government. An attempt would then be made to make a success of the new stage reached, instead of its being regarded as a spring-board for a leap into further agitation for immediate greater powers. It would avoid the fear that an honest effort to make a success of the new powers and an abstention from expressed dissatisfaction with the new Constitution renders that stage permanent and retards any subsequent offer of an increased measure of self-government.

Constitution-making difficulties

Before we proceed, however, to consider certain aspects of this constitutional progress, we must look at some of the difficulties which face the colonial constitution-maker. The most striking examples of advance to self-government are afforded by our Dominions. These have developed from small scattered communities which, later, were formed into separate colonies (each in direct association with the Mother Country) and which, by stages, achieved practically full self-government, along with similar colonial areas in the same wide stretches of territory. Ultimately, these various colonies came together to form a Dominion, with the former colonies as States or Provinces of that Dominion. This was not a very rapid process, and the Commonwealth of Australia has only been in existence since 1901, with the first settlement in New South Wales dating from 1788. But, although the process was slow, it was straightforward in Australia and in New Zealand (which developed as one unit from a Colony into a Dominion) where there are homogeneous populations composed of men and women of British descent, having the same history, language, traditions, culture and general outlook.

In the earlier case of the Dominion of Canada, where Lord Durham's work triumphed in 1867, there were two different communities, one British and one French. The history, traditions and language of the two peoples were different, but their cultural development was comparable, and they had many things in common. Nevertheless, the fact that the population of Canada has not been a homogeneous one has made difficulties from time to time, even though Canada to-day can quite properly be regarded as a unified nation.

The history of the Union of South Africa is well-known, and here again complete self-government—dating from 1910—has not yet entirely eliminated the political and human difficulties caused by the propinquity and inter-action of two European peoples different in history, traditions and language, even if they are not very dissimilar in fundamental things. And, in the background, are the Native peoples whose destiny is still to be determined.

It has to be noted, therefore, that homogeneity in a population is an important factor in the last stages preceding complete self-government, and afterwards in making it successful, and

SELF-GOVERNMENT FOR ADVANCED COLONIES 107

that diverse factors in the population make difficult that unity of outlook which has to exist to make a nation.

The position in the colonies

In many of our colonies we are faced with the problem of populations divided by race, religion and degrees of culture. And whatever may be said in criticism of our hesitations in the past, we have to face the fact that, with the utmost goodwill, and, indeed, with the strongest wish to give self-government to our colonies, it is not such a simple process in many cases as some ardent advocates of immediate self-government believe.

These diversities are of various kinds. In Ceylon they are both racial and religious. Similarly, in Cyprus, most of the population are of Greek origin, the rest of Turkish origin. In Fiji, formerly a homogeneous community, there are now 100,000 Indians forming a separate people. In Malaya, the Malays are outnumbered by the Chinese, and there is a substantial Indian population, in addition to Europeans. Indians also constitute a considerable portion of the inhabitants of British Guiana, Trinidad, and Mauritius. In other cases, there are tremendous differences in cultural levels, apart from racial divisions. Kenya could hardly be described as an advanced colony, but its British community is of a very high cultural level, and, like all British communities, has an intense desire to govern itself. In Kenya, however, there is not only a large Native population, but the situation is also complicated by the presence of substantial Indian and Arab elements. In some other of our African colonies there is a similar difference in cultural levels, which are also to be found in Seychelles and Mauritius, where most of the Europeans are of French descent. Such problems are least acute in the West African and West Indies groups, and do not exist in a colony like Malta.

What should be done?

How are the diverse elements in so many of the colonies to be treated with equal fairness in a Constitution designed to work harmoniously on a democratic basis? And is it desirable, or wise, or inevitable, where there are great cultural or racial differences, or both, to delegate Imperial responsibility and to entrust the welfare and progressive development of the more backward elements to a highly cultured minority, which may in itself be quite capable of self-government, but which may be in such economic and social relationships to the backward elements as to make a purely objective attitude to them difficult to achieve. It is, indeed, important to remember in connection with this subject of minorities, that a minority is not merely a numerical expression. The same problem arises where there is a difference in political capacity, influence, or wealth, as in the case of the Malays in Malaya, or of the Indians in Mauritius.

It is not my task to deal with colonies of backward peoples, whether complicated or not by White settlement, but with those which have advanced some way towards self-government, even though there may be present diversities of various kinds. Every effort must be made on our part to compose antagonisms arising from these diversities, and to develop a sense of common citizenship, which is an essential for the justification and success of self-government. So long as direct Imperial responsibility remains, minority communities feel themselves protected, but, as progress towards democratic self-government is accelerated, so are the fears of the minorities increased, as they contemplate themselves as being at the mercy of the majority community, with possible discriminating procedures of various kinds.

It is difficult for those who have no experience of community antagonisms, and who have grown up in an atmosphere of good-natured tolerance of different political opinions and outlook, which reflect differing conceptions of economic theory and of personal and social relationship, to realize how deep are the gulfs separating races and religions in certain parts of the world, where communities follow blindly—rich and poor together—leaders who rely on an emotional appeal to community loyalty and on traditional intolerance of those of another race or of a different faith. The only hope for success in the working of democratic institutions in those colonies where this position obtains is the breaking up of these solid communal bodies in their political activities into individuals and groups concerned with economic and social matters which will create other interests cutting across communal boundaries, and the adjustment of community and religious loyalties to their own proper spheres. There is no quick or easy way to this goal.

Education and the Franchise

Two factors making for the sense of common citizenship go together—Education and the Franchise. The same kind and quality of education should be available for all the children. We have been taking another step towards achieving this in Britain, but it is still much less of a reality in our colonies. Many children get no formal education at all, others have a few years in an elementary school, and only a privileged and small minority have access to secondary and higher education. All educated persons are not broadminded, but education does make it possible to look beyond community prejudices and to find common ground and common loyalties with other people. Just as we, in Britain, are trying to put our own educational house in order, there are gratifying signs that the Colonial Office is pressing on with efforts to give greater equality of educational opportunity in the colonies. For, if political power is given to colonies while serious educational and other inequalities exist, it does not follow that these will be early or easily removed. Class distinctions and social castes are prominent in many of our colonies, and there is no great anxiety shown by the privileged classes, who often lead the cries for self-government, to see that inequalities—educational or economic—are removed or modified. And the indigenous exploiter has often fewer scruples than his prototype in western countries.

Equal and adult franchise—without property, income or educational tests—is regarded as out of the question by many who point to the mass of illiteracy and to the general ignorance of the populations concerned. Here, again, however, it is essential that, before relinquishing Imperial control, we should see that the common people have a means of defence and are accorded political rights before we hand over these territories. Illiteracy is no bar to voting ability or to the secrecy of the ballot, as the colour-voting scheme in Ceylon has shown. Adult franchise is the quickest and best way of stepping-up the attack on illiteracy, as everywhere the demands of the common people for education are strong. It is true that the lack of political knowledge and experience will handicap the voters in the beginning, but these will not cause a revolution, as they will vote for the same kind of people as were in power before. Their standard of values will take time to change and they will only learn to use the vote by using it. They will make mistakes, as even educated democracies do at times, but they will learn something from their mistakes and gradually build up some stock of political wisdom.

Another equally vital aspect of the right to vote is that the voter—whether he uses his vote wisely or not—becomes important to the politicians, who, in the Disraelian sense, have to educate their masters. This affects not only education, but also housing, medical services, employment, transport, and all the other ingredients of civilized life. Men and women without the vote have no say in the conditions of their environment, and politicians can safely leave them out of account.

The smaller the electorate is, also, the greater are the opportunities for bribery and corruption. Adult franchise makes this old-time practice too expensive and impossible to conceal.

There is much need for franchise revision in many of our colonies where there are Legislatures, notably in the West Indies, where the new Jamaica Constitution has shown the way in this direction.

A Party System

With a higher and more general level of education and with adult franchise there is more chance of the emergence of a genuine Party system, not based on adherence to a particular community or religion, but on the approach to political problems from different economic and sociological standpoints. In our colonies to-day, even where bloc voting on communal or religious lines is not obtrusive, Members of the Legislatures are elected largely on personal grounds. Theoretically, there is something to be said for this, but, in practice, it makes the working of democratic institutions difficult. (As in earlier days at Westminster, and, to some extent to-day, lawyers are largely in evidence in colonial legislatures. There are advantages in this, but, particularly in colonies where agriculture is the most important consideration, there are also disadvantages.)

With all its defects, the Party system makes for stability, and there is an alternative governing body available if those in power fail to retain the confidence of the electorate. The Party system can be abused and become a hindrance to independent thinking if discipline is too rigidly enforced, but, with a reasonable latitude given in respect of other than fundamental matters, there is strength in combination and consequent firmness in government. And, paradoxically, there is more likelihood of a common outlook on great national issues with a Party system because of the development of a similar sense of responsibility which a common experience of governing gives.

Danger of short-cuts

Where there are minorities fearful of majority domination it is important not to take short-cuts to meet the situation. One of these short-cuts is communal representation. This was introduced with good intentions in India and was copied into some of our colonial constitutions. As already emphasized, national consciousness and a sense of pride in common citizenship are essential to justification of and success in self-government. Communal representation hinders these developments. It gives the best chance of election to extremists and deepens communal antagonisms, ultimately blocking progress to a national outlook and to a national solution of political and constitutional questions. It was abolished in Ceylon by the recommendation of the Donoughmore Commissioners, who found this made easier by the fact that the important modification of a common roll with reserved seats had been made in the previous constitutional revision. Due, no doubt, to repercussions from India, there have been demands for the restoration of communal representation by the minority communities of Ceylon, but it is to be hoped that there will be no giving way on that issue, even though the attitude of the majority community has not always been wise or tactful. A return to communal representation would kill the last hopes of a unified Ceylon, able to speak and act as a national unit.

Protection of minorities

How, then, are minorities to be protected? Many of the fears they have may be unjustified, but the fears are real and have to be met. And this problem of minorities extends far beyond the confines of our Colonial Empire and will, indeed, be a major post-war problem in Europe. It is not an acute question, so far, in our colonies, except in Ceylon, but it is one which will undoubtedly emerge in certain cases where there are different language, racial, and religious groups, as further advances are made in constitutional development. Minorities cannot be protected by any artificial grouping of electorates or weightage of representation, which is not only undemocratic in spirit and in reality, but is also ineffective, unless we go to the length of turning the minority into a majority, thus making democracy stand on its head. The demand for this artificial security to be made more substantial grows and grows, as there is never any real feeling of security, so long as a minority remains a minority.

The method introduced into Ceylon appears to be the only proper and effective one, namely, that it be made an integral part of the Constitution of the country that any proposed legislative or administrative measure which discriminates on racial or religious grounds against any section of the population, should be—*ipso facto*—*ultra vires*. The ultimate decision on any such measure should lie with the supreme law court of the country, or, it might be, with a joint-judicial authority for a group of colonies. This is analogous to the position in the United States, and it would seem to be the only sensible and effective method of procedure. It should be introduced and operated before Imperial control is entirely removed, so that confidence may be built up, while a further safeguard remains.

Proportional representation

At the same time, it is important that the voice of minorities should be heard in every Legislature. It is presumably, in that sense that there are Arab and Indian representatives (with European spokesmen for Africans) arranged for in the Kenya Legislature, and that similar arrangements are made in Fiji for the representation of Indians, i.e. as giving an opportunity for the expression of opinion rather than as a definite and permanent policy of communal representation. From this angle, Nominated Members often prove useful in intermediate stages, but they can hardly be fitted in to a fully-developed democratic system.

Although, in spite of strong advocates, proportional representation has not yet found favour at Westminster as a method of electing representatives of the British electorate, it is well worth consideration whether it should not be used in our colonies as a better and a thoroughly democratic means of securing minority expression rather than by proceeding with further risky experiments in communal electorates. Some of the objections to proportional representation put forward in connection with the working of big national Parliaments do not apply in the colonies, and to be represented and to have the ability to express grievances goes a long way towards preventing that sense of frustration which is felt when no adequate opportunity is available for the voice of the minorities to be heard. There would thus be ventilation of all points of view, in addition to the security against victimization and discrimination explicit in the Articles of the Constitution.

In countries where it has been used, proportional representation has not prevented the development or maintenance of a Party system, and it might even be considered to provide a safety-valve against a too rigid two-Party domination. It was seriously considered for Ceylon by the Donoughmore Commissioners, but it was thought that it might complicate matters at the beginning of a new system, especially with a very large increase of inexperienced voters in the electorate.

Administrative discrimination

There is, however, a further consideration. A great deal of the fear of minorities is not so much of the letter of the law, but of the way in which administration is carried out. Administrative action can achieve considerable power of discrimination in minor ways, which cannot easily be prevented by statutes or regulations, because it works within the rules The human factor always counts in the end, and minorities, entirely shut out from insight into the working of the governmental and departmental machine, suspect, rightly or wrongly, that their general interests or those of individual members of their communities are suffering injustice. Certain districts may be favoured in improvement schemes, in irrigation works, in the making of new roads or railways, in the building of schools, or in the setting up of hospitals and dispensaries and other amenities; or officials may be denied promotion or be transferred unfairly, or a bias given in various other directions. Before considering how this difficulty may be met, let us consider some of the limitations which their size and population, their geographical position or their lack of certain resources impose on the scope of colonial Legislatures.

Defence and Finance

Two considerations are apt to be overlooked by those concentrating on the desirability of all our colonies becoming completely autonomous units in the British Commonwealth and Empire. Colonial politicians, also, are apt to forget their importance. These are Defence and Finance.

SELF-GOVERNMENT FOR ADVANCED COLONIES 115

Much is being said and written on the necessity for some modification of the degree of national sovereignty if the world is to become a body of co-operating nations and peoples united by the acceptance of certain fundamental principles.

It is now obvious that few, if any, countries are in a position to guarantee their own security against physical aggression without being partners in some common scheme of defence. This is particularly true of our colonies, which are never likely to be in a position to defend themselves (or to make any great contribution to their defence) under the conditions of modern warfare. They must, therefore, be linked up with some defence system—an Imperial, or world system, or both—in the organization and direction of which, as individual colonies, though they may have some say, they can have no decisive voice. This, in itself, sets a limit, which will remain, to the degree of national sovereignty to which colonies can attain.

Finance, also, imposes present limitations in many colonies, and, in some cases, may set limitations in the future to complete independence. It is commonly believed by critics of the British colonial system that our colonies are good paying propositions for the Mother Country. No doubt there are advantages of one kind and another, from the financial and trading point of view, in the association of Britain and her colonies, but it is doubtful if, over all, the balance on the financial side is in favour of the Mother Country.

It is still less likely to be so in the immediate future, as the Colonial Development and Welfare Act of 1940 envisages large sums being spent for the provision of social services, for education and development schemes, and the present Secretary of State has made it clear that this assistance will be given on a generous scale. Not only so, but the new principle has been introduced of subsidizing, where necessary, the annual colonial budget, in addition to giving grants for capital expenditure.

Much of this financial assistance will, no doubt, prove fruitful, not only in the improved health and vigour of the indigenous peoples, but also in new opportunities for agricultural and industrial development. This will lead, we must hope, to many more colonies become self-supporting, so that subsidies and outside assistance will be no longer required.

In the case of the larger colonies, there is every reason to anticipate that this will be the position, but in a number of the smaller ones it is doubtful if it can be accomplished. So long as some measure of Imperial control remains, there is no doubt that every assistance—financial and otherwise—will be given towards the development of any colony requiring help. In so far as Imperial control is lessened, however, there will be a corresponding reluctance to provide money without an appropriate say as to its use and distribution. This situation may be met, in some cases, by the grouping of colonies, which is a likely development for other reasons, but, in the West Indies, it has been found that a prosperous colony has been reluctant to be linked up to others which were likely to be a financial liability. For a number of smaller units, therefore, it would seem to be desirable if not inevitable—and in their own interests, that they should remain in some formal association with the Mother Country.

The nature of colonial legislation

Most of our colonies have relatively small populations, and defence and foreign affairs, and, it may be, certain fundamentals of fiscal policy, are, and, probably, will continue to be (even in relation to any post-war regional organization) outside the jurisdiction, though not necessarily outside the consideration, in a consultative capacity, of the local Legislature. The result is that the matters to be decided come largely within the sphere of local government, and are concerned with housing, roads, hospitals, medical services, schools, etc. Absorbing interest is taken, not only by the whole body of Members of the Legislature, but particularly—as already mentioned—by the minority communities, as well as by the general body of the people in their administration, which, to them, is as important as the legislation itself.

SELF-GOVERNMENT FOR ADVANCED COLONIES 117

The Committee System

This position, which had made for difficulty in the working of the previous Ceylon Constitution, as it tended to bring about interference by a number of politicians and community leaders with departmental control and efficiency, was accepted as inevitable by the Donoughmore Commissioners, who decided to regularize it. They, therefore, planned a body with double functions, operating both as a Legislature, and—by means of executive committees on local governmental lines—also as an administrative body. The committees are seven in number, the aim being that on at least one of them every Member of the State Council serves, and they deal with such subjects as Health, Education, Agriculture, Labour, etc. The Chairmen of the committees form the Board of Ministers who have responsibility for finance, and for the arrangement of Government business.

The Constitution came into effect at the beginning of the slump period. The numbers in the Legislature, and, consequently, in the Executive Committees were smaller than was recommended by the Donoughmore Commissioners, and, consequently, the committees, into which the State Council was divided, were not sufficiently large to make each of them entirely representative. Circumstances which had nothing to do with the merits of the Constitution prevented some parts of it working out exactly in the way intended, and experience has shown that certain changes are necessary, some of which were anticipated by the Donoughmore Commissioners. Greater authority and wider functions should be given to the Board of Ministers, and the officers of State, designed to be advisers in the first stages of the new Constitution, should be dispensed with. The main structure of the Constitution, however, and, particularly, the committee system, has, in the opinion of many well-qualified to judge, entirely justified the belief that its main principles should be retained and be adopted in other colonial Constitutions.

There is a tendency to make superficial statements to the effect that the Constitution has not been a success, but the point to note is that it has worked, even in the absence of a non-communal Party system, and that progress in various departments, especially in social legislation and education, has been made. Although many of the elements of the Indian situation have been present, there has been no dead-lock, and valuable experience in self-government has been gained.

It is true that the Governor has had to use his veto on some occasions, and his duties in a transition stage of this kind—especially in the war period—have been undoubtedly difficult. The position of the important European community has also become increasingly strained in an atmosphere of enhanced nationalism. When the present Constitution has been modified, with features which have been felt to be undesirable removed, and increased powers are given, it is to be hoped that the State Council will find it possible to co-operate more cordially with the Governor in the exercise of such functions as remain to him, and not use criticisms of him as propaganda for a final instalment of self-government. It is a method which had some justification in former days but is not wise or helpful to-day.

There is no question of the willingness and, indeed, the keen desire of the Home Government and the British people to see Ceylon achieve its ambition of full self-government, but—as has been pointed out—the final stages of this development involve problems which must be satisfactorily solved before Imperial supervision is entirely removed. Only in this way can we discharge our full responsibilities to all the people of Ceylon.

Criticisms of the Committee System

Some critics have thought that the committee system tends to make more difficult the development of a real Party system. Experience in our own local Government, however, suggests that this is not so. The tendency has been for it to develop more and more on Party lines, and, in the largest municipal body, the London County Council, there is a fully-fledged and perfectly frank Party system, with majority and opposition whips and all the other accessories.

Another criticism, which has more substance, is that the position of the Chairman of Committees, who also form the Board of Ministers, is a difficult one. This is true, but men of character and ability have achieved considerable success as Chairmen and Ministers, even under the present disadvantage of the lack of a real Party system and in the absence of provision for a formulated Government policy. Greater powers to a representative Board of Ministers, and development on true Party lines, would eliminate many of the present difficulties, some of which are directly related to the conflicting elements in the social structure of Ceylon, which would affect adversely the working of any Constitution.

Another criticism has been made that the committee system wastes time. This comment has been made by senior officials and others in high places who have been without experience of the working of the previous system, and—one suspects—have not been familiar with the normal working of local government bodies.

Under the previous regime, there were numerous *ad hoc* advisory committees of the Legislative Council, appointed to deal with specific matters referred to them. These committees dragged on, sometimes for years. There was no system, although committees, in themselves, were obviously regarded as a natural method of arriving at agreed conclusions. Under the executive committee system, matters may certainly be referred back and decisions delayed, just as happens in well-conducted local government bodies in this country. In comparison with the previous untidy system of advisory committees, however, it cannot be denied that for comprehensive and systematic dealing with the programme of business, the present method is a great improvement. By canalizing into various subordinate channels discussions on minor points, which would not only waste time, but would, also, lower the dignity of the Council, the committee system has, in the end, saved time, and not wasted it. The record of the work done is, in itself, an answer to this criticism.

The acute communal differences in Ceylon which, as has been said, would make the working of any Constitution difficult, and provide scope for the same kind of criticisms to which the present Constitution has been subjected, would be absent in most other colonies, and would make harmonious working of the committee system a much simpler process.

A purely legislative body, serving a small population, and with certain big subjects outside its province, is too limited in its scope, and tends to become largely a debating assembly, and it is difficult or impossible to maintain the separation of function between legislation and administration. Dealing with practical administration, also, tends to cut across purely communal or racial divisions, and, therefore, helps to bring about the better way where people of the same community or race will be found on different sides on economic or social questions, when their interests or sympathies are not really the same. Progress in that direction is the only hope for the successful working of democratic institutions. It is good to see the beginning of a committee system in the proposed new Constitution for Jamaica, which could, however, with advantage, have gone much further in that direction.

General suitability of democratic institutions

There are some who doubt whether our democratic institutions are suited to other countries and peoples. Indeed, eminent authorities, whose position and experience entitle their views to respect, are convinced that parliamentary government is quite inappropriate for Oriental and African races. Even if this were true—an opinion the writer does not share—it must be remembered, as already mentioned, that all our colonies, as well as India, have derived their political conceptions from the working of the British democratic system, and it is to that ideal that their political aspirations are directed. We cannot go back along that road. It is true, at the same time, that the Westminster method is not necessarily the best or the most suitable for our colonies. The form is not the important thing, so long as the spirit of parliamentary democracy is expressed in the three essentials of a free choice of representatives, free discussion, and majority decision, and this is a method of arriving at conclusions for community purposes which is found all over the world.

The Westminster model

One of the great difficulties is, however, that in India and in our colonies, the Westminster model is regarded as the symbol and pattern of fully-fledged democracy, and anything different is regarded with suspicion as being necessarily an inferior article. This, undoubtedly was one of the reasons why the present Ceylon Constitution was looked on doubtfully by Ceylonese politicians—who include men of high culture and professional attainments, and with British university education —and why they have been agitating for a Cabinet and departmental system on Westminster lines. The Ceylon Constitution, however, was intended to provide a set of principles for colonies in a similar or in even earlier stages of development, and its joint functions are appropriate for all but the larger African colonies; and even in these, District Legislatures on committee lines might develop as the next stage in the evolution of indirect rule, as the council and committee method is quite in line with African tradition and custom.

Executive committees of the Legislature, carrying out administrative functions—subject to the approval in other than routine matters of the larger body—enable Minority Members to see how and what things are done and to have a voice in the settling of priorities, the location of hospitals, direction of roads, and similar matters. It also gives a better proportion in the subjects dealt with in the Legislature, where, otherwise, hours may be wasted in discussion of a minor point of administration.

And while committee ways of doing things are denounced from time to time by advocates of strong men and direct action, it has been found in practice that committees save time in the end, afford the best method of expressing and reconciling diverse views, and collect the greatest amount of available wisdom. Although there is not a committee system at Westminster, there is a multiplicity of committees, and there have been advocates· of advisory committees of Members of Parliament attached to each department of State. (There are already many advisory committees attached to departments, but they do not usually include Members of Parliament.)

In the devolution of some of the present duties of Parliament, forecast by Mr. Herbert Morrison and others, a committee solution has been favoured rather than that of handing over, unchecked, extensive new powers to the executive.

Many features of the United States system of government do not appeal to us so much as our own, but the committee system in Congress has admirers on this side. And there has been a strong demand in our own Parliament for a joint standing committee of both Houses of Parliament on this very subject of colonies. The war has been, on the Allied side, largely a committee war, from the Heads of States and Chiefs of Staffs downwards and outwards.

Government appointments: Civil Service Commission

The filling of government jobs of various kinds is one of the centres of controversy in our colonies and one concerning which the minorities are most suspicious. Executive committees in Ceylon may deal with minor posts, and may even make suggestions in regard to higher appointments, but it is said that this has not been found in practice to be desirable. Something in the way of a Civil Service Commission for appointments in the local Civil Service is certainly necessary. It would be best for executive committees, or any other body affected by political considerations, to have nothing whatever to do with the filling of or promotion in either minor or senior posts.

It is not, however, easy to get a body of independent people in these small colonies who can fulfil this function and who can, at the same time, enjoy the full confidence of all the communities. This is one of the most difficult of problems in colonies advancing towards self-government, and, unless some procedure is devised which gives confidence and which can become an integral part of the Constitution giving full autonomy, the relinquishing of Imperial authority is likely to result in serious friction which will imperil the whole working of self-government. It may find a solution in an area grouping of colonies for certain major functions which, as already stated, many authorities consider, for other reasons, to be desirable.

During the last stages, also, it is important that the local Civil Service should become more and more representative of the people of the colony, and this is an honourable, but not always, perhaps, an agreeable responsibility for the European members of the Service. It is difficult to render a swan song with cheerfulness. They have to try to secure, in their prospective successors, respect for the high standards of integrity which—whatever other criticisms of the British Civil Service there may be—have been characteristic of British administration all over the world, and have been the basis for the undoubted respect and admiration with which it is universally regarded. In their individual cases, just as in the case of Britain herself, they must regard the developed ability of the colonies to take over the management of their own affairs, not as a set-back, but rather as the consummation and justification of British colonial policy.

Relation of Administrative and Technical Services

There is, however, one respect in which our Civil Service, both at home and in the colonies, has not been adapted to the changed circumstances of modern Government. In former days, the preservation of public order and the collection of revenue were the main functions of government. To-day, however, the technical services are all-important, and these have not achieved—either at home or in the colonies—the status and prestige and the power of independent decision which the changed circumstances require. The test of good government in the colonies is not the ability of the Secretariat—important as that is—but the kind of hospitals and medical services, schools and teachers, agricultural provision and instruction, roads and transport, sanitation, etc., which are provided for the people. It is important that there should be a high standard in the doctors, educationists, agriculturalists, engineers and other technical and professional workers, who are recruited from this country, not only because of the immediate effect of their work, but also because of their function in training and guiding those who are to be their successors among the indigenous inhabitants. This requires some adjustment between the administrative and technical services, and greater rights of decision for the technicians in regard to their own special subjects, which would, in itself, bring to them a relatively higher prestige and status than are at present enjoyed by the technical services, and would make these services more attractive.

Promotion, also, should be made from a wider circle than it is to-day. Members of technical staffs should be recognized as suitable for appointment as Colonial Secretaries and Governors. Theoretically, they are eligible at present but there have been few instances of such appointments. Even in the Administrative Service, those serving in the secretariat have an undue preference. The backbone and strength of the Colonial Administrative Service are the District Commissioners. They know and understand the human side of administration, and are sometimes passed over because they are doing their job so well that it is said to be undesirable to change them. But it is men like these who are needed in the higher posts where the human side is apt to be insufficiently regarded. Every improvement in our administration makes it easier to secure the co-operation of the colonial peoples in their own advancement, a task in which they must share if it is to be successful and permanent in its results.

Who is to devise Constitutions?

There is a new tendency, however, to throw on the political leaders in our dependencies the main responsibility of devising their own constitutions. This may appear to be a generous gesture, and, in the case of India, it has the justification that it follows the rejection of more than one attempt from our side to provide an acceptable solution of constitutional difficulties.

In the case of our colonies, it is an undesirable procedure. With our own long experience of government and of the working of democratic institutions, we should be able to give a lead and guidance to our colonial peoples, who usually have few men of political experience or with knowledge of constitutional variations and niceties. Not only so, but where there are contending factions, how is it possible to get local agreement? Ceylon ministers have been asked to submit a scheme for a new Constitution. With one exception they are all members of the same community. Is their scheme likely to be one which will commend itself to all the Ceylon people? It will simply mean that the Colonial Office or any body delegated by it to frame a new constitution will have the invidious task of deciding between this scheme and counter-proposals, with the likelihood that the final decision will incur the antagonism and the non-co-operation of those who have not been consulted or whose invited views have not been accepted.[1]

Certainly, it is essential that local opinion of all kinds should be obtained and local needs anticipated. Commissions mainly composed of British Members of Parliament (which is, ultimately, responsible for conditions and development in the colonies) should proceed, as heretofore, without previous commitments, to the colony concerned. Such Commissions would be sympathetic and objective, and would obtain a more accurate perspective than colonial politicians who are in the midst of local controversy. These Members of Parliament could be associated with representative public men in the colony, where these were available, and, evidence should be

[1] Since the above was written, a message from *The Times* correspondent in Colombo suggests that the Ceylon Ministers may "find themselves unable to collaborate" with any Reforms Commission which the British Government now propose to send out, as the Ministers apparently resent the fact that the Colonial Office is not prepared to accept their draft without further investigation of the local position by a visiting Commission.

heard from every section of the people, official (perhaps through their associations), and non-official. It is to be hoped that, after the war—as far as the colonies are concerned—we shall revert to our former practice and discharge our full responsibility, which will be more likely to win the approval, the confidence, and the respect of our colonial peoples than the delegation of a most difficult task to local politicians.

Non-political organizations

So far, we have been discussing the purely political relationship between the colonies and the Mother Country, and the pace and character of constitutional progress. There are, however, other aspects of colonial life, which, although they have political implications and repercussions are, in themselves, non-political.

Emphasis has been laid on the need for building up a sense of national unity within which and subordinate to which, Party or community differences can be fought out. This can be assisted by securing the co-operation and the working together of representatives of diverse elements in the population on Municipal and District Councils, and on Boards or Commissions dealing with economic or social matters. In considering new Constitutions this point should be kept in mind. All the best colonial character and brains are not in the Legislative Councils, any more than all the talent of Britain is to be found at Westminster.

The importance of Municipal and District Councils in the earlier stages of colonial development has already been mentioned. These are no less important in more advanced colonies, and the more influence and scope they have, and the more they can recruit men and women of character and ability, the bigger will be their influence. Leadership is the great need of the colonies, as it is of all countries, and these councils are a good training ground. The courage, sincerity and ability required must be given every opportunity to show itself.

Such councils have not always been successful where they have been set up. One of the reasons for failure has been the fact that they have not always been properly equipped, and have had no adequate technical or clerical staff at their command. This is essential if they are to have a chance of success, and one of the causes of apparent incompetence has been this lack of adequate resources and of skilled personnel. They must also be given proper prestige and status so that good types of citizens will feel it an honour to serve on them.

These councils will not only be able greatly to assist in the day to day life of their towns or districts, but they will, also, be a balancing factor to the Legislative Councils, especially if, as in this country, they have associations which can represent to the Government and Legislative Council the views and needs of their citizens on projected Government measures. Many of our difficulties in colonial constitutional development would have been avoided if local government on a liberal scale had been an integral part of our programme for every colony. Our own Parliamentary system developed from our local government, but many of our colonies have been expected to make laws before they were entrusted with the duty of making regulations and bye-laws.

The technique of local government, however, was outside the ken of most of our Governors and administrative officials, and they could not be blamed for not pushing something with whose organization and working they were unfamiliar. An authority in local government is now Permanent Under-Secretary of State for the Colonies, and since his appointment, a leading expert has been visiting a number of our colonies and advising on this subject. So, even if late in the day, progress in this connection is being made.

Co-operation in administration

An important aspect of the activities of such councils is that they make it possible for men and women of different political views to come together for practical administrative work and thus promote unity of outlook and co-operative working. During some of the worst days of political tension in Palestine, the municipalities of Jerusalem and Haifa, consisting of Jewish and Arab members, were discussing their local problems and carrying out their administrative functions with a substantial degree of co-operation. The multiplication of such councils and the enlargement of their scope in regard to rating and other matters in Palestine and in other difficult territories would, at least, help towards a realization of common interests, which—it cannot be too often repeated—is essential for successful self-government.

Other bodies

In the same way, commissions or boards might take over subjects like transport, wireless, port facilities, etc., on the same lines as our London Transport Board and B.B.C. Not all colonies would give great scope for this, but, if they could be extended from the few at present in operation, it would enable men and women of judicial temperament and of public spirit, who would not be willing to go into the hurly-burly of political life, to give service with members of other communities or races. Their scope might even be extended to collaboration, for specific purposes, with adjacent colonies, or even with non-British neighbours, without questions arising of any constitutional amalgamation. (The Anglo-American Caribbean Commission is a good example of the latter kind of co-operative effort.)

There would, of course, be an ultimate authority in the Government and Legislative Council, but the day-to-day administration would be carried out in a non-political atmosphere. Public utility companies for electricity, gas, etc., are other forms of enterprise which help to provide common ground and better understanding between members of opposed political groups. The modern trend towards public enterprises, and the functional approach to self-government, should find full application in our colonies. The development of trade unions, with a composite membership, is a hopeful feature in many of our colonies, and, if these are set off by similarly mixed

SELF-GOVERNMENT FOR ADVANCED COLONIES

groups of employers, that, also, will help to break up the solid masses of community blocs in which individuality is lost and national unity is endangered.

Difficulties of democratic government

Democratic government is not easy, and greater sympathy should be extended to those colonial politicians and peoples making their early efforts in this sphere. British people and British administrators are apt to believe that corruption, intrigue and inefficiency have always been absent from our parliamentary system, but a little acquaintance with history, and with the works of Dickens, will remind us that our own progress to rectitude was slow. Many eminent voices in these former days proclaimed the unsuitability and the danger of a real democracy in our own country. Too censorious judgments should not, therefore, be passed on stages of political development in our colonies which will be found to have relevant parallels in our own Parliamentary history.

Conclusion

It will be seen that there is no lack of problems and difficulties in the later stages towards self-government. Nothing has been said of the relation of the colonies to the needs of the world, in connection with which Britain has undertaken certain obligations and proclaimed certain general principles, for example, in regard to access to raw materials. The taking over and the ways of implementing such obligations will be another matter for discussion before complete autonomy is granted, though it may be that some international agreement will be worked out in this connection.

Progress to self-government must be made as rapidly as possible. It is, however, clearly undesirable that the control of the British Parliament and electorate should be removed from any colony until all its people have full civic rights and are adequately equipped—through a variety of representative and democratic institutions—to go forward on their own in economic, educational and social progress as efficient and prosperous units in the British Commonwealth of Peoples.

NOTE.—The personnel of the Donoughmore Commission, on whose recommendations the present Constitution for Ceylon was set up, was as follows: The Earl of Donoughmore, who was at that time Chairman of Committees in the House of Lords and an expert on Parliamentary procedure. The late Sir Geoffrey Butler, a brilliant member of a distinguished family, Member of Parliament for Cambridge University and lecturer in that University on Diplomatic History. He was a recognized authority on constitutional practice at home and abroad. The late Sir Matthew Nathan was an experienced Empire administrator, having been Governor of Gold Coast, Hong-Kong, Natal, and Queensland, and was specially well-versed in problems of local and national government. Sir Drummond Shiels, at that time Member of Parliament for East Edinburgh, was the fourth member of the Commission.

Language and the African
by IDA WARD

The compact mass of the continent of Africa often tempts us to overlook both its size and its diversity. We consider Europe, even when thinking in terms of a United States of Europe, as a number of countries each a political, cultural and, as a matter of course, linguistic unit, differing widely from its neighbours, but we are apt to consider the continent of Africa as one entity and to expect a unity or a possibility of unity which we should not dream of looking for in Europe. In no aspect is the diversity of Africa better illustrated than in language, and in no aspect, perhaps, are the implications of this diversity so little understood. It may be well to look at the picture briefly.

Lord Hailey's *Survey of Africa* gives the number of African languages as over seven hundred. This is a conservative estimate and some scholars say there are close on a thousand, but the exact number is not known, nor do we know precisely where a dialect ends and a language begins. We have a good deal of general information about African languages, however, and detailed knowledge of some. We know, for example, that a vast family of languages, known as the Bantu[1] family, fills the huge section of the continent south of a line running roughly and somewhat irregularly from Duala in the Cameroons to the coast of Kenya, with the exception of the enclaves of Bushmen and Hottentots in the south-west, and the Masai enclave in East Africa. There is a strong family likeness in grammar and construction in all the members of this family and a phonetic relationship is readily traceable. Dr. Doke, Professor of Bantu languages at Witwatersrand University, classifies them into "zones," such as North-Western, Kongo, South-Eastern, South-Western Bantu, etc., and each of these zones into "clusters" and "groups." He uses the term "cluster" to refer to languages of

[1] The name "Bantu" was given to this family by Dr. Bleek in 1869. The word means "people" in this language group.

the same philological type, and "group" to divisions of the cluster. People speaking one language of a group, the smallest of Doke's sub-divisions, can easily learn to understand those who speak another language of the same group.[1]

North of the Bantu area in a belt south of the Sahara, stretching from the Atlantic coast to the Anglo-Egyptian Sudan, is the Sudanic family of languages. These languages, doubtless connected distantly with the Bantu, are, however, of a very different type. They possess certain characteristics of construction in common, but are not so apparently related to each other as are members of the Bantu family. Indeed, so diverse do they appear that it is only comparatively recent research that has made clear any affinity among them. Within this wide field again, are divisions and sub-divisions each containing an unnumbered collection of languages, and it is the regular thing to find that speakers of neighbouring languages of this area do not understand each other's speech. North and East of the Sudanic area lie the Semitic and Hamitic languages on which we have more information. The Nilotic and Nilo-Hamitic languages form two other groups and are classed with the Bantu and Sudanic languages as Negro languages. There are also border-line languages, between and within the Bantu and Sudanic areas and "mixed" languages such as Hausa which is Hamitic in structure and mainly Sudanic in vocabulary. Arabic has influenced some of the languages in the Bantu and Sudanic areas, such as Swahili and Hausa which have had considerable infiltration of Arabic vocabulary. The Bushman and Hottentot languages of South-West Africa belong to an entirely different family, according to the latest classification, the Khoisan family. The well-known "clicks" are a special characteristic of these languages, and have been borrowed by some of the South African Bantu languages.

A large proportion of Negro languages are, in varying degrees, tonal, i.e. variations in the pitch of the voice may, and frequently do affect the meanings of individual words and are used to

[1] Compare, for instance, the fact that Swedes, Norwegians, and Danes with some effort can understand each other's languages.

express different grammatical constructions. Some of the West Coast languages have perhaps the most elaborate tonal systems, but present-day research is revealing the existence of regular tonal patterns in most of the Bantu languages also. An example will illustrate the difficult element of speech. In Yoruba (spoken in Nigeria,) the word ọkọ means *husband, canoe, hoe, spear*, according to the pitch of voice of the two syllables.[1] *Omi tutu* may mean *the water is cold*, or *cold water* according to tone.[2] In Twi (spoken on the Gold Coast) *ontie* with different tones means, *he does not listen*, and *let him listen*,[3] i.e. the difference between negative and subjunctive is tonal and tonal only.

The numbers speaking an African language—not dialect—vary from the many millions who speak Hausa[4] as their mother-tongue, to a few thousands or even hundreds speaking some of the smaller tribal languages.

It will be evident that this multiplicity of languages presents serious problems in the development of African colonies; indeed schemes for such development, whether social, educational, economic or political, have linguistic implications which need careful examination. For most of these schemes, we take for granted that within a measurable distance of time, the population will be literate: the extension of school education is planned and mass education schemes are in active preparation. One of the first questions we have to ask is what part the African's language is going to play in these plans, in education, in propaganda for better health, for the establishment of better social conditions, for economic and political development and to introduce him to the modern world.

The development of a people should spring from deep roots in the people themselves, and a superstructure without such roots will lack stability. There is nothing more fundamental than the

[1] Represented graphically these are ọkọ (- -) *husband*, ọkọ (_ _) *spear*, ọkọ (- ¯) *hoe*, ọkọ (- _) *canoe*.

[2] Omi tutu (- ¯ - _) *The water is cold;* omi tutu (- - ¯ _) *cold water*.

[3] Ontie (- _ _ -) *He doesn't listen*, ontie (¯ ¯ ¯ ¯) *let him listen*.

[4] In N. Nigeria, N. Territories of the Gold Coast, French Sudan.

mother-tongue, and it would appear axiomatic that, for the African, as for other individuals, the mother-tongue should form the basis of his development and his means of self-expression, "The mother-tongue is the true vehicle of mother-wit." "A man's native speech is almost like his shadow, inseparable from his personality." "Only through wise use of the mother-tongue can clearness of thought, independence of judgment, and sense of individual responsibility be developed at the start, and only thus can the creation of new classes of native society, separated from the vast mass of their fellow countrymen by loss of contact and ready communication with those who have no knowledge of English, he avoided."[1]

It is interesting to note that in a small book recently printed in Nigeria, publications in 54 languages of this colony are listed: there are many other languages in Nigeria, however, especially in the pagan areas of the Bauchi plateau in the north, and in the Niger Delta, which have no literature at all. The writer went to a training centre in Northern Nigeria and in a class of thirteen men, there were thirteen languages represented. Some of these may have been so closely related as to be considered dialects, but many of them were different languages and not mutually understandable.

Let us examine what has happened up to the present time, and see if, in the light of the new ideas that we are looking to implement, any change in attitude or action is desirable or possible. In this way, we may perhaps arrive at an estimate of the part that vernacular languages may play in the immediate future of African development.

There are wide divergencies in language policy as between Britain and France or Portugal, for example. France and Portugal make use of French or Portuguese only in administration and education in the territories for which they are responsible, not only teaching these languages in school, but using them as the medium of instruction from the start. They leave the vernacular either to remain a home language only or gradually

[1] In the Calcutta Report on Education, 1919.

to be superseded by the metropolitan language. Britain, on the other hand, has had the avowed policy of using the vernacular for the beginnings of education, introducing the teaching of English at a fairly early stage, and making use of it as the medium of instruction in secondary and higher schools, and in some cases, even in the upper classes of the primary school. Christian missions in British territory, which are responsible for a large part of primary education, have made considerable use of the vernacular. Missions in French, Portuguese and Belgian territory use the vernacular for religious instruction. Belgium seems to follow a policy lying between that of France and Britain: more attention has been paid to vernaculars in recent years and in the Belgian Congo three official vernaculars are recognized. We are credibly informed, too, that the attitude to the vernaculars in French territories appears to be changing, and that the late M. Eboué, Governor-General of French Equatorial Africa, showed keen interest in them.

At the present moment we have not enough accurate information to make an adequate comparison between the two types of policy as holding in British and French (or Portuguese) territories, with respect either to the place of the vernacular or the skill of the Africans in the use and understanding of the European language. For instance, we do not know if in French or Portuguese territory, the African can read and write his own language, as well as French or Portuguese; nor do we know the degree of literacy or the numbers literate in either the vernacular or the European language, or if the French colonials—or Portuguese—have produced literature in any degree in these languages or in their own. We do know, however, that there must be a body of men who have helped in the translation of the Bible and who consequently must have a certain competence in their own language, and the Missions have probably taught reading in the vernacular. Information is also wanting as to whether the teaching of French or Portuguese tends to make a rift in the home between the younger generation and the older people, who have not had these opportunities of education. Similar questions need careful and factual examination in British colonies[1] and under the different conditions prevailing in British East Africa and in West Africa. We want to know not only the practical results of these policies, but their influence on the development of the Africans themselves.[2] This and other accurate information is necessary not only to check certain sweeping assumptions and generalizations, but to provide material for constructive modern developments.

There are, indeed, many practical difficulties in African language questions, and these have tended to obscure the fundamental right of every man to adequate expression in his own language. Even where, as in the British colonies, the recognized policy of Government has been to begin education in the vernacular, there seems always to have been in the background the feeling on the part of the teacher and taught that this stage must be got over quickly in order to reach what was thought to be the main purpose of schooling—the learning of English. It is true that, in the West at any rate, many children in the past have been sent to school for the sole purpose of learning English, and any attempt to put weight on the vernacular has been received as a threat "to keep the African back." It is also true that knowledge of a European language opens the door to money-earning jobs: early settlers, traders, missionaries and government officials needed clerks, and too often "education"

[1] An African from the Gambia recently stated to the present writer that the stress laid on English in school to the virtual exclusion of the vernacular very definitely caused a rift in those families where the parents knew no English. As he put it, "We can't discuss at home the things we have been learning about in English; we can only talk of trivial things."

[2] At a recent meeting in London, an American anthropologist, Dr. Margaret Mead, pointed out that the transition from the spoken to the written language should be made and established in the mother-tongue, the language in which the child is cherished and loved and scolded. Otherwise there is likely to be disorientation. She instanced the example of American Indians whose capacity for dealing with the English language, particularly the written language, was below their general intelligence; this, she said, was mainly due to the fact that they had not written their own language.

has been equated with the power to read, write and speak a little English. British policy for many reasons has been interpreted variously and in many areas no steady line of language development pursued. Lip service has been paid to the basic principles underlying the use of the vernacular, but a lack of conviction or a feeling that the difficulties of the situation are overwhelming have often led to little more than lip service.

There are, of course, other reasons, very easily understandable underlying this attitude. There is a strong and sincere belief on the part of many Britons that the best we can do for the African is to teach him English and let him learn everything he needs through English. And it is true that Africans are drawn into a new current of life and ideas through the learning of a European language, especially if they go far enough to read with understanding and appreciation the best of English literature. There are also fields of knowledge that are at present closed to them without a European language and which under the best of conditions would remain closed for generations to come. Some of the practical difficulties, too, are such that to the "teach 'em all English" school this has, on the surface, seemed not only the easiest but also the most sensible way out. These beliefs have been shared in the past by numbers of Africans, though among them at present there is a reaction in favour of vernacular study. We return to this point later.

Language questions do indeed bristle with difficulties; some of these are too detailed to be discussed here, but we must consider those of general application which can be appreciated by the reader who is not a specialist in either linguistics or education. The number of African languages and the relatively small numbers of people speaking some of them makes it an economic impossibility to develop all into languages of literature. Miss Wrong deals with this aspect of the problem in her essay, where she describes the conditions upon which such development must depend. To help in the decision as to which languages can most usefully be developed we need more linguistic information: surveys of particular areas to find out which are likely to become dominant languages, whether a lingua franca is possible or not, which dialect of a group has the widest "spread" and would therefore be the best to adopt as the literary form. Questions of this kind often involve the dominance of political groups, the trading activities of certain tribes and what may be called the vested interests of the missions whose workers have written down a language and translated into it the Bible and other books. We owe a great deal of the work that has been done on African languages to the missionaries, and in many cases this has been of the highest order. It has sometimes happened, however, that by the chance of the place of mission settlement, a dialect has been written down which does not adequately serve the larger language group to which it belongs, and by the mere fact of writing down it has achieved a prestige which its qualities and the extent of the area over which it is spoken do not justify. At some later period, a branch of the tribe, becoming more politically conscious and receiving wider education, rejects this as unrepresentative of its language and demands its own written language. Such a situation needs careful handling to reach a satisfactory solution: it is obvious that to have several written forms which are fundamentally one language is undesirable from every point of view. The basis of such settlement must be unbiassed research. Similarly, surveys of those areas where a choice can still be made are essential to avoid multiplying these difficult situations. We can draw certain parallels with the dialect situation in European countries; for instance we have many dialects in Britain and only one written form. But the conditions which established the literary tradition in England cannot be artificially created, nor can we wait on time for a solution.

Parallel with the dialect question is that of orthography. The variety of methods which have been used to write down African languages is exceptionally large: not only have writers of different European languages used their own systems, differing in many details, but those of the same home language have used widely differing devices to represent African sounds, often in the same language. An attempt at simplifying and systematizing African orthographies was made by the International African Institute as one of its first activities,[1] and the Institute's suggestions have been accepted and introduced wholly or in part for over sixty languages. There are still some outstanding anomalies. It is, of course, impossible to make an orthography that will suit all languages, and modifications have to be made: it is noteworthy, however, that in those areas where the "Africa" orthography was introduced with little difficulty, the greatest progress in the development of literature has taken place.[2] We all know that questions of dialect, spelling and pronunciation start wild controversies and rouse sharp antagonisms and we cannot expect Africa to escape these. Patient examination and explanation of the problems, however, should go far towards settling them.

Another of the general problems affecting the use and development of African languages, again the result of the multiplicity of languages, is the problem of school education in areas where more than one language is spoken. What is to be the medium of instruction in a class of children that are divided among two or more vernaculars? It is true that these languages are usually closely related and it is not very difficult for speakers of one to learn the other vernacular. But it does present an added difficulty in education.

The points just touched upon are examples of practical problems which must affect language policy, however high our ideals may be. There are others which may interest the general reader with regard to the languages themselves. There has been a tendency among Europeans to consider African languages as "primitive," to think they have a small vocabulary, that they are incapable of expressing anything beyond the simplest ideas, and incapable of development.

This attitude has transferred itself to educated Africans

[1] *Practical Orthography of African languages:* Memorandum I of the International African Institute; second edition, 1930.
[2] In the Gold Coast and in South Africa (Zulu and Xhosa) for example.

who have despised, or affected to despise their own language. In both cases, that of the European and the African, such an attitude is based on ignorance. Neither knows the capabilities of the vernaculars. Again it is a question of sweeping assumptions without adequate factual background. Many of the African languages have large vocabularies, and are capable of expressing extremely fine shades of meaning.[1] It is true that they have not the means of expressing abstractions as have many European languages, nor have they the vocabulary ready-made to deal with modern inventions and ideas. But this does not mean that such powers will never develop. We need only remind ourselves of the history of the English language to illustrate how borrowings and adaptations have taken place and are indeed taking place in our own day and generation. Such borrowings and adaptations are being made in a number of African languages to-day.[2]

Nor should it be thought that Africa stands alone in these problems. The situation in Africa may be compared with that in Europe when Latin was used as a universal language for education and for general communication. The local European languages were despised as barbarous and clumsy, and unfit for literary purposes, just as many people have judged and are judging African languages. If the "barbarous tongue" of Britain had not been strong enough to withstand the attacks made on it from the Continent of Europe, the treasury of English literature would have been lost to the world. Fortunately, it was strong enough, and while holding its own as a language, showed a power of absorbing and transmuting what it wanted out of the languages of the conquerors. Latin in many European countries was rejected, and when accepted it was modified and became French, Spanish, Portuguese. The comparison between this situation in Europe, and the present conditions in Africa cannot, of course, be carried out rigidly; it needs some qualification owing to the different world we live in to-day. The general

[1] Much of this is conveyed by tonal patterns.
[2] See R. East *Modern Tendencies in the Languages of Northern Nigeria: the problem of European words*, *Africa*, vol x, No. 1, 1937.

speed of life, the greater mobility of people, rapid means of transport and communication, as well as the more universal demand for education, make the picture somewhat different, but the principle is the same.

We need not go to the past only for a parallel either. Situations comparable with those in Africa are found to-day in the less advanced areas of Europe and Asia. We have heard much recently of the progress made in Russia towards literacy in the local languages and in Russian.

We have said that the African tended to despise and neglect his own language. This attitude now appears to be changing and a new approach to the whole problem of the relationship between the vernacular and English is showing itself. This is part of a bigger thing, the desire to preserve and build upon the best in African culture. It may be based on a new national spirit which is a development to be expected, but there are signs that it has a deeper significance. Educated Africans, men and women educated to a high degree in western ideas, are the main forces behind some of these movements, and it would appear that having reached the place where they can fully appreciate European history, literature, art and science, and knowing how these are shared, in some measure, by all classes and types of people, begin to search for similar possibilities for their own people. And they find it in their languages, in their own history and traditions, in the philosophy as expressed in their proverbs, folk tales, tales of heroes and praise-songs, and in their arts and crafts.

This movement is probably a reaction from the former attitude of "everything English," and it also arises from a desire to have a historical past upon which to build which can foster a self-respect that could not thrive when Africa was regarded as the "dark continent," and the Africans as everything barbarous and uncivilized.

Nor is the attitude of these men confined to the study of the past. They know that the great mass of the illiterates must be raised to a level of education which will enable them to take an honourable part in some form of democratic government, and that this can only be done in the vernacular. Film and radio will play important parts in these mass and adult education schemes, but a literate population is necessary to carry out anything more than a superficial raising of the standards of living and of knowledge. A vast mass of reading material is necessary for the general advancement of the people. This side of the question is dealt with by Miss Wrong in her essay on "Literature and Literacy in African Colonies." But we may say here that it involves a deeper and wider study of the vernaculars by both African and European; it means that Africans must write and must learn to write. In our opinion no need in Africa is more urgent than the training of African writers to undertake the task of putting into the minds and hands of their people the modern tools for general development, material, social, political and spiritual.

We cannot envisage the question of language and the African without considering the place of English in the British Colonies. Does the increased weight on vernacular study we have suggested imply the neglect of English? By no means. A European language and the vernacular are not mutually exclusive: bilingualism is not impossible. There is an example of satisfactory bilingualism in Africa itself: Afrikaans and English are used in South Africa. In Canada many French are bilingual: in Switzerland the people are frequently tri-lingual, and in Russia there are many races in the eastern section of this vast territory that speak and read their own language and Russian. Both are taught and used in the schools. These recent experiments in Russian education should be examined and their results carefully observed: there is little doubt that we could learn much from them that could be of use in Africa.

In the British territories, to be able to speak and read English is likely to be an essential qualification for all men and women with any pretension to an education beyond that of the simplest primary grade. And a simple English can be taught in the primary schools if this does not mean neglect of the mother-tongue.

It is our firm conviction that the more careful the study and use of the vernacular is, the better and wider will be the English work, since language and its powers will be learnt on familiar ground, the mother-tongue: this discipline will then be transferred to the learning of English with much more satisfactory results.

A further practical use of English lies in its place as a general or auxiliary language for use in the joint activities of different tribes of one colony, and in the different colonies of one area. A united West Africa will need one general language. There are Africans to-day who, reacting against the domination of English, wish to see Hausa as the general language. To the present writer this would appear an unlikely development. It is true that Hausa is spoken as their mother-tongue by several millions of West Africans, and that the Hausa are traders making settlements in all the larger towns of the West Coast. But this does not constitute a lingua franca and the difference in structure between Hausa and other West African languages would probably militate against its general use. English is a more likely medium owing to the start it has had, and as it brings direct touch with the modern world.

In the East African territories the story is reversed. Swahili is considered as a lingua franca which can be used over very large areas, and as such its use has been advocated as the best second language of instruction. It is also so closely related to other Bantu languages that it is not difficult to learn. This policy has been firmly resisted in many areas where the mother-tongue is used in the first stages of education, and, where a second language of instruction is called for, an insistent demand has been made for English. What the final outcome of this controversy is likely to be is difficult to predict: there appear to be signs that the demand for English must be met.

What conclusions can we come to after these "reconnaissance sweeps" over the field of African languages? Miss Wrong's essay deals with some of the urgent practical moves and we may, I think, add a few generalizations here. First and foremost is the fact that the vernacular is likely to be one of the most effectual tools of immediate progress. This is becoming increasingly realized by African and European alike. From this it follows that every encouragement must be given to the development of the main vernaculars: further research into the languages themselves is a sine qua non of such development, and as Africans will be the main wielders of this tool, they must be drawn in with Europeans to investigate and analyse their languages on modern principles. Moreover, Africans must write, since a literary standard will only grow by writing, and writers do not sprout overnight; they need assistance, advice and training. Linguistic training therefore, comes in the first line of needs[1]; such personnel as this training can provide will form the nucleus of centres of study in Africa where, at institutions like Achimota, Makerere, the Rhodes-Livingstone Institute, in training and higher colleges and wherever universities may be established, departments of vernacular languages should in time be set up.

The second conclusion we come to is a psychological one. When the African realizes that, instead of the past of pure barbarity he has been led to look on his heritage, he has elements of culture on which to base his contribution to the modern world, his natural pride is roused. He no longer feels himself as having one foot in two cultures and neither very sure, with all the attendant feelings of frustration and insecurity. The study of his language is part of this development, for his language enshrines the wisdom and philosophy of his people. And when Europeans share this study—as they do—his pride is enhanced, and the psychological effects of this are called into play with limitless possibilities.

[1] As this article goes to press, it is announced that ten scholarships have been offered to Africans this year for linguistic study in England. Four Research studentships, not confined to Africans, are also to be awarded. Both classes are financed from the Colonial Research Fund.

Is Literacy Necessary in Africa?

by MARGARET WRONG

Political, economic and social development in the modern world makes necessary the spread of education to the whole population. Without the education of the people the foundations of democracies are insecure, as is recognized in the inscription over the entrance to the New York Public Library, which reads: "On the diffusion of education among the people rests the preservation of our free institutions." In totalitarian states also popular education is promoted in the interest of planned political, economic and social development.

A condition for the spread of popular education is the spread of literacy. The goal of universal literacy is in sight in the U.S.A. and Great Britain. The U.S.S.R. claims that whereas in 1897, 69 per cent of the population were illiterate, to-day only 10 per cent are unable to read and write, and Japan reports a literacy rate of over 99 per cent. But in spite of the fact that during the past twenty years great advance has been made in the spread of literacy in many states, the goal of universal literacy is still distant. Statistics are inadequate, yet on the basis of those available it is estimated that 62 per cent of the peoples of the world are still unable to read and write.[1]

We know that in British Africa the majority of the people are still illiterate. We must consider whether the spread of literacy is necessary for the political, economic and social development promised them by the Imperial Government, which is committed to their progressive advance towards self-government by "a series of pronouncements carrying an authority as complete as any which our constitution affords."[2] In addition to this, Britain is committed to economic and social advance which shall provide the peoples of British African territories with

---
[1] Literacy figures from *Towards a Literate World*, Laubach.
[2] Hailey, *Britain and her Dependencies*, p. 39.

improved standards of life,[1] for it is argued that self-government and the impartial rule of law alone is not enough to ensure freedom. "Effective freedom . . ." says Professor Hancock, "also signifies economic progress, a healthy diet, decent medical services and good educational opportunity." He adds that "progress towards self-government in British colonies might have been quicker if the Colonial Office had been aflame with a passion to wage total and unremitting war against poverty, disease and illiteracy."[2] What ground is there for the thesis that literacy is a condition of "effective freedom" for African peoples?

Can self-government be attained while the mass of the population are illiterate? It is true that some illiterate African chiefs and elders in council have in the past ruled over their illiterate subjects with a large measure of popular support. But the merging of tribal units under a central government which uses reading and writing as instruments of communication puts these illiterate rulers and peoples at a disadvantage in relation to the central administration, to other units in the British Commonwealth, and to the rest of the world. Under feudal African rulers—such as the Emirs of Northern Nigeria—the illiteracy of the mass of the people is a barrier against the gradual circulation of new ideas necessary for orderly evolution from feudal to more popular forms of government; for a large illiterate population which is easily swayed by rumour increases the likelihood of violent political change through sudden contact with the outside world and in particular through the return of men now serving in the forces whose education has been advanced and outlook broadened by their experiences. Then, too, when the masses of the population are illiterate it is difficult, if not impossible, to protect them from deception by unscrupulous persons who can deceive them about the purport of written regulations, and extort bribes for access to chiefs and officials to whom the people, by reason of their illiteracy, have no access through writing.

[1] *Statements of Policy on Colonial Development and Welfare*, Cmd. 6175.   [2] Hancock, *Argument of Empire*, p. 47.

In areas of white settlement in East and Central Africa the spread of literacy among the African population is an essential condition of advance to self-government, for to grant self-government while the majority of the population is isolated and hampered by illiteracy in response to pressure from a European minority means domination by that minority. This domination is feared by African peoples who ask in no uncertain terms to remain under the protection of the Imperial Government until there has been an advance in their educational attainments which will enable them to share political responsibility with the European minority.

The fear of domination by this minority has been plainly shown in African opposition to the proposed amalgamation of the Rhodesias and Nyasaland. To quote an African of Nyasaland: "It may be possible to argue that amalgamation might benefit the European community but it will never benefit the Africans. The natives are content to be under the protection of His Majesty's Government, and . . . do not wish any amalgamation with the Rhodesias. . . . Amalgamation would put an end to the development of self-administration. Nyasaland is a small country for Africans, protected from raids and civil wars by the British. The position is that of a small boy going a journey with a big man. The small boy (Nyasaland) does not want to go on the journey with the big man (Rhodesia) lest the big man overrule him and lest he lose interest in protecting him." Another African correspondent writes: "If we are far from civilization, it is the duty and responsibility of our missionaries and education department to see that we are being brought up step by step to the highest attainments in this world. We are protected by the Home Government, so we should remain for evermore."

For the sake of "effective freedom," the advance of education of the African population must be taken into account in fixing the date for the granting of self-government. Without this advance, it is impossible to ensure adequate representation by Africans in the legislature and adequate participation by

Africans in the administration. The spread of literacy among the people of British colonies and dependencies in Africa is a necessary step in the advance to self-government.

Nor can the economic development necessary for "effective freedom" be achieved without the spread of literacy. This development includes increased industrialization and mineral exploitation requiring the labour of African peoples. The illiterate African is condemned to remain an unskilled worker and is debarred from the wages and higher standard of life of the skilled worker. He is also in more danger of bodily harm than is the literate worker because he is unable to read warning notices and safety regulations. Illiterates have been killed at railway crossings and injured by machinery because of this disability. Then, too, the illiterate is easily deceived because he cannot read labour contracts, or the destination printed on the railway or bus ticket he buys. That Africans require both trade unions and co-operative movements is recognized by the British Government and steps are being taken to foster these,[1] but they cannot be established on secure foundations in the modern world with a membership isolated by illiteracy from the circulation of information and ideas, and from contact with other workers. So illiterates are debarred from skilled occupations and from participation in the control of economic development.

A large illiterate population is also a bar to the economic development of whole territories for it is not only the illiterate worker who labours under a grave disability, but the whole society. In Kenya, for instance, there are signs of a growing conviction among far-sighted Europeans that in the interest of the entire population the standard of life of Africans must rise, for 3,000,000 Africans living at a low standard limit consumption and retard the development of local markets. The spread of literacy undoubtedly fosters a desire for higher standards of life and increases the demand for commodities. This is indicated

[1] Cp. *Labour Supervision in the Colonial Empire*, 1937–43. Colonial No. 185, H.M. Stationery Office.

by the following letter of an African published in the newspaper *Baraza*, in Nairobi: "Modern education has undeniably brought about a standard of civilization among the Africans which calls strongly for a departure from that primitive state in which they were to a higher level of living and thinking, and to be able to respond to this irresistible call it is necessary to bring about a definite improvement on the material side of their existence." A European business man in South Africa stated a general truth when he said: "A Native who can read and write has a greater economic value to the community and commands a higher wage than one who cannot; indeed, the manual work in shops and stores and factories could not be carried out without this qualification."[1]

Africa is predominantly an agricultural country and the conservation of the soil and development of scientific agriculture is of primary importance for the wellbeing of the inhabitants and for the supply of products needed by the rest of the world. But erosion, wastage of the resources of the land, and the destruction of forests have reached menacing proportions. To conserve and develop the resources of the land, the co-operation of the people is essential, but adult illiterates bound by custom and ignorance are suspicious of new methods, and are slow to co-operate. In the report of the Native Affairs Department of Northern Rhodesia for 1938 it is stated: "It has been the subject of every report that improvement in the present rather deplorable conditions rests with the education of these peasant farmers by trained agricultural instructors, both white and black. It is also noticed that natives do not plough, cultivate, fertilize or do dozens of other things they should do properly, but what chances have they to learn?" The Soil Conservation Officer of Kenya writes: "Unfortunately, it has long been a tradition that agriculture is a suitable mode of life for the fool of the family. Africa is tending to adopt this European fallacy. But the land, in which society is rooted, demands the services of some of

[1] *Report of Native Economic Commission, Union of South Africa*, 1930–32, para 649.

the best men which society can produce if it is not to fail to nurture that society.[1]

In both industry and agriculture the full economic development of African colonies and dependencies is therefore impossible without a determined assault on illiteracy, for illiterates are debarred by ignorance from making their full contribution to that development.

Social advance also depends on the spread of literacy for in this sphere, too, illiterates are barred from full co-operation which alone will achieve success. For instance, the battle against disease cannot be won on the clinical front alone; preventive medicine on a grand scale is a condition of victory. The prevention of disease requires a growing understanding of scientific cause and effect on the part of the African population. A doctor with long experience in Africa points out that "the science of preventive medicine, based on scientific facts of cause and effect, has no ideas in common with African belief that health and disease are dependent on external enemies, human or spiritual, who can invoke magical powers if necessary. These deep-rooted beliefs about health and disease remain unshaken even where western medicine appears to have been accepted. Hospital drugs are known to cure the symptoms of certain diseases, and therefore are applied for, but at the same time the patient is paying the local 'doctor' first to find out the source and agent of the evil which is causing the disease, and secondly to remove it. There is also a large group of potential diseases for which the African never seeks aid at hospital; those which he believes threaten him on the breaking of a tribal sex taboo, and for which he must buy 'medicine' in order to protect him from the consequences of the lapse."[2]

In improving social conditions, the spoken word, films and broadcasting can arouse interest and introduce new ideas, but these have to be supplemented by the written word which can

[1] Colin Maher: "The People and the Land: Some Problems," *East African Agricultural Journal.*
[2] Janet Welch, *Health and the Home*, p. ix.

IS LITERACY NECESSARY IN AFRICA?

be constantly referred to if the new ideas are to bear fruit in action. When Africans recognize that knowledge relevant to improved conditions of life can be made available through the written word they make the effort to learn to read. In gatherings of African women in remote areas those who were barely literate have asked for health charts and printed material on the care of children in order to teach other women "the new wisdom which will keep death from our huts." There is abundant evidence that literacy must spread in order to wage total and unremitting war against disease.

In the report on *Mass Education in African Society*[1] adult literacy is regarded as "an essential means of achieving all-round progress," for the following reasons:

(*a*) It has been proved that the attainment of literacy makes people aware of the need for social and economic improvements, and therefore they will co-operate more readily with welfare and other agencies working on these lines.

(*b*) The rapid changes in family and village life make it imperative to give the people every possible means of understanding and controlling what is happening among them. Health measures in the home and village, enlightened training of children, correspondence with absentees, budgeting and account keeping—all become possible and in time acceptable to a literate people.

(*c*) In order to progress towards self-government in the modern world colonial peoples must learn to read, and to understand, not only about their own local affairs but those of wider import. If control in local government is to be on a wide and democratic basis, it cannot nowadays be in the hands of a mass of ignorant and illiterate people.

Therefore this report urges that African Colonial Governments

[1] *Mass Education in African Society*, Colonial No. 186, H.M. Stationery Office, 1s., 1943.

should "submit as soon as possible their proposals for the elimination of illiteracy within the next two or three decades."

What degree of literacy exists in British African colonies and dependencies to-day? It is impossible to give accurate statistics, for census returns do not furnish the necessary data. Rough estimates may be made based on education reports giving the number of children in school, and the length of school life, but records of adults who learn to read outside school are lacking. The extent and quality of elementary schooling, the adult education given by missions which make ability to read the Bible a condition of full church membership, and the degree of contact with European towns and industrial centres are factors that have to be taken into account in forming estimates of the extent of literacy.

We know that there are many obstacles to be faced and overcome if literacy is to spread. These obstacles fall roughly into three categories—lack of revenue to develop juvenile and adult education, lack of conviction about the need of universal literacy, and opposition on the part of certain groups and interests to its spread.

Revenue has been lacking for the establishment of compulsory, school education. Missions have initiated and are to-day carrying on the bulk of educational work with varying degrees of financial assistance from government, but they cannot meet the educational requirements of whole territories. In many parts of Africa schools are overcrowded or lacking. In some, children are being turned away for lack of room, for example, in South-Eastern Nigeria there are Christian schools with from 250–1,400 children in attendance, and demands for more which cannot be met. It is estimated that in British African colonies and dependencies only from 10–30 per cent of children between the ages of 6 and 10 years are in school. Many of these children have only two years in sub-standards, and it is doubtful how many of these achieve literacy. Africans are beginning to demand compulsory education and, like Europeans, to expect that those who pay taxes to the State should have education provided by

IS LITERACY NECESSARY IN AFRICA?

the State. Only in a few districts has it been possible to establish compulsory elementary education.

But compulsory elementary education alone will not make the population literate within a reasonable time. To achieve this the development of adult education must go hand in hand with the expansion of the school system. This, too, requires increased expenditure. The Colonial Office and local colonial administration are unlikely to be "aflame with passion to wage total and unremitting war against . . . illiteracy" unless revenue for this warfare is found.

If the public are "aflame with passion" to wage this warfare there is more hope of finding revenue, for the pressure of popular conviction is needed to speed up discovery of ways and means. The attendance at schools and the efforts made by many Africans to support and develop juvenile education indicates a growing desire for literacy, as does the effort made by many adults to learn to read. Reasons for this effort include the desire to read the Bible—the first book in many African languages—and strong economic incentives, specially among men and boys who go to work in European towns and industrial centres and become convinced that they are handicapped by illiteracy. The desire for literacy also spreads among women. A group of women in South-Eastern Nigeria gave the following reasons for wishing to become literate: desire to read the Bible, to have access to knowledge gained by their children in school, and to be able to read and write letters.

During 1943 experimental literacy campaigns, organized by missions in selected villages in Sierra Leone, revealed a growing demand. The report on these campaigns states:

> The first three or four weeks were spent in the preparation of posters, syllable charts, and lesson cards, etc. We met the Paramount Chief and Headmen and they showed themselves very interested and willing to help in any way possible. . . . Posters were nailed to the walls of houses in the town, some giving news items, some stating the ad-

vantages of being able to read (particularly with regard to health matters) and others being drawings. We were assured later that it was chiefly these latter that had persuaded so many to try to learn to read.

We instructed two young men and three young women in the teaching of the new lessons.

Within a few minutes of reaching the town on the morning of the opening day of the campaign, seventy men and women had bought copies of the first lesson, and by the late afternoon the number had reached one hundred. During the next few weeks the number reached two hundred and ten, out of an adult population of three hundred and ninety. The consequence of such a response was that the teachers were besieged by pupils as was any other person in the town who could read. Later in the day when the children came out of the town day-school they also were pressed into service.

One of the organizers of this campaign writes, "We have only just made a beginning and now requests are coming in from tribal authorities in other parts of the country as to whether they can have a campaign in their districts. . . . The astonishing thing, contrary to all our previous experience, is that in some places the number of women to learn is only a little less than that of the men. . . ."

Educational work in the forces is also spreading literacy and increasing the desire for it. A European writes of this work in African units: "We are doing as much as we can to give them a rudimentary education in literacy with a view not only to increasing their efficiency as soldiers but also to assist them in adapting themselves to post-war conditions." He adds that the men "are extremely keen on improving themselves educationally and our efforts are greatly appreciated by them." Men who have made the most of these educational facilities in the army when demobilized will return to their homes as apostles of literacy.

Though the demand for literacy is spreading among Africans,

ignorance and isolation still breed among many of them complacency with things as they are or inertia and frustration. The result is closed minds and lack of initiative. Many of the older people think they cannot learn to read. This belief can only be overcome if confidence in their ability to learn can be fostered, and the effort of learning brings benefits. A man of seventy in Nigeria wanted to become a census clerk but did not believe himself capable of learning anything. His struggles with the A, B, C depressed him and his teacher. Then he discovered that he was the best mathematician in the class and "after that he was full of confidence, mastered even the A, B, C with his shaking hand, and became one of the chief census clerks."[1]

Besides indifference, and lack of conviction about the need of literacy, there is opposition to its spread on the part of some Africans and some Europeans. Feudal rulers such as the Emirs of Northern Nigeria, are not necessarily anxious to promote literacy which will result in the spread of new ideas and questioning of the present political pattern. An educated African, for instance, who proposed starting adult reading classes in one place in Northern Nigeria, met with a warm response from illiterates but no encouragement from the Native Administration. In Muslim communities in particular, many men are not anxious that women should be literate, for in the words of a Muslim worthy, "If a woman learns to read she is disobedient to her husband, and if she learns to write she writes to other men."

Some Europeans who sincerely desire the advancement of African peoples, lack conviction about the need of universal literacy. Some regard literacy as dangerous because ability to read means access to evil as well as good. Others—usually without first-hand knowledge—think that broadcasting and films are substitutes for the written word and that literacy for all is unnecessary.

There are other Europeans, including some farmers, industrialists, and skilled white workers who oppose the spread of literacy because they fear it will interfere with a supply of

[1] Joyce Cary, *The Case for African Freedom*, pp. 91-2.

cheap African labour. Literate Africans demand higher wages, show more initiative, and are more likely to compete with white labour. These opponents of the spread of literacy agree with the late Professor Malinowski, that "to educate a man is to raise not only his knowledge and skills, but also his hopes and his ambitions, his claims for full citizenship, and the sense of his personal dignity,"[1] and they see literacy as a step in this direction, so unless literate Africans are necessary for the performance of some work required by them they are against its spread.

In the long run, obstacles to the spread of literacy will be overcome by the determination of the people to learn to read. Literacy will spread as it becomes evident to them that there is information in books which will enrich their lives. Religion has been, and is a powerful incentive to learning to read. Both Muslims and Christians are "People of the Book." Learning to read the Koran in Arabic is a religious duty for Muslim men, and among many Christians, reading the Bible in the mother-tongue is a powerful spur to literacy. Economic opportunities available to the literate are another powerful incentive. Salaries of teachers and clerks are sought after to-day for—in the phrase of an African schoolboy—they offer "a little cure for my financial influenza." There is also a growing desire among the rank and file for access to knowledge found in books, whether it be on health or on other subjects, and the desire for information about the rest of the world and its customs grows with contact. An old African elder, for instance, in a central African village, asked for "a book in my own tongue which tells how England is governed and why white men do what they do." The conception of recreation through reading is still limited to a minority, but is spreading, and favourite English authors range from Shakespeare to Ethel M. Dell.

It is evident that women are coming to see the value of literacy because they realize that literacy helps them to deal more efficiently with a difficult environment and to pass on what they

[1] B. Malinowski, *Native Education and Culture Contact*. International Review of Missions, October, 1936.

know. "Write down the recipes you have taught me," said an African woman to a European. "for I want to remember them and teach them to other women in my village." The war strengthens the desire of women for literacy, because they wish to write to and to read letters from sons, husbands and sweethearts with the forces.

The incentive for the spread of adult literacy is lacking if printed material available is unintelligible or irrelevant to the life and interests of adults. It is useless, for instance, to expect the adult to be spurred on to making the considerable effort required if the books available for the first stages of acquiring this new skill are only children's primers. Dr. Laubach points out that "the illiterate has a sense of inferiority and is very apprehensive lest he may not be able to learn," and that "We must find a rather powerful motive for study before we can overcome this fear of failure." So in successful adult literacy campaigns teachers of adults emphasize the advantages—political, social, economic, material and spiritual—to which the literate has access. The final page in one primer for adults used in the Philippines reads in translation:

> Now you are very happy, for you have learned to read.
> This is good luck for you.
> It is like your release from prison.
> You are coming into a new world.
> The wisdom of the world has been collected in books.
> You will become very wise if you read these books.
> If you do not read, you will soon forget what you learned.
> Now you must read every issue of the *Lanao Progress*
>   (a simple periodical).
> We are printing secrets from all the world.
> We are searching through a thousand books and a
>   hundred magazines to find these secrets for you.
> If you read every page you will become wiser.
> Some day you will be a leader in Lanao.
> If you read the laws we publish, you will become clever.

You will be able to read all epics, lyrics, sacred stories, romances, news, and wise counsel.[1]

It is obvious that to spread literacy a growing literature of interest to the people is required, but in what language shall that literature be produced? In all British colonies and dependencies there is a strong desire for English, for Africans consider that without a European language they are at a disadvantage in the modern world and are cut off from its life and thought, and from economic advancement. Literature in simple English must therefore be included in plans for spreading literacy. But English is not enough. The whole population will not become literate in a foreign tongue; and in any case, as Dr. Ward points out in her essay, "The mother-tongue is the true vehicle of mother-wit." She also shows that a rift is caused in families where the older generation is illiterate or literate in a language with little or no literature, while the younger generation depends on reading English as the source of new ideas. For this and other reasons elaborated by Dr. Ward, the necessity of a growing literature in African languages is pressing, even though the practical difficulties of developing such a literature are many and include multiplicity of languages and dialects, and selection of a lingua franca as a vehicle of literature in areas where language groups are small and local. For this development of literature in African languages the encouragement of African authors is essential.

What publications in African languages exist? A count based on information available in London, which was made in 1938,[2] notes publications in 302 African languages. A bibliography recently compiled in Nigeria lists publications in 54 languages of that territory. In a few African languages there is a growing literary development, but in others there are only one or two booklets and no additions have been made for many

---

[1] F. Laubach, *Towards a Literate World*, p. 45.
[2] *A Survey of Literature in African Languages*, Books for Africa, January, 1939.

years. Publications fall under three headings: religious books, school books, and general literature, the majority being literature on Christianity and textbooks. The Bible, or portions of it, has been printed in 290 African languages. Since 1938 a considerable number of publications in various African languages have been added and the response to literary competitions indicates a growing interest among educated Africans in the development of literature in their own tongues.

Though literature in most African languages is still at an early stage, an examination of published material by African authors in a number of languages includes folk-lore, proverbs, songs, customs, history, biography, religion, poetry, drama and fiction. The fostering and guiding of this literary movement is of the first importance, for the supply of literature is obviously inadequate. The teaching of reading has greatly improved, but what is the good of that if there are not publications of interest to read? If literacy is to spread, a movement to produce literature in selected African languages on a scale not yet attempted is required.

Once literature is produced, it has to be efficiently distributed, both in centres of population and in lonely places. For this a variety of channels have to be created. Missions have been the pioneers in setting up bookshops and depots. Mission stations and schools have been centres of distribution. These facilities need to be increased. In great African markets and traders' stores most commodities but books can be obtained. Mobile units and colporteurs are few. Libraries are small or more often non-existent. A number of efforts to establish libraries have failed. A promising beginning in a big West African town had in 1939 dwindled to a single case of dusty novels in a municipal building, and before it sat a tax collector, as though the unattractive collection in itself was not enough to hold a would-be reader at bay! The usual cause of failure is that the interested founder has died or gone away, and there are not trained African librarians to guide and encourage reading and to make the library a centre of adult education. Fortunately, a new day is dawning in British West Africa, for a library school is being started there under the auspices of the British Council.

Once we admit that the spread of literacy is an essential condition for the political, economic and social advance to which Great Britain is committed in African colonies and dependencies, we admit the magnitude and the urgency of the task waiting to be done, a task which includes the creation and distribution of literature, as well as teaching whole populations to read. This can only be accomplished by the united effort of Africans and Europeans "aflame with a passion to wage total and unremitting war against illiteracy."

Some Problems of Tropical Economy
by J. S. FURNIVALL

1. *Definition*. It is my privilege in this paper to suggest for consideration some problems of tropical economy, by which I mean the economic aspect of tropical society. The study of tropical economy has, I think, been unduly neglected. Much has been written on the political problems of the tropics: on Dominion Status, Trusteeship, the Dual Mandate, Direct and Indirect Rule, Assimilation and Association, and so on; but students of tropical *politics* tend to disregard the *economic* aspect of social life. Much has been written also on the economic problems of the tropics: on the development of their physical resources and their human wealth, on progress and welfare; but students of tropical *economics* tend to disregard the *social* and *political* aspect of economic life. Much again, during recent years, has been done by students of tropical anthropology to draw attention to the economic significance of social relations and customs; but their main interest is in race and culture, and these can best be studied where least contaminated by European influence. Tropical economy touches, but is distinct from tropical politics, economics and anthropology; it has an interest of its own, and is most interesting where European influence is strongest.

The subject is as wide as the tropics—world-wide, and co-extensive with humanity. One's outlook on it is necessarily coloured by one's experience. My own experience has been in Burma and the tropical Far East. But the main problems of tropical economy arise out of contact between two contrary principles of social life under conditions generally similar; everywhere therefore they are much the same. Under native rule the social order rested on personal relations, with the tie of kinship, reinforced by custom, imposing duties sanctioned by religion; even where some form of territorial organization had emerged, the personal nexus still remained the basis of society.

Both social and political relations were personal, not legal; and authority was based on Will and not on Law. Law, indeed, was conceived as superhuman, religious, like *kismet* or *dhamma*. In Europe, on the contrary, a civilization derived from Greece and Rome under the vitalizing force of Christianity has, during the past four hundred years, shown an increasing tendency to base economic and social relations upon reason, and to apply law—no longer superhuman but an instrument of social will— to the assertion and protection of rights. Wherever Europe has gained any measure of control over the tropics, contact has been established between these two contrary principles: between the tropical system resting on religion, personal custom and duties, and the western system resting on reason, impersonal law and rights. Ordinarily control has been established for the economic advantage of the colonial power, and the general result has been the domination of tropical society by economic forces.

I wish, first, to illustrate the working of these forces in the external and internal relations of tropical society; then to show that they had created a society *different in kind* from that of Europe. with a characteristic tropical economy raising problems distinct from those of Europe; and then to invite your attention to some of these problems.

2. *Evolution of external relations.*—If we examine the evolution of colonial relations, we can hardly fail to notice the close correspondence between colonial policy and the economic advantage of the colonial power. Starting from the seventeenth century we may distinguish four stages. During the first stage the objective of colonial policy was tribute. This could be obtained with least cost and trouble by utilizing and strengthening the authority of native chieftains on a system of *indirect rule*. The Industrial Revolution introduced a second stage and, during the nineteenth century, the object of colonial policy was to open up markets for European manufactures. This required the rule of law through native assistants, no longer native chieftains exercising authority on native lines, but trained in western schools to work on western lines. The system adopted was one of *direct rule*, and

SOME PROBLEMS OF TROPICAL ECONOMY 163

there was a beginning of western education and self-government. The third stage may be dated from about 1870 and the opening of the Suez Canal. It arose out of the growth in Europe of large-scale enterprise needing vast supplies of raw materials from the tropics; native enterprise was inadequate to the demand and there began the direct development of tropical resources with European capital. European employers wanted intelligent and healthy labour and technical assistants; and we find a new interest in native uplift, and especially in primary and technical instruction and in hygiene. Concessions, and to some extent labour, could most conveniently be obtained through native chieftains and, outside the mines and plantations, a poor and scanty population could afford only a cheap administration along native lines. We find, accordingly, a reversion to indirect rule, but with one eye on uplift, as exemplified in the doctrine of the *dual mandate*. Soon, about 1900, there followed a fourth stage. In Europe the growing power of capital was countered by the labour movement; but in the tropics capitalists could obtain cheap and unorganized labour, and there set in a trend towards industrialization in the tropics. This brought little change in tropical administration, except that capitalist production had found most scope in rural areas and, with industrialization, the centre of interest shifted to the towns, where indirect rule was inconvenient and aroused criticism. But we find something new in Europe. The Labour Party and Socialists wake up, quite suddenly, to their material interest in the tropics and to their imperial responsibilities; there appears the germ of a conflict in colonial policy along class lines.

An attempt to cover within a single paragraph the history of three hundred years up to this day necessarily leaves holes to patch and points to criticize. But I am attempting merely to illustrate in broad outline the parallel between colonial policy and economic interest. I do not suggest that other factors were wholly inoperative. National policy reflects ideas transcending economic ends. These ideas have an independent vitality, and men accept them even to their prejudice. Liberty, Democracy,

Nationalism: with each new god we fashion, we trust him though he slay us. But in colonial policy ideas suffer a sea change. Take for instance education. So early as 1793 Wilberforce was urging on Parliament the duty of providing instruction in India; the first missionaries reached India only a few years later, and in 1815 the Governor-General expressed his sympathy with the ideal of general public instruction. As yet education was only a humanitarian ideal. But cheap cottons were just beginning to reach India, and twenty years later western education was becoming a practical necessity. In 1835 the Government passed a Resolution to promote education, and this was confirmed as a main head of policy in 1854. Yet it was only with the improvement of communications and the opening of the Suez Canal that commerce and education went forward hand in hand with giant strides. Idealists had created an atmosphere favourable to the cause of education, but instruction spread only so far as economic circumstances were propitious. Even so, humanitarian ideals went awry in application. The ideal was the uplift of the masses by general primary instruction. Yet schooling remained the privilege of the few, who sought it not on cultural grounds, but with a view to make a living; and the schools were not a medium of culture but narrowly vocational and material, even when conducted by missionaries. Only during the present century, under the pressure of nationalism and with the demand for more intelligent labour, did primary instruction begin to make notable progress. Here, I suggest, we have an illustration of the general principle that in colonial relations humanitarian ideas do not control but are controlled by economic circumstances, and that in modern tropical society economic forces are abnormally and unhealthily predominant.

3. *Evolution of internal relations.*—Turn now to the evolution of internal relations, as illustrated by some sketches of social life in Burma. We conquered Burma in three stages during the nineteenth century. In 1826 we took over two outlying coastal provinces; in 1852 we linked these together by the occupation of Lower Burma; and in 1886 completed the absorption of the

country by annexing Upper Burma. During the nineteenth century the main object of our colonial policy was to obtain markets for our manufactures, and in Burma we introduced the system appropriate to this policy, direct rule through native assistants. The two oldest coastal provinces were, and until recently remained, thinly peopled and unprofitable. Lower Burma in 1852 was a waste of swamp and jungle but, after the opening of the Suez Canal in 1870, was rapidly brought under cultivation by immigrants from Upper Burma growing rice for export. Upper Burma was the centre of an old oriental civilization. Upper and Lower Burma provide an instructive contrast; the former illustrates the impact of western rule on an established social order, and the latter a society built up under western rule.

A typical village in Upper Burma was rather like a large family, with its life centring round the Buddhist monastery and the soil. It was not self-contained after the Indian pattern, and caste was unknown. In the monastery all the boys, rich and poor alike, learned their letters, their national traditions and the rudiments of their religion; any lad of promise might aspire to the highest positions in the land, but mostly they continued on the land, as owners or cultivators. The land round the village was worked with a variety of crops on a system evolved through long experience as most convenient to the general social welfare of the village; waste land was common to all, for grazing, fuel, etc. The people cultivated mainly for home consumption, disposing of their surplus largely by barter; money was little used and hardly needed. Petty trade was the province of the women, who enjoyed many privileges that until recently were exceptional in Europe. Social and economic life were regulated by village custom and *social demand prevailed over individual demand*. The general pattern of social life was summarized in a proverb, "Cultivation gives place to houses, and houses to the monastery"; religion came first, man next, and money last. Life had, of course, its darker side. Their world was small, and life and property were insecure against war, oppression and scarcity; but they had a civilization with many pleasant features and, on the whole, it gave them what they wanted.

Western rule upset the balance by substituting the rule of law for the rule of custom. For example, in one tract chillies were cultivated. The profits in a wider market tempted a few people to cultivate them on land reserved by custom as the catchment area of rice fields. There was no law against this, and appeals to authority were ineffective. Before long the rice land was thrown out of cultivation. A few people were richer, but the village as a whole was poorer; individual demand had prevailed over social demand. Again, on irrigated land elaborate customs provided for an equitable distribution of the water. One man would take to cultivating onions. There was no law against this, but it upset the system of distribution and the rice fields were destroyed. Similarly encroachments over the waste put an end to common rights of fuel and grazing. The cultivators produced more crops for export, and could buy more European manufactures, but gradually, everywhere, in all aspects of life, *individual demand prevailed over social demand*. The process was more rapid where Europeans, Indians, and Chinese came in as merchants and middlemen, but it penetrated in some degree to the remotest village, with a corresponding dissolution of society into a mass of individual atoms.

Turn now to Lower Burma. Here, after the opening of the Suez Canal, immigrants by the hundred thousand poured down from Upper Burma to grow rice for export. The reclamation of the swamp and jungle was costly, and they had to borrow money. The only people with access to capital were Indian money-lenders and, ordinarily, by the time the land was cleared it had to be made over to the Indian money-lender for debt. Gradually there evolved what has been officially described as a "system of industrial agriculture organized for the export market."[1] The land was owned by absentees whose sole concern was to get as much rent as possible by letting it annually to the man who offered most. Tenants, shifting ordinarily from year to

[1] *Indian Statutory Commission*, XI, p. 18 (H.M.S.O., 1930).

year, cultivated large holdings with hired labour employed separately for each agricultural operation; some of these operations were performed by Indian coolies. Thus, by the economic process of natural selection by the survival of the cheapest, the countryside was converted into a factory without chimneys. The pattern of economic—one cannot say of social—life was further diversified by the presence in the larger villages of Chinese, selling liquor or general stores and often illicit opium. Among the shifting rural population there was no possibility of social life, and individual demand in its crudest form prevailed over social demand.

The present century saw a further development when European capital was applied to the working of oil fields, mines and plantations with foreign labour. But the foreign elements were most conspicuous in the towns. For, by the working of economic forces, the activities of the Burmese were restricted almost exclusively to agriculture, while urban occupations were in the hands of Indians and Chinese, who functioned as middlemen between the Burman and the Europeans, round whom the whole process centred. The general result was that the organization of the community for social life, characteristic of a Burman village under native rule, was transformed more or less completely into an economic system organized like a factory for production.

In other dependencies, where indirect rule has prevailed, as in Malaya, the dissolution of native society has been more gradual and less complete. But, in proportion as the people are protected from the adverse effects of economic progress, they tend to be shut off from its stimulating influence. In either case, under direct rule, the final result of social evolution is a plural society in which economic forces are abnormally and unhealthily predominant.

4. *The plural society.*—It is this plural society that I suggest is characteristic of the modern tropics. One finds there a society in which two or more groups live side by side but separately within the same political unit. All the members of all the groups

are subject alike to the economic process of natural selection by the survival of the cheapest, and all respond in greater or less degree to the economic motive, the desire for individual material advantage. But that is all they have in common. Each group holds by its own religion, its own culture and its own ideas and ways of life; the members of each group mix with those of other groups only in the market place, in buying and selling. These conditions have economic and political implications.

From the economic standpoint one distinctive feature is the lack of organic unity within each group; each group tends to consist of an aggregate of individuals, with individual demand prevailing over social demand. Again, taking all the groups together, there is no common standard of welfare and no common standard of general welfare. This is true also as regards production. The European has his own standards as to what "is not done" in business; so have the other groups. Each group has its own idea as to what is right and proper, but they have different ideas. The most obvious character, however, is that the tension existing everywhere between classes with conflicting economic interests is aggravated in a plural society by a corresponding cleavage along racial lines.

That reacts on political stability. The groups together form a business partnership rather than a family concern. But it is a business in which a dissolution of the partnership would involve the bankruptcy of all concerned. Few recognize this fact, and most see that on many points their material interests conflict. At these points economic forces are always tending to create friction, and the plural society is in fact held together only by pressure exerted from outside by the colonial power; it has no common social will.

Here then are the main points of difference between tropical economy and that of Europe. In the political affairs of Europe we can take a common social will for granted, and our concern is how best to ascertain and give effect to it; in the plural society of the tropics we must first create a common social will. On the

SOME PROBLEMS OF TROPICAL ECONOMY

economic side of life, in Europe we can take demand for granted, and our concern is how best to organize supply; in the plural society of the tropics we must first organize demand.

5. *Problems of tropical economy.*—Now, if this analysis of tropical economy be accepted, it must be taken as a basis for any restatement of colonial policy. In attempting any such restatement two points must be borne in mind. One is that, however unsatisfactory the result, nevertheless extensive readjustments of native society were needed, not merely in our interests, but in the interests of the peoples themselves. They were inevitable. "No man liveth to himself alone," and it was not merely inevitable but good for the people to make contact with the modern world, however unwelcome, even at the expense of foreign rule, however unpleasant. The other point to bear in mind is that present conditions have not arisen out of statements of policy in the past. There was no deliberate choice between indirect rule, direct rule and the dual mandate. They were dictated by economic circumstances; they happened. Again, there has, on the whole, been little encouragement of foreign immigration; on the contrary, it has been discouraged, sometimes even by massacres. The plural society was not planned; it happened.

The path to it was indeed paved with good intentions. A generation of Liberals proclaimed the doctrine of economic freedom; their Imperialist successors assumed the "white man's burden" of developing the tropics; the modern catchword is —shall we say—"world welfare." Each generation claims new and higher ideas of its imperial responsibilities; but because it has one eye on its material advantages the high ideas go wrong in application. The Liberals gave freedom of opportunity—to manufacturers; the Imperialists gave freedom of opportunity—to capitalists; does world welfare imply more than freedom of opportunity to a tacit combination between European manufacturers, capitalists and wage-earners? I find it impossible to study the history of colonial relations without thinking of Jack Horner, who sat in a corner, eating a Christmas pie. He put in his thumb and pulled out a plum, and said "What a good boy am I!" In the interest of world welfare we desire that tropical dependencies shall be free and prosperous. Good. If free, they will not involve us in war. If prosperous, they can afford to buy our wares rather than cheaper goods from, say, Japan. If tropical labour is well paid and well regulated it will not compete unfairly with European labour. We urge reforms in the interest of world welfare and the tropical peoples; but they are also in our own interest. There is no harm in that. But it should make us look to our motives, and to the methods in which we propose to give effect to them. Are we merely turning a new page in the history of Jack Horner, or are we really turning over a new leaf?

I think that, if we examine the programmes of colonial policy now commonly put forward, we shall find that they would tend to our advantage rather than to the advantage of the dependent peoples; that they would tend either directly to make tropical society more unstable and less capable of independence, or would have the same effect indirectly by giving freer play to antisocial economic forces. Jack Horner has not yet pulled out all the plums. Will he finish the pie before he turns over a new leaf?

Everywhere, not merely in the tropics, there is an unceasing conflict between economic progress and human welfare, between individual and social welfare, and between social and political welfare. But, finally, political welfare is the condition not merely of social and individual welfare, but also of economic progress. In colonial relations there is an unceasing conflict between our interests, or what we take to be our interests, and the interests of the people, or what they take to be their interests. But, finally, world welfare is a condition both of their interests and ours. That, however, is an article of faith, resting on the evidence of things unseen; economic progress on the contrary appeals to universal common sense.

In the light of this analysis, then, I will venture to offer for consideration four propositions with regard to tropical economy, each presenting a corresponding problem of colonial policy.

SOME PROBLEMS OF TROPICAL ECONOMY 171

I. The plural society has come into existence because the only factor common to all groups and members has been the economic factor. Trying to cure its defects by purely economic measures is like casting out devils in the name of Beelzebub. *The first* problem is to find some principle transcending material ends, some moral principle, that *all* can accept as valid.

II. The economic factor predominates because the colonial power, exercising political control, is primarily concerned for its economic interests. The *second* problem is then to dissociate so far as possible economic and political control; to find some moral and not solely material authority.

III. The predominance of economic forces is prejudicial to social and individual welfare because these forces sacrifice social to individual demand. The *third* problem, accordingly, is to devise some machinery for the organization of demand.

IV. The plural society is inconsistent with political welfare because it is unable to stand alone for lack of a common social will. The *fourth* problem therefore is to devise some means of creating a common social will.

6. *Nationalism.* To solve the problem of finding a principle transcending the sphere of economics we must turn to religion. We can find such a principle in Christianity, in Islam or in Buddhism; but it is valid only for those who hold the same religious faith. This limitation applies also to most of the modern religions or quasi-religions: Socialism, Communism, Fascism, Nazism. One such principle, however, makes a general appeal— the principle of Nationalism. One need not be a Scotsman to accept the principle of Scottish Nationalism, and if a Scotsman tells us that he drinks whisky instead of water because it is the national beverage, we may not believe him, but we can accept his statement politely as an explanation and not merely an excuse. As this illustration suggests, there can be nationalism without a nation. In Burma we have Shan and Karen nationalism; tribalism would come under the same head where tribal peoples have not yet risen to the concept of a common nation. In nationalism, then, we have a moral principle that all can accept as valid, and

that furnishes a criterion of policy other than the criterion of individual advantage.

7. *Control.* But nationalism, dangerous everywhere, has peculiar dangers in the plural society of the tropics. For it not only sharpens the edge of antagonism between the groups, but sets the large native majority against the Government representing the colonial power, weakening instead of strengthening society, and encouraging the Government to make unreal or unwise concessions, and to rely more actively on division as a principle of rule. But the dangers and difficulties are due chiefly to the fact that the interests of the colonial power are, or seem and are thought to be, closely identified with one group in the plural society, the group representing European capital interests. The solution lies in separating economic and political control.

That, however, is merely an old problem in a new form. So long as officials in the tropics were mercantile employees they preferred their private interests above their public duties; only by dissociating their private and official interests, by converting them into civil servants, was it possible to secure uncorrupt administration. Again, so long as chartered companies combined government and commerce, they looked to profit rather than to public welfare; only by imposing State supervision was it possible to make them govern even well enough to avoid financial ruin. Now the same problem takes the form of establishing international supervision over national colonial relations.

Suggestions to that effect have often been propounded recently. Some go so far as to advocate international administration; but it should hardly be necessary to argue that this is impracticable, as impracticable as interchanging the English mayor with the French prefect or the Dutch burgomaster. Others, more plausibly, suggest international control. But that, even if accepted by the colonial powers, might lead not improbably to a still more formidable domination of Europe over the tropics. A system of international supervision however, would be merely a stage further in a process that has been operative for some sixty years. My purpose now is to state problems rather than to provide solutions; it is difficult, however, to state problems effectively without illustrating them, and possible solutions afford convenient illustrations. But it is the problems rather than the solutions that I ask you to consider. Let me then illustrate how international supervision over colonial relations might work.

Presumably an Allied victory will lead to a reconstitution of the League of Nations along new lines, with a special branch for colonial relations and a regional committee for each major area. I suggest that each political unit should submit annually to the appropriate regional committee a report on the *measures adopted*, and *progress achieved* in respect of *individual, social* and *political* welfare. That may seem a small matter. But it is, I think, all that is immediately practicable, and I wish to show that no more is immediately necessary. The regional committee would exercise a *moral* authority superior to that of particular colonial powers, resting on a *moral* principle superior to particular economic interests. The submission of annual reports would *confirm* colonial powers in their professions of good will, *encourage* mutual emulation between them in well-doing, *assist* them in restraining anti-social economic forces, and *tend to allay* nationalist suspicions as to their good faith. But *its most important function* would be to serve as a school of comparative tropical economy, where all could learn from the achievements and mistakes of others. Science is nothing if not disinterested; but in colonial relations we believe what it suits us to believe and prove what we want to prove. The regional committee might in some degree *transfer colonial relations to the realm of science*; it would help us to find out what we ought to do and, until we know that, we may always, with the best intentions, do more harm than good.

8. *Individual and Social Welfare.* Next to indifference, weakness of good will, it is the lack of knowledge that hinders the promotion of individual and social welfare in the tropics; we do not know what to do, or how to do it, or how best to provide

the necessary funds. There are three aspects of the problem: aims, machinery, finance.

(*a*) *Aims*.—In the past many useful experiments have been made in the promotion of tropical welfare; some successful, others no less instructive because they failed. Such experiments and their results would come to light and be available for general information in the annual welfare reports to the Regional Committees. The annual reports would also reproduce local statistics and, when subjected to critical examination, the insufficiency of these would immediately become apparent. It is not merely that tropical statistics are often inadequate and inaccurate; many dependencies compile masses of statistics of meticulous accuracy—and quite useless. In general such statistics convey information about economic progress, but otherwise are mainly of departmental interest—if any: they tell very little about welfare. For example, during the past twenty years, political reforms have purported to confer greater power on the natives both in Burma and in Netherlands India; yet from an analysis of the trade returns it would seem that, during the same period, the economic position of foreign capital has grown stronger and that of the natives weaker. So far as economic power reacts on political power the political reforms appear to have been ineffective. That is the kind of information which the regional committees would require; at present it must be dug out of the figures by laborious research, but the scientific study of welfare would place it in the foreground. It is not sufficient to collect more, and more accurate, statistics, unless they are correlated with the constitution of tropical economy and its problems. In this *organization of knowledge* the regional committees might play a leading part.

The organization of *knowledge*, however, avails little without a corresponding organization of *thought*. Tropical affairs receive little attention in Parliament or in the Press. More has been done recently to meet the need for the consideration and discussion of such knowledge as is available, but in the Netherlands much more is done; the periodicals devoted to colonial affairs are not only more numerous but better informed. Here we depend largely on retired officials like myself, twenty years behind the times, or on missionaries, who usually know little of administration, or on natives who, too often, may know little of their country. Very few people know much about tropical economy except officials who come in contact with it in their daily work. In Netherlands India officials may discuss and criticize Government policy freely both in speech and writing, and this goes far to explain the remarkable progress of the Dutch in tropical administration during the present century. But, on the English tradition, officials are muzzled; they cannot even bark. In view of the need for informed discussion and of Dutch practice and its results, the possibility of allowing greater freedom to officials generally might well engage the attention of the suggested regional committees. Here again, however, my purpose is to state problems rather than to provide solutions, and *the better organization of knowledge and thought* is one of the great problems of tropical administration.

(*b*) *Machinery.*—If we could know what to do, it might seem easy to do it. But the thing is not so simple. Welfare projects may relate *either* to individual *or* to social welfare. Projects of *individual* welfare may depend *either* on individual *or* on co-operative effort. Projects of *social* welfare all require co-operative effort; some the people will *approve*, to many they will be *indifferent*, and some, many will *oppose*. Let me give a few examples.

At the beginning of the century the cultivation of groundnut was unknown in Burma. Government distributed seed. For some years the experiments were unsuccessful and the ill-success was attributed to the conservatism of the people, the easy and acceptable explanation usually put forward when welfare projects fail. Then a cultivator happened to hit on the right soil and appropriate methods of cultivation; he got a paying crop and within a few years groundnut spread over many hundred thousand acres. By their *individual* efforts cultivators could make a profit and nothing more was necessary for the crop to spread.

A few years later millers offered a premium for a certain type of paddy. The Agricultural Department tried to popularize it. But the millers could not afford to pay the premium unless they could obtain supplies in bulk. That implied co-operative production over large areas where most of the cultivators were shifting tenants holding their land for no longer than a year. The cultivators would have welcomed higher prices for their paddy, but co-operative effort was impracticable. Again, in some parts of Burma cultivation is liable to damage by erosion. In the early stages this can easily be prevented by local co-operation, and the people can easily be made to understand the importance of preventing it. But ordinarily it escapes notice and people remain indifferent until simple remedies are no longer feasible. Moreover, it is often due to the cutting of fuel for boiling palm sugar, and measures to stop the practice will be unwelcome to those who manufacture sugar.

All these illustrations, which could be multiplied indefinitely, are drawn from agriculture, where the popular idea of welfare ordinarily coincides with ours. But in other matters their ideas and ours are often different. If they prefer showy but insanitary houses, or palatable rather than nutritious food, how can we help them? One finds suggestions that everything can be done by education or compulsion. Can it? I remember visiting a school during a lesson in hygiene. The teacher was instructing his class from the approved text-book, and he was surprised and aggrieved when I suggested that the best lesson in hygiene would be to clear away the dirt and cobwebs in the schoolroom. That was not his job. His job was to get his pupils through an examination qualifying them for various appointments, including appointment as—sanitary inspectors. Again, when plague first came to Burma, Indian coolies, ignorant of Burmese, were sent round some of the towns to whitewash the interior of Burman houses. That was done with the best intentions, but it did not make the Government more popular, it did not teach the people sanitation and, incidentally, tended to spread rather than to prevent plague. These examples of education and compulsion

SOME PROBLEMS OF TROPICAL ECONOMY 177

are not encouraging. But both education and compulsion bear intimately on welfare projects and deserve further examination.

On no matter, perhaps, is there so general agreement as on the value of education, and especially of primary instruction. This, it is suggested, will teach the people to improve their agriculture, to shake off the bonds of the money-lender, and will open out wider horizons and lead them towards autonomy. I must confess to scepticism. Over large parts of the tropical Far East literacy has long been more widely spread than it was in Europe until the last part of the nineteenth century; yet it did not help the people to improve their cultivation, or protect them from the money-lender, or enable them to preserve or regain their independence. Moreover, the practical difficulties of general primary instruction are often under-rated. Parents will do their utmost to send their boys to school if this will help them to earn a livelihood. But so far as primary instruction makes for *social* rather than *individual* welfare, illiterate parents will not send their children to school except through persuasion or compulsion; there is no demand for it. And who shall decide whether primary instruction is their greatest need. Nationalists prefer the extension of technical, vocational, scientific and other forms of higher instruction as more essential to national advancement. Here again we come up against the problem of demand. It is a commonplace of modern educational policy that such instruction should not be given in excess of the demand; the demand is limited, and therefore instruction, it is argued, must be given sparingly. But why is the demand limited? Are lawyers or doctors most needed in the tropics? Doctors. And for which is there a demand? Lawyers. There is a demand for lawyers because all classed in the plural society must employ men trained in Western law. But each group has its own tradition of healing, and native doctors trained on Western lines cannot make a living outside Government service. So there are many lawyers and few doctors. Natives generally have adopted a few European drugs, such as quinine. Persuade them to *want* Western medical assistance, make it available on terms *within their means*, and doctors will soon be ten times as numerous as lawyers. It is the lack of demand that hinders the spread of western hygiene and the enforcement of labour regulations. The people do not believe in them and do not want them. You will not create a demand for these things by teaching them in school, through teachers who have no faith in them. Much might be done by adult education, but that is merely one form of organizing demand.

What, then, about the other alternative—compulsion. Of late years it has often been suggested that we are justified in employing compulsion—strictly, of course, for the welfare of the people; much as the Inquisition employed compulsion for the welfare of the heretic. But the Inquisition looked to spiritual welfare, whereas we look to material welfare, and cannot avoid a side glance at our own. The Dutch justified the use of compulsion under the Culture System as promoting the welfare of the people; but this did not secure their acquittal from a later Liberal generation on the charge of self-interest. Now we advocate primary instruction—for the welfare of the people. Also it will make them "easier to control and govern" and will teach them the dignity of manual labour, sanctity of contract, and the duty of working harder, longer, more honestly and more continuously —for European employers.[1] Moreover, expenditure on primary instruction will leave a smaller margin for higher education that will fit the people to run the country for themselves. In whose interest is the new enthusiasm for primary instruction—theirs or ours? Labour legislation in the tropics is a matter on which Labour and Capital have much in common. It will protect wage-earners in Europe against unfair competition; it will protect European firms in the tropics against oriental or native firms with different standards and ideas of welfare; it may hinder the growth of a native middle-class competent to run their land on modern lines. In whose interest is the new enthusiasm for labour legislation—theirs or ours? Let us claim all the credit that we

[1] Mayhew, *Education of India*, p. 226; Mayhew, *Education in the Colonial Empire*, p. 141.

can, and take all we can get, welfare by compulsion will still expose us to unworthy suspicions. And, finally, compulsion will fail to create welfare. You cannot make people wise or well against their will. Compulsion for any constructive end is effective and, I would suggest, legitimate, only where it is employed to enforce the common social will on a recalcitrant minority; it is merely one method of organizing demand. Better education, better health, like better agriculture, depend on the organization of demand, and for that compulsion is no substitute.

These illustrations will, perhaps, suggest the kind of machinery needed for the promotion of individual and social welfare. First, though not most important, comes the departmental expert, in agriculture, irrigation, education, sanitation, and so on. Consider the function of the expert with reference to the simplest case of all—the spread of groundnut. An agricultural expert should be able to show that groundnut cultivation pays; provided that he knows enough about local soils and native methods of cultivation and local agricultural economy. He may, gradually, acquire a knowledge of local soils, but native ways and native life lie outside agricultural science; they are not his *pidgin*. He can breed a more paying type of paddy; but he cannot make it profitable for people to cultivate it. Or take your sanitary expert. He will insist on fly-proof doors and windows for a meat stall; but he cannot make the people close them. The expert is a specialist in his own subject, but not in native life. He tries to adapt native life to scientific principles; welfare requires the adaptation of scientific principles to native life. But that is not his job. Again, the expert looks at life through departmental blinkers; but health, wealth and happiness are inseparably interfused, and life cannot be cut up into little departmental sections. The expert does not see life whole, nor does he see it steadily; for one expert rapidly succeeds another and what one does another undoes.

For the promotion of welfare then the departmental specialist needs the assistance of a specialist in native life. The Dutch have recognized the need for this, and like to regard their tropical administrators as social engineers. This implies that tropical administration is a science, and that candidates for this profession, whether European or native, should be trained accordingly. At present in British dependencies this training is neglected, and one of the problems of tropical economy is to make responsible authorities understand that it has problems needing special study.

But our machinery is not yet complete. I touched on erosion. In the early stages that can easily be stopped. But who is to notice it? Not your transitory civil servant. Some one is needed, therefore, who has local knowledge. And one thing, perhaps the most important, still remains. About 1,800 Burmans discovered and took readily to inoculation against small-pox; about twenty-five years later we introduced vaccination. They still prefer inoculation to vaccination. Why? The usual explanation is their conservatism, the old familiar story. How was it, then, that they welcomed inoculation so readily? One could suggest several reasons for their distrust of vaccination, but it can be overcome only by the personal influence of some one whom they know and trust—by what the Dutch call "gentle pressure." Besides the expert and the social engineer, there is a need therefore of welfare officers with a knowledge of local conditions and the local people. I would suggest then as essential to the administrative machinery of welfare the departmental expert, the social engineer, the welfare officer with a knowledge of local conditions, and the leader with influence among the local people.

(c) *Finance*.—All this will cost money. How can we raise the capital to pay for welfare? Capital is needed for small-scale private enterprise, for large-scale Western enterprise, and for public utilities.

For small-scale private enterprise co-operative credit is often advocated. But co-operation is most difficult where most needed, and easiest where least needed. Where needed least, it tends to substitute the bond of private economic interest for that of general social welfare, and is most dangerous, therefore, where easiest. Its limitations and its dangers are often overlooked. If people can get money, they will readily swallow co-operative doctrines, but, for co-operation to succeed, they must digest the doctrines. Successful co-operation, like other forms of welfare, depends on the organization of demand. That is a slow process, and cannot meet the urgent and general need for petty capital. Co-operative enthusiasts confound a social and an economic problem, and make both more difficult. State banks and State pawnshops seem necessary, with co-operation as an adjunct.

For large-scale enterprise many advocate the raising of foreign capital. The Liberals regarded economic progress as a guarantee of welfare. They proved mistaken, but many still regard it as a *means* of welfare. Western capital, they say, will pay for native welfare. But this implies an increase of capitalist control, making the plural society more complex and unstable. Some prefer to raise the capital through the State with a wide extension of State enterprise. But where will the money come from? Europe. Where will control lie? Europe. Will that enhance or diminish local autonomy? Most will be raised in boom years, leaving for lean years a heavy burden of debt and possibly default. Will that foster good feeling? Who will decide how the money shall be spent, and see that the enterprises are well run, and, so far as possible, in the native interest? The same government that depends on them for revenue. In Netherlands India, at the height of the "ethical" movement, the Government could not afford to abolish the penal sanction on State mines. In Burma, when local bodies were managed by officials, one heard nothing of their defects; when they were made over to the people, one heard of nothing else. And will it be easier to make over government to the people if we complicate it with profit-seeking enterprises? I agree that Governments might be more active in enterprise than in British dependencies at present, but, under suitable conditions, private capital may be less dangerous.

Similar considerations apply to the raising of capital for public utilities. But such projects raise further questions as to the nature of welfare. What about the large sums thrown away on railways?

Where, by the organization of demand, people can be persuaded that their welfare is concerned, much may be done, as suggested by Dr. Hinden in her *Plan for Africa*, with "local brains, local labour and local capital"; and where the natives are apathetic or adverse, vast sums will be required and vast sums wasted. Thus, in the provision of funds, as in the invention of machinery, the fundamental essential to projects of individual and social welfare is the organization of demand.

9. *Political welfare.*—Lastly we come to political welfare, the organization of a common social will, so that the plural society can stand alone, capable of independence and of choosing freely whether or no to remain associated with the colonial power. Space allows me to do no more than touch on some of the chief problems which this raises; that, perhaps, is all that can usefully be attempted now.

The Government will have two main functions: to restrain antisocial economic forces, and to create a new social order. Both require a strong Government with intimate knowledge of local conditions and the local people; strength and knowledge both necessitate continuity of government in a single person. Frequent changes every few years, in accordance with general usage at the present time, will be fatal to success.

With a stronger Government wielding greater power for a longer period, how can we provide against a misuse of authority? In a plural society with no common social will, Government cannot be made responsible to the people on the lines of western democracy because there is no people to which it can be made responsible. Democratic forms will only make the society more unstable and less capable of independence by giving voting power to one group while leaving economic power with others. It would seem necessary to attack the problem indirectly. Two lines suggest themselves. A plural society resembles a Confederacy. One step towards creating a common social will would be to convert it into a Federation. The other line of approach is to foster nationalist feelings among the capitalist groups, and to develop capitalist interests among the natives.

SOME PROBLEMS OF TROPICAL ECONOMY 183

Thus, by stages and degrees, the reintegration of society might be possible. Some few years, however, must elapse before we have sufficient knowledge to formulate a plan of action. When we know better what to do, we shall know better what form of government can do it. Until the plural society should become capable of independence, the Governor would be responsible for its political advancement to the moral authority exercised by the regional committee on behalf of the world conscience embodied in the League of Nations.

Here then I have tried, very baldly, very inadequately, but I hope intelligibly, to suggest some of the problems of tropical economy. I can offer no cut and dried solution. It has been suggested that all could be solved by adopting the principles of the French Revolution: *égalité, liberté, fraternité*. Equality—no colonial power has gone further than the British Empire in applying the doctrine of equality before the law. But, as Blake remarked when this tremendous formula was first re-echoing through Europe: "One law for the lion and the ox is oppression." But, you may say, we do not mean equality in that sense; we mean that all men should be equal in the sight of—Marx. Words, I fear, mere words. Others suggest that Socialism would provide the solution; it would be sufficient to abjure all profit. But are the natives also to abjure all profit? It is easy enough to renounce the world, the flesh and the devil on behalf of others. Godparents do it every day. Are we to baptize the whole world compulsorily in the name of Marx? Words, idle words, I know not what they mean. How *can* you introduce Socialism where there is no society? Again, what will happen to the mines and oilfields and plantations of Burma after the War? The Burmans do not know how to run them; they have never had the chance to learn. Are they to be left to some picker-up of unconsidered trifles? Those are facts, not words, and it is facts that I have tried to face. All Socialists hold, I suppose, that we are all members one of another; that individual welfare depends on social welfare, political welfare on world welfare. But the organization of world welfare raises immense problems of which not the least formidable are those facing us in the tropics. Their solution will demand a sympathetic understanding, taxing to the utmost human knowledge and good will and calling for wide co-operative endeavour. It is as a contribution towards understanding them that I have here tried to present what seem to me some of the major problems of tropical economy.

Land Hunger in the Colonies
by C. W. W. GREENIDGE

Introduction

"To whomsoever the soil belongs, to him belongs the fruits of it. White parasols and elephants mad with pride, these are the fruits of a grant of land." This is still as true a saying as when an Indian Rajah embodied it in his land grant a thousand years ago.

Nature's blessings of air, sunlight, water and soil are the basis upon which all life is built. The application of human effort to the soil and the action on it of air, sunlight and water provide man's first needs: food, clothing and shelter. With civilization man's wants grow beyond the bare necessities, until they reach a state when very many other products of the earth also become necessary to his comfort and happiness. These include minerals which are found below the ground, and they are wanted in a skilfully manufactured form. Millions of people in the advanced countries have acquired the necessary skill and are engaged in manufacturing those products, and so have become divorced from the land. But in most parts of the globe the land is still the sole economic asset of the people, and there the whole social organization and the coherence and persistence of community life are bound up with the possession of land. To them nothing is of greater importance than the right to occupy land. The first thing almost any writer on African questions will tell about the African is that what he most wants, is most anxious over, most suspects the white man's dealings with him about, is land. That is not confined to Africa, but is common in other colonial territories.

The colonial people must have enough land of reasonably good quality to provide for their present requirements and for an improved standard of living. That an improved standard of living is urgently necessary cannot be denied. Unfortunately, European nations had acquired control of most of their dependencies before serious attention was given to the predominant place which occupation of land holds in the economy of non-industrialized countries. The special relationship of backward people to their land was not understood until the researches of anthropologists in recent times established its supreme importance. It was not until then that the recognition of native rights in land became part of British colonial policy. Meanwhile, a great deal of injustice had been done, and so far little effort has been made to repair it.

Historical

To understand the causes of this injustice, one must make a brief historical retrospect.

The earlier commissions granted in the Middle Ages by Popes and Princes to navigators and discoverers, charged them "to conquer, subdue and reduce to perpetual servitude pagans and other enemies of Christ and to occupy and possess their lands." The right to do this was vigorously debated by jurists and theologians over a long period, and resulted in a persistent preponderance of juristic opinion in favour of the proposition that lands in the possession of any backward people who are politically organized ought to be regarded as belonging to them, and not liable to seizure by a nation which acquired sovereignty over such people. This principle was followed by the English, Dutch and Swedes during the earliest period of the colonization of the New World. Friendly North American Indians were protected in possession of the lands they occupied and were considered as owning them by a perpetual right of possession. The tribes inhabited the land, not as by the right of individuals located on particular spots, but as common property from generation to generation. But as European colonization spread, and the demand for land and labour grew, human ingenuity worked to satisfy that demand.

Methods of acquiring Native Lands

Two principal methods were evolved by which the indigenous

inhabitants of backward countries were deprived of their lands and forced to work for wages. The earlier method was to assume that a native chief was in the same position as a European landowner, and possessed the right to alienate the land of his tribe. This assumption was unfounded because the conception of individual ownership of land is seldom found among primitive people. Land is usually owned by them communally, and individual tenure of a part of it is a usufructuary right personal to the occupier, dependent upon the goodwill of the community represented by the chief. Tenure may be conditional on proper use. In the early days of colonization savage tribes in uncolonized parts of the world, unfamiliar with the institution of individual ownership have often been willing to allow Europeans to occupy part of their lands, believing that they were granting only the right to use the land so long as the particular grantee required it. Many large tracts of land have been acquired in this way for a totally inadequate consideration, such as a few cases of gin or gaudy clothing, and have been converted into ownership in perpetuity. The European grantee, in accordance with his accustomed practice, secured his tenure of the land by a written instrument couched in the language of European land law, the meaning of which the grantor seldom, if ever understood, but on which he made his mark as requested. The validity of some of these grants has been questioned by litigation, but rarely has the native been able to get redress for the iniquity of his position under the white man's law.

By far the most usual method of depriving natives of their land has been the nationalization and sale method. Strangely enough, this had its origin in the realization of the need to protect native holders or occupants of land from fraudulent or unscrupulous purchasers. In order to achieve this, a doctrine was propounded that the fee simple of native lands was vested in the Crown by right of conquest, subject to the communal right of possession by the natives, described above, and that individuals could not purchase native lands without the consent of the Crown. The uncultivated, or at least the unoccupied lands of the colonies were assumed to be Crown Lands held in trust for the benefit of the public in some of the public's many manifestations. So far, so good. It is, unfortunately, the case that laws which in their terms appear to do justice to natives are sometimes administered in such a way as to defeat that end. An opinion crept in later that where tribes or communities were occupying an inordinately large extent of land merely for hunting or even for pasturing flocks and herds, there was no just reason why some part of it should not be taken and put to more productive use. This, however, was subject to the qualification that sufficient land should be left to the original occupants for their sustenance. Thus arose the policy of reserving definite areas for the exclusive use of the native inhabitants—the Native Reservation system. Disastrous mistakes have been made in the determination of the practical question as to how much land ought in a given case to be left to the native inhabitants, and how much should be made available for non-native settlement or exploitation.

But whatever the theory of the trust, in practice it has usually been held without any definite policy save the dominant idea that the development of the colony must be the first object of the governor, and the best way to achieve that development was to sell to all-comers proprietary rights in the land. In some colonies improvident alienation of large areas to Europeans has reduced the native inhabitants to the condition of a landless proletariat. It is improbable that any colonial Power would to-day dispute the proposition that the native people under its sovereignty are entitled to be secured in the possession of a sufficient quantity of land to enable them to obtain an adequate subsistence in the circumstances of their condition. There is clearly a duty cast upon these Powers, who subscribe to that proposition, to see that just legislation results in sufficient land being made available to the natives under their sovereignty to secure them fair and tolerable conditions of living. It is of little use taking credit for the abolition of chattel slavery if we allow economic slavery to take the place of the old, worn-out form of compulsory labour. There is a slavery which locks up men's bodies; and there is a freedom which indeed sets men's bodies free but locks up all they need for sustenance. It is not to this sort of freedom that we ought to condemn the people in our colonies.

The following pages will illustrate the effect of alienation of the lands of natives to Europeans (individuals and corporations) and to educated natives in creating land hunger among the mass of people which exists in many colonial territories to-day.

The term "colony" is used here in its extended sense to include some territories which are now self-governing dominions but were colonized from the Mother Country, as well as colonies and protectorates for the administration of which the Crown is still responsible.

The Commonwealth of Australia

M. F. Lindley, in his book *The Acquisition and Government of Backward Territory in International Law*, says:[1] "Australia has usually been considered to have been properly *territorium nullius* upon its acquisition." To the same effect, the Select Committee of the House of Commons on Aborigines reported in 1837: "Such, indeed, is the barbarous state of these people and so entirely destitute are they even of the rudest forms of civil polity, that their claims, whether as sovereigns or proprietors of the soil have been utterly disregarded." This happened 150 years ago in a country in which the indigenous population has been estimated by some authorities to have been at least 300,000 and by others at as many as a million at that time. To-day, there are about 50,000.

The story of the colonization of the Continent of Australia from 1788 onwards is painful reading. So widespread was the practice of shooting or otherwise destroying the aborigines that in 1838 the Governor of New South Wales issued a proclamation forbidding indiscriminate slaughter. In 1838, in Tasmania, the

[1] Page 40.

Island State of Australia, the aboriginal inhabitants, numbering about 2,000 were driven into a narrow peninsula and set upon by an armed force superior in numbers and shot. The remnant were then placed on a small island, where they lingered, steadily declining in numbers, and the last died in 1876. It is now known that the belief that the Australian aborigines were destitute "even of the rudest forms of civil polity" was erroneous. They were organized under a very simple, but strict rule of law into little tribes or groups scattered far and wide throughout the Continent. The expropriation of their land was therefore founded on a false assumption.

The remnant of the aborigines have been driven into reserves. Professor Wood Jones, Anthropologist and Professor of Anatomy at Melbourne University, says: "The aboriginal reservations in Central Australia are a bitter joke and a good exercise in political bluff." Mr. Stacey, M.P., said in the Australian House of Representatives in March, 1943: "The Aborigines have been given a raw deal. Land had been taken from them and used for huge cattle stations. It was the Government's duty to see that some of the land was restored to them so that they could live under conditions that God had made them to live." And Dr. Charles Duguid, another writer of authority on the Australian aborigines, in a recent pamphlet, "The Future of the Aborigines of Australia," describes various reserves which he mentions as reserves of sand almost devoid of water or game, beyond an odd rabbit, and concludes with the question, "What is the future of the tribal natives still with us?" which he answers, "Their future depends on land."

The greater part of the Continent of Australia is unproductive desert. There are parts in which rain does not fall oftener than once in two years. European settlement has covered the more fertile lands of the east and southern coasts, and the aborigines have retreated into the waterless central and north-western parts of the Continent. The greatest number of aborigines are in Western Australia. They were 26,605 in 1940, which is more than half of the total surviving. The above will show that a race is approaching extinction by starvation resulting from expropriation of its land by a dominant race.

There have been human-hearted men and women in Australia who have protested all along against this inhumanity, and have worked to awake the national conscience to its guilt. Unfortunately, the responsibility for the Australian aboriginal has been parcelled out among the States of the Commonwealth and each State has left the native question in the political background. Happily, the tide seems to have turned, and it is now recognized to be a national responsibility. At a recent Constitutional Assembly of the States, it was decided that the Federal Government should assume control of the "welfare of aborigines" for five years after the war. This augurs well for the future, for the skill and insight shown by the Federal Government of Australia in the administration of native affairs in the mandated territory of New Guinea, have earned high praise.

The Union of South Africa.—Like Australia, the Union of South Africa contains large areas of land which are so barren, rainless and scantily habitable that they may be left out of account as suitable for human habitation. There are in round figures 7,000,000 Africans and 2,000,000 Europeans in the Union. Of the Europeans only 696,000 were rural inhabitants in 1936, the latest statistics available. The proportion of the African and European rural population is therefore 10 to 1. Yet European ownership covers 14/15ths of the land, leaving about 7 per cent or 23,000,000 acres for African use. The European holds 43 acres for every one acre held by the African. That the amount of land available for African use is grossly inadequate has long been recognized. To-day, approximately 30 per cent of the 250,000 families living in the Transkei are landless. A Commission which investigated the matter reported that an additional 17,700,000 acres should be set aside for Africans. The Native Trust and Land Act, 1936, purports to implement that recommendation and authorized the expenditure of £10,000,000 on the acquisition of additional land, but, up to November 1937 (the latest figures available) only 824,900 acres had been acquired at a cost of £1,304,000. Not only are Africans denied the right to buy land outside the Reserves, which have been declared by the Land Commission to be inadequate for their needs, but a European who lets land to an African is liable to a heavy fine unless the African works for him at least six months a year; thus Africans are even restrained from becoming tenants on non-native lands.

Southern Rhodesia.—The land in Southern Rhodesia climatically suited for general farming, whether by Africans or Europeans, is definitely limited. Southern Rhodesia has made more generous provision of land for its African population, than either the Union of South Africa or Kenya. It has, however, committed itself to the policy of segregation as that term is understood in the Union and it is planned to divide up the country between black and white. 74,000 square miles have been alienated to or set aside for alienation to Europeans and 48,000 square miles have been set aside as Native Reserves for the Africans in communal ownership. A further 19,000 square miles, known as the Unassigned Area, has been set aside for sale to Africans in individual ownership. While the area available for the two races, namely, 74,000 and 67,000 square miles respectively, does not show such marked disproportion, we must not overlook the fact that while there are 1,500,000 Africans, there are only about 70,000 Europeans. In other words the allowance per head is 40 times as much for Europeans as it is for Africans. Lord Hailey says in *An African Survey*,[1] "large areas of the land set aside for purchase by Africans are infested with the tse-tse fly and other parts are deficient in water," and the Report of the Bledisloe Commission says of it that subject to the development of the necessary water supplies, it is capable of providing only 20,000 individual holdings. There are 350,000 Africans outside the Reserves in need of land. Allowing that the average family would number five persons, these landless Africans would need not 20,000, but 70,000 holdings or $3\frac{1}{2}$ times the area allocated for them.

[1] Page 737.

Northern Rhodesia.—The total area of Northern Rhodesia is about 185,000,000 acres. Area, however, means little, as the greater part of Northern Rhodesia is covered by poor soils requiring enrichment by fertilisers if cultivation is to be more than temporary. Of the 185,000,000 acres, 35,000,000 acres are in Barotseland and that is, by treaty obligations with the Barotse, reserved both from alienation and prospecting for minerals. Of the remaining 150,000,000 acres only 35,000,000 acres are Native Reserves. A corollary of the setting up of Reserves is that the native population is moved into them and kept there. In 1938 the European population was 19,588 and the African population was 1,366,425, of which 550,000 were in Barotseland. There was thus one European for every 120 Africans. Sir Alan Pim, in his Report on Northern Rhodesia, says that there is definite overcrowding in some of the Reserves, and that in none of the Reserves can the position be regarded as satisfactory, and he recommends enlargement of them. With more than 100,000,000 acres of unoccupied Crown lands, it is difficult to understand why the Reserves are overcrowded. Northern Rhodesia has had many Land Commissions, but they have not yet resulted in action to relieve the land hunger of the people.

Kenya.—The total area of Kenya is 140,000,000 acres of which some three-fifths is arid and relatively worthless, leaving 56,000,000 acres of more or less useful land. This is the only area which can properly be taken into account for cultivation. Kenya is one of the few British territories in the tropics which has an extensive area of land, with an invigorating climate suitable for permanent residence by Europeans. This is due to its elevation. The area is called the Highlands.

There has been a fair amount of settlement in Kenya by Europeans and the European population is about 20,000, of which, however, only about 2,000 are farmers. The African population is 3,000,000 and the Indian about 60,000. Of the 56,000,000 acres of useful land, Native Reserves comprise some 30,800,000 acres and 10,688,000 acres have been set aside for alienation to Europeans. This 10,688,000 acres includes 2,528,000 of Forest Reserves. The rest of the 56,000,000 is Forest Reserves. Some 7,000,000 acres have been alienated to Europeans. Only about 1,300,000 acres of this is said to be suitable for cultivation and in 1943 there were 864,000 acres under cultivation. The balance of unalienated land reserved for Europeans is 704,000 acres. Before 1912 alienations to Europeans were in freehold tenure, but since that year leasing has been the practice. Between 1934 and 1938 no less than $1\frac{1}{2}$ million acres of leased land was surrendered to the Crown and in 1938 the area in cultivation had shrunk to 546,604 acres, which indicates that in normal times settlers had not found farming profitable. War needs and guaranteed prices of produce have stimulated cultivation.

Many Commissions have examined the land problem of Kenya and each of them has stressed that many of the Native Reserves are overcrowded. Lord Hailey has remarked in *An African Survey*[1] that "Land Commissions in Kenya have proceeded on the principle that they were precluded from making any recommendation which would result in a material reduction in the area reserved for Europeans." Does this imply that he regards that as a possible source from which land might be found to satisfy the land hunger of Africans in Kenya? It seems that some 704,000 acres more than they need were reserved for Europeans, and it is time that they were restored to the Africans from whom they were taken. There would still be ample room in the area alienated to Europeans for an extension of European settlement. In 1934 the size of the average holding was 2,534 acres, of which the average in cultivation was 234 acres. In 1943 there was a shortage of food in Kenya for the African population, and another is forecast this year.

In other parts of Africa under the British flag the position is very much better than in the territories mentioned above. Of them, Canon G. W. Broomfield says in his book, *Colour Conflict*:[2] "Land policy has been influenced very little—in some cases

[1] Page 751. [2] Page 30.

hardly at all—by the demands of white colonization and alienation of land has not interfered with African life and prospects of advancement."

The Seychelles Islands

The Seychelles Islands are an archipelago in the Indian Ocean, few of which are inhabited. The total population is 30,000, of whom 22,000 live in the island of Mahé, in which the capital is. Coconut production is the chief industry and the inhabited islands with one exception—La Digue—are owned by coconut planters. Among the 22,000 inhabitants of Mahé there are only 150 rural landowners and the coconut planters control the labour market and keep wages at a low level. The stranglehold which plantation owners have on the land is the chief cause of the poverty of the people in the Seychelles. The average wage of a male labourer is 15s. a month and of a female 9s. These meagre cash wages are not supplemented by free rations, as in many of the African colonies, nor even by free vegetable plots, and the labourers are able to grow only very little of their food. Except in the island of La Digue, in which there has been division of land into small holdings, the people are dependent on the sufferance of the large landowners even for the lots on which their huts stand. It is not to the interest of the planters that they should grow their food and they do not let them have much more land than house lots. The Government decided just before the war to divide about 500 acres in Mahé into small holdings. The scheme was suspended on the outbreak of war. Since then imported food has become very scarce and dear and the need is now urgent to press on with this scheme as well as to extend land settlement generally.

The West Indies

The outstanding racial feature of the West Indies is that their population is predominantly African in origin, descended from slaves imported from Africa. In most of the island colonies the aboriginal inhabitants have either completely disappeared or all but so. It is somewhat different in the two continental colonies, although even there the population is predominantly African or East Indian in origin, the latter being descended from indentured coolies imported from India. In British Honduras, there are about 14,000 Mayas of the ancient race of Central America, and in British Guiana there are 8,800 aboriginal South American Indians. In the colonies in which sugar is the sole export product the land is for the most part held in large estates and the coloured population is chiefly employed at wages. This is especially the case in Barbados, Antigua and St. Kitts. In the colonies with a more varied agriculture this is less so. In Jamaica rather more than one-third of the arable area of the island is divided into holdings of under 50 acres. In Trinidad, Grenada and British Guiana about half of the alienated land is in small holdings and in Tobago, St. Vincent, St. Lucia, Dominica, Montserrat and Nevis the proportion is higher. In Barbados and Antigua only one-fifth of the cultivable area is in small holdings. In Barbados, of a total of 106,000 acres, 19,228 acres are owned by 18,805 people in a population of 210,000. In St. Kitts there are hardly any rural landowners. The 7,400 labourers who work on the sugar estates are allowed to plant 2,500 acres of inferior land in vegetables on condition that they work on the estates when required. In British Honduras, a country as large as Wales, there are among 57,000 people, less than 2,000 landowners, which includes owners of house lots. One landowner owns a sixth of the total area of the colony.

The two most pressing economic problems of the West Indies are redistribution of land and securing a price for sugar sufficient to enable adequate wages to be paid. Until land is redistributed and made available to the majority of people to grow a substantial part of their food, the people of the West Indies will continue to be wage earners and to live in want during the three or four months every year when there is little or no work on the plantations. The wages paid are hardly sufficient to maintain more than bare subsistence and do not permit of saving for the slack season. The poverty of the people of the West Indies is acute, and Royal Commissions have repeatedly urged as a principal remedy and reform the settlement of the people on the land. The Royal Commission of 1896–97 observed that "no reform affords so good a prospect for the permanent welfare in the future of the West Indies as the settlement of the labouring population on the land as small peasant proprietors; and in many places this is the only means by which the population can in future be supported." The Olivier Commission of 1930 on the Sugar Industry, reported a generation later: "We are convinced that while schemes of land settlement cannot relieve the present emergency (the threatened collapse of the sugar industry) the increased settlement of labourers on the land as peasant proprietors offers the best prospect of establishing a stable and prosperous economy in the West Indian colonies. We regret that with exceptions to which we refer more particularly elsewhere, so little has been done to carry out the strong recommendations of the 1897 Royal Commission in this direction." The West India Royal Commission, 1938–39 also made the following recommendation: "The outstanding agricultural need in the West Indies is the more intensive use of land with increased production of food in order to support a rapidly growing population. The most urgent need is the development of peasant agriculture" and elsewhere, "The Government should take powers for the compulsory acquisition of agricultural land needed for land settlement and similar purposes."

The Colonial Office has tried to put these recommendations into practice in several of the colonies, but the apathy or penury of the local Government and vested interests have frustrated these good intentions, and the recommendations of the Royal Commissions have not been carried out in adequate measure.

The British community recognizes its general obligation to the less-developed peoples under its control, but it is under a very special obligation to the negro population of the West Indian colonies. In the words of the report of the West Indian Royal Commission of 1897:[1]

"The black population of these colonies was originally placed

[1] Paragraph 513.

in them by force as slaves; the race was kept up and increased under artificial conditions maintained by the authority of the British Government. What the people were at the time of emancipation and their very presence in the colonies at all, were owing to British action or to the action of other European nations for the results of whose policy the United Kingdom assumed responsibility on taking possession of the territories in question; we could not, by the simple act of freeing them, divest ourselves of responsibility for their future which must necessarily be the outcome of the past and the present. For generations the great mass of the population must remain dependent upon British influence for good Government and generally for the maintenance of the progress they have made hitherto. We cannot abandon them and if economic conditions become such that private enterprise and the profits of trade and cultivation cease to attract white men to these colonies or to keep them there, this may render it more difficult for the British Government to discharge its obligations, but it will not in any case diminish the force of them. We have placed the labouring population where it is and created for it the conditions, moral and material, under which it exists and we cannot divest ourselves of responsibility for its future."

The Emancipation Act of 1833 was a just and humane measure. England, however, was grievously at fault in imagining that, by setting the slaves free and paying £20,000,000 compensation to their former owners, the mischief of slavery had been or could be abolished. The effects of two centuries of demoralizing treatment are not so easily and cheaply undone. The slaves were set free and thrown on the labour market without any bargaining power, and their descendants are still for the most part landless wage-earners who have to take what they can get or starve. A Government spokesman, commenting on the riots in Trinidad in 1937, stated that the labourers on the sugar plantations were living in economic bondage. Wages have increased since then, but they are still below what is required to maintain a decent standard of living. In a recent broadcast the Governor of

LAND HUNGER IN THE COLONIES 199

Barbados said that Barbados could not support its population in decency. Land should be made available to the mass of people in the West Indies with security of tenure on which to grow their food. Opinions differ as to whether tenure should be individual smallholdings or large, collectivized farms. Investigation must determine that.

An interesting experiment in re-distribution of land, initiated by the United States Government in Puerto Rico through a department called the Insular Land Authority, merits examination. Plantations have been bought by this Authority and are being run as proportional benefit farms, designed to preserve the advantages of large-scale operation and skilled management with the sharing of profits between the workers on the farm.

Ever since the last quarter of the last century when the price of sugar collapsed, there has been in the West Indies a poverty which has hampered and crippled the administration and oppressed and destroyed the people. For more than a century they have waited for private enterprise to develop sufficient industry to employ all of the population at wages which would maintain them at a decent standard of living. That private enterprise has not been forthcoming. It is time that the Government intervened in West Indian industry and supplied the initiative and energy which has been lacking from private enterprise.

The Converse.—While there is land hunger in the colonies already mentioned, land policy in British West Africa, thanks largely to the statesmanlike foresight of Lord Lugard, has safeguarded native interests in land in those dependencies by controlling alienation of land to non-natives, as a result of which there is very little ownership of land by non-natives. There is one part only of Nigeria in which there is land hunger. That is the Ibo country of Western Nigeria, in which the average density of population is 200 to the square mile, although in some parts it exceeds 400 and in some places reaches 1,000. The Ibo country is the most thickly populated region in tropical Africa, and the soil has become so impoverished by over-cropping that it will not yield sufficient food to sustain the population. This congestion is, however, not due to European intervention but to increase in population, now numbering about 3,000,000 on an area of land too small for their needs.

Land Policy in Uganda, Tanganyika and Nyasaland has also safeguarded native interests. In the two South African Protectorates of Basutoland and Bechuanaland non-native landowning is insignificant. Up to 1943, land policy in Swaziland left much to be desired. This country contains 4½ million acres. Two-thirds of the land had been alienated to Europeans, 40 per cent of whom were absentees, and about 1,000,000 acres were used only for grazing sheep in the winter months. The remaining third was insufficient for the needs of the Swazis, numbering 153,270. Representations were made in 1942 to the Secretary of State for the Dominions (then Mr. C. R. Attlee) by the Paramount Chief Sobhuza II, supported by sympathizers in this country, with the result that an investigation was instituted and it was found that 27,000 Swazis were landless squatters on the land of Europeans. With a grant of about £250,000 from the colonial development and Welfare Fund, enough land has been bought to settle all of these 27,000 Swazis and to build roads and provide housing, water supplies and schools and employ officers to supervise the methods of cultivation and grazing used by the occupants and to see that the land is not misused. Investigation established that 60 acres is necessary to maintain each family in Swaziland.

The Colonial Office has also shown signs of appreciating the gravity of this land question in the colonies, for which it is responsible. Last year a large area of land in Northern Rhodesia was acquired by the Government from the North Charterland Company, which, it is believed, will be made available to the African population. Within the past few months the Colonial Office has also announced a grant of £500,000 for land settlement in Jamaica, and of £85,000 for land settlement in the island of Antigua in the West Indies.

Conclusions

There is no problem of greater urgency and significance to the colonial people than that of providing them with sufficient land on which to grow their food, wholly or in part. In many tropical colonies work is seasonal, depending on the rains, and employs the people for only six or eight months each year. Their poverty is acute in the slack season when they are entirely dependent on wages for a living. To them, land on which to grow food is a pressing need.

In 1940, the Colonial Development and Welfare Act was passed, which authorises a maximum expenditure of £5,000,000 a year from the Imperial Treasury for ten years on colonial development and welfare. Up to the 31st March, 1944, only 10½ per cent of the money available had been spent. The explanation given is that men and material are not available during the war to carry out the development contemplated by the Act. A Minister of the Crown has stated that any part of the £5,000,000 a year not spent in a financial year lapses to the Treasury. Up to the end of March, 1944, some £18,000,000 had lapsed. Could this not be re-voted and spent on buying land in colonies where the need for re-distribution of land exists? In some cases, such as Kenya, the Seychelles and British Honduras, there is enough land, but it is mal-distributed. In other cases, such as Barbados, and the Ibo country of Nigeria, there is an insufficiency of land for the congested population, and the remedy there will lie in mass transfer of population.

Nothing would convince the people in the colonies more forcibly of the repentance of the British Government for its past neglect of them than acquisition of land with which to satisfy their land hunger.

The British West Indies
by HAROLD STANNARD

Just as the Channel Islands are the relics of a lost English Empire in France, so the older West Indian colonies are what is left of the great expansion of England across the Atlantic. Insular and continental settlement began simultaneously in the first quarter of the seventeenth century. Cromwell fostered the newly founded Empire both by legislation and by conquest, and in the Seven Years War England made large gains of territory at the expense of France and Spain alike in the Caribbean and on the mainland. The Napoleonic period saw a further diminution of both French and Spanish power in the New World, but by Napoleon's day island and mainland conquests had ceased to be connected. The War of Independence had cut off the British West Indies from their natural hinterland and had left a heritage of economic strain. When the United States concluded her first commercial treaty with Britain in 1795 West Indian trade questions proved specially thorny to negotiate. Moreover, the West Indies did not, like the American colonies, gain the compensating advantage of unity. Conquests during the Napoleonic wars did, indeed, enlarge the spread of British power in the Caribbean, but the opportunity of organizing a coherent West Indian Empire had been lost with the restoration of Cuba to Spain in 1763. That great island might have been anglicized at least as completely as Trinidad, which did not become British until 1797, and the other islands would have centred themselves upon it much as the Leeward Islands centre upon Trinidad to-day. But the prospect of Cuban sugar finding a market in Britain was distasteful to the powerful sugar planting interest, and Cuba, left in Spanish hands for another century and a half, was in no case to become the focal point of nineteenth century West Indian life.

This historical background needs to be recalled now when, after a century of quiescence, the Caribbean is again becoming prominent in the world's affairs. The leasing of the bases has established the United States inside the British area, and the progress of the war has steadily increased American influence throughout the whole region. The words "colonial system" have an unpleasing sound to American ears but the essence of the colonial system—a governor appointed from Britain and not responsible to the local legislature—is what Americans find in the West Indian colonies. Nor is the record of constitutional progress likely to impress American observers. British minds find something attractive in the fact that Bermuda, Barbados, and the Bahamas still operate constitutions granted in Stuart times, partly because British minds are respectful of tradition, partly because they see in these constitutions the beginning of the process which culminated in the Statute of Westminster. These considerations are, however, lost upon Americans, who note that British rule has ignored the changes of three hundred years and draw inevitable inferences.

Contacts with Americans are far too frequent throughout the West Indies for this critical American attitude towards British institutions to be without effect on West Indian minds. Nevertheless, the probability of the Caribbean passing wholly into the American orbit appears much less strong to-day than when the construction of the Panama Canal was put in hand nearly forty years ago, and for this there are three reasons. First, the revulsion, on allegedly patriotic grounds, from everything British is declining throughout the United States and has vanished from responsible circles. American policy in the Caribbean now aims at co-operation with the British and the establishment of the Anglo-American Caribbean Commission is symptomatic of the changed attitude. Secondly, the war and the extraordinarily rapid industrial development that it has brought about has caused Canada to look beyond her own boundaries and to realize the full significance of the Caribbean interests she has developed since the Ottawa Conference, with the important consequence that the West Indies are again becoming linked with an American hinterland still under the familiar flag. Thirdly, there has been a notable stirring of West Indian thought, which is no longer content to regard the West Indies as the natural prizes of power, but is, on the contrary, beginning to claim that West Indians can and should determine their own future.

This last development, tentative though it is, is clearly of the greatest importance. When I first visited the West Indies in 1938 I found that though poverty was everywhere the cause of rising discontent, the belief obtained that the British possessed the secret of government. West Indians could express their grievances, but the remedies must come from the Colonial Office. In the last six years this conception of the British official as possessed of some special and exclusive political virtue has wilted away. No longer will West Indian feeling explode into riots by estate labourers deprived through the fall in sugar prices of the pittance on which they had lived. It will express itself rationally in a demand for autonomy and particularly in an insistence that West Indians are capable of occupying the major administrative posts which, in the larger colonies, are still reserved for officials sent out from home.

This new political consciousness has asserted itself with particular strength in Jamaica, thanks mainly to the work of Mr. N. W. Manley, the most distinguished figure in British West Indian history. Mr. Manley set himself to break the vicious political circle created—surely to its shame—by close on three hundred years of British rule. The masses of the people of Jamaica are poor, ignorant, unhealthy and hag-ridden by superstition, and until quite recently the authority responsible for their condition pointed to it as proof of their unfitness for self-government. What else could be expected of such people, if they were given a vote, than that they should prefer a coloured man to a white, or, at best, consider political issues in the merely personal terms that have long been the curse of Jamaican politics?

Mr. Manley dealt with this situation by setting himself to create a political party in the British sense—an organization, that is to say, deriving from the realities of local life, making them the source of principles of betterment and converting those principles into the terms of a realizable programme. The People's National Party proclaims its goal by its idealistic title; for the Jamaica in which it began its work could produce mobs but not a people, was possessed of a certain insular pride but had no national consciousness, and was without parties because it was without the political sense which creates them. Nor can it be said that the People's National Party has yet realized its aims. The defects which it seeks to remedy are still only too apparent. But it has caused Jamaicans to think who had never thought before in their lives and has taught other Jamaicans to think constructively instead of querulously. It is the strongest influence operative in Jamaica since the missionary enterprises in the early days of emancipation; and like them its influence has been above all things educational.

Mr. Manley's work is full of lessons for the British West Indies in general, but little is known of it outside his own island and his glowing patriotism is itself Jamaican rather than West Indian. The mutual ignorance and lack of contact between these colonies is a serious obstacle to their progress as a whole. In the past they could hardly be blamed for their insularity. British possessions in the Caribbean extend in an enormous arc from Honduras on the mainland in Central America through the Windward and Leeward Islands to Trinidad and Barbados and thence to British Guiana, the English-speaking world's one outpost or bridgehead in South America. The Bahaman archipelago lies outside this system, separated from Jamaica by the great island of Cuba and adjacent to the coast of Florida. Sea communications between these scattered colonies have been rare and slow, local jealousies were active and the larger colonies felt themselves nearer in spirit, and, indeed, often in fact, to England than to one another, the more so as French or American possessions lay between them.

Air travel has transformed this situation. A few years ago the journey from Trinidad to Barbados involved a steamship voyage of twelve hours or longer; now the plane has cut the time down to seventy-five minutes. The cost of air travel is likely to prevent frequent intercourse between the more distant colonies, but the fact that the long journey from Jamaica to Trinidad can now be done in a day makes it worth the while of busy men to meet and confer and enormously extends the area which educational facilities can cover. Such institutions as the Imperial College of Tropical Agriculture in Trinidad, or the recently established Social Studies school in Jamaica will be inter-colonial in the future as they could never have been in the past, and will contribute, in the course of time, to the formation of a common West Indian outlook. Already the Anglo-American Caribbean Commission has organized a conference attended by delegates from the possessions of both Powers. Already, too, the Dutch are arranging to participate in the Commission's programme of research work and French co-operation may also be expected when conditions in Martinique and Guadaloupe become more normal.

The development of a sense of unity throughout the Caribbean, which is geographically one though politically diverse, is to be welcomed. But of all the cultural influences operative in a region in which British, American, French, Dutch, Spanish and Portuguese ideas all meet, the British has long been the strongest and the most widely extended. All the British West Indian colonies have learned the great lesson of British experience that whereas religious, social, and sometimes economic differences do not admit of argument, politics can be discussed and political progress made on terms acceptable to all, or nearly all. There is every reason for the British example to retain its force at a time when the colonies are becoming politically minded, and on this ground it is desirable that men and women from the various colonies should look to conferences in Britain as a means of strengthening their common British tradition, as well as to the local Anglo-American conferences for the promotion of the general welfare of all the Caribbean. Arrangements, for example, to bring over to this country every summer a group of schoolmasters drawn from every West Indian colony for a refresher course would have a powerful effect in promoting inter-colonial unity and would make Britain more than a great but distant name. This is but one instance of the administrative development which improved communications, and especially air travel, will make possible. The whole subject needs to be thought out in advance so that the new facilities are put to good use as soon as they become available.

There is another force, the more notable because it is human and not mechanical, which is also promoting West Indian unity. The Royal Commission of 1938, whose recommendations, though not its report, have been made public, was struck by the almost complete absence of modern social services in the West Indian colonies and the obvious inability of the local treasuries to provide them. It therefore recommended that they should be established at the cost of the British Exchequer, and that an officer of ripe administrative experience should be appointed for the purpose. The Colonial Office brought this recommendation into harmony with the general plans for colonial betterment set out in the Colonial Welfare and Development Act of 1940, and it is under this Act that Sir Frank Stockdale has been appointed to the new post of Comptroller of West Indian Welfare and Development. Sir Frank and the very able group of specialists associated with him are far indeed from wishing to impose upon the colonies a cast-iron set of policies taking no account of local conditions. Their plans for each colony have been drawn up on the spot but they are necessarily tending to bring the various colonies into step with one another. Particularly is this the case with the new social services now in course of establishment by Professor Simey, the Comptroller's Social Adviser, whom the University of Liverpool, where he holds the Chair of Social Science, has lent to the West Indies.

Professor Simey found in Jamaica an institution not only without parallel in any other West Indian colony but without precedent in Jamaica's own history. This is the remarkable organization known as Jamaica Welfare Limited. Like so much else that is vital and progressive in Jamaica it owes its initiation to Mr. Manley. The development of the Jamaican banana industry has given the United States Fruit Company important interests in the island and Mr. Zemurray, the head of the concern, himself began in a very small way indeed. Mr. Manley invited him to help the poor cultivators from whose ranks he had risen, and Mr. Zemurray agreed to a cess of ½d. on every branch of bananas exported from Jamaica. Before the war this levy was bringing in about £20,000 a year and Jamaica Welfare, with Mr. Manley as its chairman, was formed to administer the fund.

The mere establishment by West Indians of a body prepared to undertake bold social experiments was something new in West Indian history, the belief in the superior political flair of the British official having previously left all initiative in his hands. The new institution justified itself by breaking new ground and here again it defied tradition. In every West Indian colony there is a small minority of local men who have made their way up the educational ladder and established themselves in the professions. Their work usually brings them to the local capital and once there they have been reluctant to maintain any contact with the poor labourers of the countryside whose condition reminded them too sharply of their own ancestry. Six years ago I had frequent occasion to tell my Kingston friends that unless and until they made themselves the associates and leaders of the barefoot workers on the plantations, they would never really count in Jamaican politics. They might stand for election to the parochial boards and the Legislative Council, and would get the cultivators' votes because they were Jamaicans and not Englishmen, but they would not win the cultivators' confidence, and would therefore be unable to rely on their support for a constructive programme. Thanks to Jamaica Welfare, such language would be out of place now. It has brought some of the best brains in the island to bear on policies of village betterment—policies essential to social progress since about four-fifths of the population lives in villages. Moreover, in developing its activities, Jamaica Welfare has had the courage to ignore the colour line and has recruited for its service some of the most experienced European social workers in the island.

Jamaica Welfare has made mistakes. Realizing the need of village community centres, it began by putting up an elaborate building which the peasants were at first frightened to enter. But it has always been quick to profit by its errors and the later community centres—there are now about thirty—were genuine village growths, most of them with the village school as their headquarters. Seeking support where it was most likely to find it, Jamaica Welfare addressed itself first to lads in their teens and formed them into 4-H clubs. The name and the model are American, the 4 H's standing for head, heart, hand and health, but the clubs themselves are akin to the Young Farmers' Clubs of this country. The success of the 4-H clubs, of which there are now about two hundred, aroused the interest of the young married men. These were formed into groups of Pioneers, whose title—to say nothing of their theme-song, "We're out to build a new Jamaica"—indicated their purpose. These too were successful and created by their success the need of a yet more comprehensive organization. It took the form of a Co-operative Movement, rudimentary enough in that it had to make the bare idea of co-operation intelligible, but very powerful because it appealed to the tribal consciousness of the people, latent since their ancestors were taken out of their social setting in Africa and given nothing to replace it in their new homes. By co-operation workers had begun to build houses and were cultivating a largish estate and the movement had made such strides that, while I was in the island,[1] it attracted the sympathetic attention of the Government.

The war was a disaster to Jamaica Welfare. The export of bananas ceased and with its cessation funds dried up. Application for assistance was made to the Comptroller who found himself able to recommend a grant of £30,000 for five years.

[1] I was in the West Indies from August 1942 to August 1943, and during those twelve months visited the four major Colonies—Jamaica, Trinidad, British Guiana and Barbados.

This is generous help but a price has to be paid for it. The money will reach Jamaica Welfare through the local Government and the directorate has been enlarged from seven to eighteen in order to admit members of the Legislative Council. The pioneering work of Jamaica Welfare has thus been brought to an end and it has become an official agency of betterment. But the danger that enthusiasm and initiative would be driven out of it has largely been averted by Professor Simey's action. He has used his influence as the Comptroller's Social Adviser to recommend Jamaica Welfare's example to the other colonies. A project for a Trinidad and Tobago Welfare has been carried through and a Barbados Welfare is in operation. This last is a remarkable achievement. Nowhere in the West Indies is the colour line drawn with more strictness than in Barbados, and Barbados Welfare is among the few instances in the Colony's history of white and coloured people voluntarily meeting on terms of equality and subscribing considerable sums of money for the common good.[1] Further, Professor Simey has already held in Jamaica the first of his projected courses on social work, based on the experiences of Jamaica Welfare and attended by students from the other colonies as well as by Jamaicans. All these Welfare movements, including the transformed parent body, have still to justify themselves in action, but they are of the utmost promise both in their plans for social betterment and in their power to arouse and canalize local enthusiasm. As such they deserve more notice than they have yet received in this country. They are the first expression of the new will of West Indians to determine their own future.

The nascent political consciousness of West Indians and the breaches in local insularity are the two most potent influences now modifying West Indian life. If they persist, the future of the Caribbean will be different from its past. But the past still overshadows the present, dominating it socially, yielding with

[1] British Guiana was also planning a Welfare organization at the time of my visit but there it was proposed to make it a part of the Youth Movement.

reluctance economically, giving ground politically only because London is forcing the pace. In Trinidad and British Guiana franchise reform is under consideration by *ad hoc* committees; in Barbados the pressure of progressive elements has at last proved strong enough to bring it about; and in all three colonies feeling has been stirred by the grant of adult suffrage in the new Jamaican constitution. The old Jamaican franchise was not ungenerous. There were about 100,000 voters in a population of approximately 1,250,000, about half of whom are under 21. The transition to complete democracy will increase the whole number of voters at least sevenfold, and the number of women voters perhaps a thousandfold. This vast extension of the electorate has confronted Jamaican politicians with new problems as well as with new opportunities and has already led to the formation of new parties. The West Indian mind is generous and with the issue of the new constitution a sponge has been wiped over the past; but the English observer cannot but regret that this great step forward was only taken after a previous failure to satisfy Jamaican aspirations, after a period of considerable tension in local politics and after pungent American criticisms of British institutions. If one half of the Caribbean knew how the other half lived, it would profit by these warnings and would hasten to complete its franchise revision which, particularly in Barbados, has proceeded at a snail's pace.

The greatest benefit that will follow from closer and more regular contacts will be that each colony will become aware of the other colonies' experiences and will consider their possible bearings on its own affairs. There are, indeed, West Indians who would expect much more and that quickly; but those who talk glibly of federation have not realized the practical difficulties involved nor the strength of the prejudices to be overcome. Federation is the consequence of a common will based upon common thought, but there is no such community in the West Indies, where public opinion is only just beginning to form. Moreover, in spite of all that concurrent social legislation and the impulse towards more intimate contacts may achieve, there cannot be so much uniformity in the West Indies as will permit more than the loosest kind of federation. Indeed, to use the idiom of American politics, confederation rather than federation should be the goal because all the colonies differ profoundly from one another.

They differ not only in their soils, but, to a surprising extent, in their climates. The rainfall of each island depends on the height of its central mountain, so that two islands actually in sight of one another may grow different products. They differ in their histories; Barbados has never been in other than British hands whereas Tobago, less than a hundred miles away, claims to have been taken and retaken twenty times in the years when Britain and France were fighting one another all over the world. They differ in cultural background; Jamaica, for example, being purely British, whereas St. Lucia was French until 1815 and still clings to its patois. They differ markedly in religion. Barbados, with its English past, reflects the sectarian differences familiar at home; Trinidad, Spanish till 1797, is predominantly Catholic; Jamaica presents a dismal picture of religious chaos. As many as fifty-eight different sects were thought worthy of separate mention in the recent census, and the number of minor sects may well run into hundreds, most of them being manifestations of a tribal consciousness forced to express itself in a religious idiom for want of any other.

Above all, the colonies differ in racial composition. Barbados has the simplest racial structure, its elements being either British or African. It is a disturbing feature of Barbadian life that the colour line is drawn more rigorously than in any other of the larger colonies. This is because the island became a place of refuge or deportation for Royalists in the Civil War period, and received ship-loads of indentured labourers, mainly from Ireland. Such men lacked the resources of the planters in the other islands, and their descendants form a class of poor whites whose members have nothing but pride of race on which to base their claim to the respect of their black neighbours. It may cause surprise that this class should have been able to enforce the rigid social conventions of the colony; but the whites stand together, are in control of the island's economic resources and are numerous enough to form a society of their own.

At the other end of the racial scale is Trinidad, whose population constitutes a mosaic of peoples deriving from Europe, Latin America, Asia and Africa, with elements—French as well as British—from the smaller islands to the North. Trinidad is one of the two major colonies in which the presence of a large East Indian element, in this case one-third of the total population, adds to the difficulties of government. The East Indians were brought to the island to supply the cheap labour required after emancipation under a system of indenture which was allowed to continue until 1917. Many of these East Indians have remained humble folk, unassimilated, illiterate, with no desire beyond saving money to buy land. But now that coolies have ceased to be brought from India and the children of the earlier immigrants go to school, the community's standard of life is slowly rising. Already a good many of its members have entered the professions and the claim for fuller East Indian representation in the Government is persistently urged. Here too, national consciousness is beginning to develop and is bringing with it a livelier interest in Indian affairs. There is general sympathy with Congress's claim for self-government, but next to none with its demand for secession from the Empire. Against this tendency to racial separatism must be set the unifying influence of the oil refineries. Alone among the British West Indian colonies, Trinidad has a substantial body of workers, drawn from every element in its population, employed in mechanical processes.

In British Guiana the East Indians, numerically about equal to their fellows in Trinidad, constitute the largest racial element in the population, outnumbering the Africans by a few thousands. In British Guiana, as in Trinidad, East Indian interest in public affairs is fairly recent, but its development has led the Africans to fear that the East Indians may claim the full rights of a majority and seek to Indianize the colony; and this fear has found confirmation in occasional indiscreet East Indian utterances. As a consequence, relations between East Indians and Africans are distant and full of mutual suspicion. As additional bar has thus been erected on the darker side of the colour line, and the texture of the hair is as effective a cause of social division as the colour of the skin. In Jamaica yet another form of cleavage is apparent. Here the several racial elements would be swamped by a majority of African descent with a variable admixture of white blood, were it not that the Colony's economic structure has shaped itself on racial lines. Every village grocery store belongs to a Chinese, the clothing trade is in the hands of Syrians, and only the courts, the schools, and the hospitals are open to all Jamaicans without distinction of origin.

Each colony thus confronts problems of its own which it must solve for itself. What is common to all is the patent need of social betterment. Slavery has left behind it a terrible heritage. Family life, as Europeans understand the word, has never established itself, and fully two-thirds of the children born in the British West Indies are officially illegitimate. How far the official classification corresponds to the facts is matter for dispute, often fairly heated. There are those who point to cases of permanent concubinage—known in Jamaica as "common law marriages," which is just what they are not—and those who cite examples of women having half a dozen children by as many different fathers. Full light on West Indian social conditions can only be thrown by competent social surveys, for which Professor Simey's work is preparing the way.

Not since the days of the Greek city states have there been communities in which the fundamental problems of human society present themselves so clearly, so intensely and in so personal a form as in the West Indies. The parallel is not fortuitous. The Caribbean is the only region in the modern world in which Europe, Africa and Asia meet. In the ancient world they met in the Aegean and there issued from their meeting the superb civilization of Greece. Who can say what lofty Caribbean destiny is now beginning to weave itself on the loom of time?

An Anthropologist's Point of View
by M. FORTES

Social anthropology is a branch of social science. Hence anthropologists are bound to approach their subject matter in a spirit of detachment and ethical neutrality. As citizens they have their private political opinions, and share to a greater or lesser extent the ethical and cultural values of their society. They may be impelled to study a particular problem by these values. But they must not allow these values to bias their interpretation of the facts of social life, as they study them in the field. This is the chief distinction between the anthropologist's approach to colonial problems and that of the practical man, whether he be merchant or missionary, government official or social reformer.[1]

Social anthropologists are concerned with the *how* and *why* of human behaviour in certain forms of human society. Their chief aim, at the present stage of development of the social sciences, is to contribute to our understanding of human social organization. They are not colonial experts. The problems of colonial expansion come into their sphere of interest as special aspects of the contemporary social environment of the peoples they study. Colonial expansion is, to an anthropologist, simply a special case of a world-wide phenomenon, the spreading of Euro-american civilization. This phenomenon is of particular importance for modern anthropological research as it represents the most powerful force of social evolution among the so-called "backward" societies.

The types of societies social anthropologists have given most attention to are variously called "simpler," "preliterate" or "primitive" societies, by contrast with a modern industrialized society. Most of these societies are far simpler in their total social structure than a modern nation-state or even a modern

[1] Cf. Raymond Firth, *Human Types* and "The Future of Social Anthropology" in *Man*, 44, January-February, 1944.

city. Their outfit of goods and services is smaller, often infinitesimal compared with that of a Western European society. But the crucial difference lies in the fact that they lack the art of writing and all that has become possible through that art; and, more significantly, that they lack the knowledge, the institutions and the technical processes rooted in experimental science.

Most of these societies are very small in the scale of their political and economic organization compared with the smallest European states. Even where their economy includes a market mechanism it is commonly based on production for subsistence. Their social philosophy, generally expressed in religious and mythological forms, is insular both in time perspective and in geographical view. But there are many borderline cases which defeat rigid classification. Throughout the Far and Middle East, as well as in Eastern Europe, there are states and territories comparable in scale of political and economic organization, in territory and population, to advanced West European societies. In every aspect of civilization except the possession of experimental science and its applications, some of these Oriental countries had, at the beginning of this century, attained a level of excellence comparable to that of any European country. But their lack of experimental science puts them more on a par with some African and Oceanian societies in many respects. From the point of view of their standard of living, their technique of production, and the legal and social context of their life, Chinese, Balkan, and Northern Nigerian peasants stand on much the same footing.[1]

A hard and fast line is still more difficult to draw when we think historically. Modern Euro-american civilization is only about two centuries old. The life of the masses in sixteenth-century Europe probably bore a closer resemblance to that of an African peasantry of to-day than to that of a modern English countryman. And at the other extreme of the historical scale

[1] This can easily be checked by comparing Fei, H. S., *Peasant Life in China*, Nadel, S.F., *A Black Byzantium*, and Warriner, D., *Peasant Life in Europe*.

there is the phenomenon of Nazism. The black sheep of a family is, nevertheless, of the same blood and bone as his virtuous brethren. To say that Nazism is a brutal and insane perversion of Euro-american civilization does not absolve its enemies from some share of responsibility for its emergence. War, rapine, and brutality are commonplaces in the history of some African and Oriental peoples. But simply because of the small scale of their social organization and their lack of science, no pre-scientific people now extant can match the record of destruction and death wrought in Europe by war.

When we turn from the massive and material aspects of social life to the individual the differences between primitive man and Euro-american man reach vanishing point. Physically and psycho-physically all mankind is a single species. There is no incontrovertible scientific proof that inborn mental abilities and dispositions are positively correlated with skin colour. The available evidence, in fact, points in the opposite direction. That does not mean that there are no differences of quality or quantity in the expression of mental dispositions, or in the application of inborn abilities, between people of different races. Reputable anthropologists are unanimous in ascribing this to differences of training, of economic and social outlets, and of cultural standards. This generalization applies also to most of the popular racialist beliefs emanating from Europeans who have practical dealings with non-European races. The extreme racialist ideologies are typical instances of the function of mythology in social organization. They are obvious by-products of a competitive economic struggle and irreconcilable cultural patterns. They constitute a combination of defence mechanism, rationalization, and magical belief serving to maintain unity of purpose and cultural solidarity among the caste or class that holds them. Hence scientific refutation rarely has any effect. They can be eradicated only by political or economic action designed to overthrow the gross inequalities in the bi-racial social system.

Less virulent, but still insidious, varieties of these mythologies occur in areas where the economic relations of the ruling race and the subject race tend to be complementary rather than competitive and where for historical and climatic reasons, the former exercise political power in a spirit of trusteeship. In such a setting it becomes necessary both for utilitarian and for moral reasons to throw open the gates of European culture to the natives of the country. Racial myths appear on both sides as a protective screen for the cultural values of each race. They are defensive myths, symptomatic of divided ideals and interests, not aggressively used to bolster up unwarranted privileges.

Among these fallacies is the belief that non-European races are lazier than Europeans. This is nonsense. Leaving aside defects of physique and health, due in part to defective nutrition, we have enough objective data to prove the contrary. The impression arises from experience of non-Europeans in wage labour doing work without the slightest social meaning for them. Inside their own social system, or working for ends they accept as worthwhile, these men are often more industrious than Europeans. Environment, technical shortcomings and cultural standards may impose a different rhythm of work and rest from ours. Or, for the same reasons, their output might be less than could be expected. But this does not imply a disinclination to work.[1] Indeed, the surprising thing is that indentured plantation labour, or men driven to the mines by economic and legal pressure, do any work at all.

Another fallacy of the same kind, often heard in Africa, is that the natives are "routine minded" and "lack initiative." This, one is sometimes inclined to suspect, is nothing but a

[1] This question has to be studied against the background of the total native economy of a particular people. Cf. for example Firth, R., *Primitive, Polynesian Economy*, 1939; Richards, A. I., *Land, Labour and Diet in Northern Rhodesia*, 1940; Nadel, S.F., *op. cit.* Evans-Pritchard, E. E. *The Nuer*, 1940. In this connection it may be noted that the zeal and industry of African schoolboys is notorious. They have to be forced to relax.

projection.[1] Experience shows that non-European peoples have no lack of commercial enterprise, inventiveness or adaptability.

The belief that Africans and other non-European races are by nature improvident deserves closer scrutiny. Research has shown that thrift, foresight, and economical use of resources are common among non-European peoples in the context of their native economic systems. But there is no place for capital accumulation in a subsistence economy; saving is merely postponed consumption. This outlook is carried over into production for the world market and into wage labour in the European sector of a colonial economy. It is encouraged by the whole structure of colonial economy, with its barter-like exchange of European goods and services for colonial raw materials and labour. And on the other side there is the insatiable demand, typical of undeveloped countries poor in material goods, for every conceivable kind of consumer's goods. There is little doubt that the propensity to save, in our sense, will assert itself when the basic consumer's wants are satisfied and when incentives and opportunities for it arise.[2]

The balance of scientific evidence and of practical experience shows that non-European races are not radically different from us in their fundamental psycho-physical make-up or in their educability. Differences in performance arise from differences of economic, social, and cultural conditions. We must first ask what are the social and cultural forces behind

---

[1] Projection—a psychological process by which a person attributes to others socially disapproved character traits he himself has.

[2] This is already apparent among the salaried classes and the better off wage earners in West Africa. A great deal depends on the incentives. West Africans will stint themselves in order to provide an education—valued both as a path to lucrative employment and as an open sesame to the white man's culture—for a son, or to buy land. But no other form of investment as yet open to them has the same combination of high security and high prestige value. Long term industrial or commercial investment calling for a large sacrifice of immediate consumption would not, at present, meet with a significant voluntary response.

such differences of performance in a particular situation before admitting other explanations.

Social anthropology differs from, say, economics and jurisprudence in that it is concerned with society as a whole and not with one functional system in isolation. This approach is perhaps easier in a primitive society where the interlocking and interpenetration of the different functional systems that make up a social structure are more obvious than in our society. Social organization and the life of the individual are not so departmentalized as with us. Economic activities, domestic life, religious practices and beliefs, legal and political institutions, are all interwoven. The basis of this is a wide-spreading network of kinship ties which tends to bring the same groups of people together for all the various purposes and tasks of social life. A pervasive scheme of reciprocal rights and duties upheld by religious and moral sanctions supports or takes the place of explicit legal institutions. Political power and authority go hand in hand with wealth and economic leadership, but these are counterpoised by equivalent duties and responsibilities. Despotism is not a common feature of primitive political organization; and with all its vices—which are many—class rule or government by privileged groups or military autocrats has seldom reached such depths of perfidy and malignancy as is familiar to us from the history of Europe. The general tendency, in fact, is for political responsibility and initiative to be broadly based and widely distributed. This is related to the pre-capitalist economic structure and pre-scientific technical equipment of primitive societies. This results in a great degree of economic equality. Thus it is seldom possible for a class structure based on wide discrepancies in the ownership of the means of production, or on the possession of specialized skills, to become permanently entrenched.

This is a highly simplified picture. For there is, of course, a very wide range of variation in primitive social structure. In the most homogeneous and compact primitive societies the social structure has a high degree of stability and internal

AN ANTHROPOLOGIST'S POINT OF VIEW

equilibrium. The common interest, backed by powerful religious sanctions, usually prevails when internal conflicts arise. At the other end of the scale are groups like the large African native kingdoms. Their social order is more analogous to ours and their political and economic institutions resemble those of earlier stages of our society. Wars of conquest and civil wars have shaped their political forms and established the sanction of military force as the supreme sanction of law and order. A fairly complex occupational division of labour makes for a diversified economy. Social stratification by rank or by status, associated with political, religious and productive functions is found: and an extensive system of internal and external trade, involving a wide range of inter-tribal intercourse, was often found long before the European conquest. Yet even in these societies the tendency towards an internal equilibrium is marked and revolutionary changes in the social structure, especially at the level of the territorial sub-divisions or the kinship groupings of the society were exceptional in the past. The dynamic of social change tended to work within existing channels.[1] The kind of contradictions found in the structure of modern capitalist society do not arise.

In trying to get a view of the total structure of a primitive society as it is developing to-day, all the forces operating within it and impinging on it from outside have to be considered. That is how anthropologists come up against the effects of colonial expansion.

Anthropologists attach special significance to an aspect of primitive society that the practical man is apt to notice only when it becomes a source of obstruction. This is the culture, or the qualitative make-up of a people's way of life. There are many analogies between the social structure of some primitive societies, under present conditions, and earlier stages of European social evolution. But there is a great gulf between the qualitative make-up of most primitive societies' way of life and Euro-

[1] Readers may be referred to the literature already cited for fuller discussions of these points.

american civilization. Literacy and science are distinctive items of Euro-american culture with a long tradition. They have a high social value for us irrespective of their particular use or abuse by a class or a State in any historical period. They not only directly shape our technology and economic structure but dominate our social philosophy and our patterns of values. So also modern Euro-american civilization has distinctive legal and ethical codes, specific most-favoured patterns of family life, education, religious belief and political theories whose roots go far back in the history of this civilization. In spite of shifts in the balance of economic and political power and of tremendous changes in social structure, there has been an essential continuity in Euro-american culture since the Middle Ages. The pluralistic character and contradictory currents of Western culture must not blind us to this.

Primitive cultures are generally conspicuously homogeneous compared with ours, and the different provinces of culture are more interfused. Sound empirical knowledge, the fruit of generations of trial and error, blends with magical belief in the techniques of production. Religious, moral and legal sanctions together make up a single fabric. A chief is at the same time political, judicial and religious head of his community. Primitive cultures often differ profoundly from ours in content, too. Institutions such as matrilineal inheritance as the basis of the law of property, polygamy, ancestor worship, divine kingship, annual tribal festivals, and so forth, are the rule rather than the exception. And they are as deeply rooted in the past—though it be an unrecorded past—and as completely incorporated in the present social system of a primitive people as is our culture in ours. From the standpoint of social evolution the important thing about culture is its value aspect. A people's culture embodies the values by which and for which they live. It defines the common ends in pursuit of which social unity is maintained and the private ends for which men will work and make sacrifices. And, as with us, these social values and ends are framed in non-utilitarian terms. They are, for a primitive people, matters of ethics and morals, of religion or art or political sentiment, felt to be the *vis a fronte* of social existence. Earning a livelihood is felt to be only a means to these ends. Thus we find that the centre of gravity of the equilibrium characteristic of a stable and homogeneous primitive society lies in its scheme of cultural values; and that a primitive people undergoing rapid social breakdown are apt to become a rabble of acquisitive or exploited individuals and the prey of irrational[1] mob impulses if they cease to have common cultural values.

It cannot be too strongly emphasized that these are generalizations of facts and not statements of values. No trained anthropologist is so naïve as to believe that primitive societies are paradises on earth.[2] But it is also not deniable that very many primitive societies had a way of life that was satisfying and supremely worth while to them before they came into the orbit of Euro-american civilization. The destructive effects of Euroamerican contact on these societies has been repeatedly emphasized not only by anthropologists but by Royal Commissions, journalists, government officials and bodies like the Fabian Society.

Whichever way we look at it, Western civilization, whether

---

[1] I.e. violently inconsistent with the theories of human life, nature and the supernatural most widely accepted in that society as well as devoid of objective validity in the situation in which it arises. Racialism among Europeans and mass conversions to Christianity among primitive peoples, are examples.

[2] The curious myth that anthropologists want to "preserve" untouched native societies as "museum pieces" is so absurd that it hardly deserves comment. Those who put it about merely show their ignorance of modern anthropological research work, as well as a shocking lack of understanding of the historical processes of our times. In fact, nostalgia for the "unspoiled savage" is usually found among those who get their living from breaking up primitive societies and "corrupting" the savage—government officials, traders, missionaries, etc. The myth is a good example of the scapegoat myth. Sometimes it serves to cover up failure in the face of the intractable realities of native life, which it is the business of anthropologists to understand. In other cases it serves to confuse potential critics of unrealistic panaceas advocated for the colonies.

in the form of naked capitalist exploitation of land and labour or in the benign forms of legitimate commerce, missions and government, comes into the life of colonial peoples as an alien revolutionary force. The effects of this have been too often described to need recapitulation here. But it must be pointed out that the worst excesses of the white man's rapacity in the tropics, no less than the more constructive enterprises of European capital, technology and missions are all part of the same institutional fabric of Western civilization; that a money economy has a similar social impact on a pre-scientific people among the free cocoa farmers of the Gold Coast and in the South African native reserves; that Western education and missions produce similar results in Samoa and in West Africa. It is this that justifies the anthropologist in trying to analyse what happens in terms of a "clash of cultures" or an "impact of Western civilization on primitive society." The effect of this impact is to bring about the disorganization of native society to a greater or less degree.

It has been thus throughout the history of European colonization. In the extreme case, among extant colonial peoples, the disintegration is almost catastrophic owing to the physical disruption of native society by an excessive drain on its manpower. This has happened in Nyasaland, for example. In the most benign cases, as in Northern Nigeria, where contact is practically limited to commerce and a paternalistic administration, the effect has been merely to set up new strains in the social structure and to start a slow process of social erosion. In the intermediate case, as in the Gold Coast Colony, the internal contradictions due to contact are more acute and the process of social dis-articulation has gone far. Contradictory patterns of wants and economic opportunities engendered by the entry of West Africa into the world market and the adoption of a money economy result in indebtedness and excessive litigation. Political conflict between the traditional native authorities and new social classes brought into being by the new social and economic forces at work in the country is kept in check only by the vigilance of the British administration. Last, but most important, there is an insidious conflict of cultural values. The freedom of movement, speech and enterprise maintained by the force of British government is the main source of this change. But missionary activity, education, new legal and political ideas and the general ferment of social change play their part. The religious and legal sanctions of right conduct have become ambiguous, and the common symptoms of a maladjusted social system—crime, prostitution, corruption, and unbridled acquisitiveness—have become prominent to an extent never known in the traditional social order.

Supplementing these changes within the native societies composing the artificial administrative unit called a colony are equally significant changes in their inter-relations with one another. The White Man's peace (and that only) makes possible an unprecedented movement of individuals to take advantage of the opportunities thrown open by the White Man's commerce. There is a great and haphazard mingling of people of widely different culture, and no common interests other than pecuniary wants, especially in the new commercial and industrial centres. New economic roles—from that of unskilled labourer to that of the professional man—open the road to hitherto undreamt-of occupational mobility. A class structure based on differences of wealth, occupation, and the prestige of literacy grows up outside or in opposition to the traditional social structures. New types of social personalities come into existence—the absentee landlord, the money-lender, the commercial middleman, side by side with the school-master, the clergyman and the doctor. In the new towns the symptoms of social maladjustment are more widespread and acute than in the tribal areas. For, however far social disintegration has gone in the tribal areas, there still remains a skeleton of community organization and a remnant of common cultural values. These are lacking in the new urban centres, whose sole *raison d'être* for all its inhabitants is the iron compulsion of pecuniary need, and whose sole value for them is the opportunities offered for pecuniary ambition. There is no such thing as a civic conscience or civic pride, no sense of unity or social purpose in the heterogeneous commercial-cum-administrative centres of African colonies.[1]

This well-known situation is susceptible of various interpretations. It is arguable that such a state of affairs is historically inevitable in the transition from a primitive social structure to a complex modern organization. History can be quoted in support of the theory that so radical a change in the whole structure of a society must be paid for in sweat, blood and tears, in disruption of established modes of thought and conduct, and in much socially costly trial and error. On this argument, assuming the continuation of the present governmental and economic structure of the colony to serve as a stable framework, the process of historical evolution can be left to work itself out. And the process might be helped on and to some extent guided by "planning" and by an intensification of all the existing processes of westernization—for that is what proposals for increasing education, medical services, industrialization, etc., amount to. The avowed goal in this line of thought is "raising the standard of living" of colonial peoples, and it is implied that the achievement of this goal in itself will produce a magical transformation for the better in the entire social life of colonial peoples.

The achievement of this economic goal depends largely on the amount of resources and effort devoted to the task. The response of most colonial peoples to new economic opportunities, opened up to them without a corresponding demand for

---

[1] This is, in fact, the typical picture of what J. S. Furnivall calls a "plural society." His book, *Netherlands India*, and his various papers on Far Eastern problems, in particular "Progress and Welfare in the Tropical Far East," published by the Institute of Pacific Relations deserve the most careful study by those who are concerned with problems of colonial development. But it is perhaps as well to remind the reader that Furnivall's picture of the Far Eastern dependencies does not apply entirely to Africa or Oceania. The sector of intensive Euro-american penetration is small in West Africa relatively to the total native population, and the impact in East and South Africa is in some ways more disorganizing than in the Far East.

heavy temporary economic sacrifices, will be great. But it is difficult to believe that the cost in terms of social disorganization can be avoided. It has not been hitherto, in areas of rising standards of living. And it is still more difficult for an anthropologist to believe that this is the infallible panacea for all colonial problems.

Where social evolution is concerned the margin of unpredictability is enormous, even in our own society. In the colonies, owing to the neglect of social research in the past, lack of data makes prediction still more chancy. Thus the kind of colonial social structure that may emerge as a result of such a policy is anyone's guess. It is a wise precaution that makes the most zealous colonial planners refrain from venturing too far into the political, legal and social implications of their schemes.

The cliche "self-government" is no answer to the questions what kind of Government? what system of law? what patterns of ethics? what quality and standards of cultural values will the new colonial society have? But this is the crucial question to an anthropologist. He can testify from observation that equality in a state of common material poverty, dirt and danger from disease, where it goes with equality of rights and duties and deeply held common cultural values is not a disorganizing force in society. On the other hand, a high average standard of living and health, where it is associated with wide discrepancies of wealth, political power, and social privilege, in a society lacking vital common purposes and values, may have results only too lamentably familiar from our own history.

Economic development may be regarded as an end in itself, with the implicit assumption that the social structure most appropriate for every stage of economic progress will, with a little guidance here and there, crystallize out in the historical process. It is as well, then, to be aware in advance of the price that will certainly have to be paid for this. If, on the other hand, raising the standard of living in the colonies is regarded as a means to social and political ends, it is desirable that these ends should be defined and the tactics of economic development closely related to them.

This ties up with the important problem of the driving forces of progress. Economic progress is deceptively easy to bring about in an undeveloped country. In a colony it can be imposed by the suzerain power. But it comes from outside. The avidity with which individuals in a colony respond to new economic opportunities does not mean that there is any social impetus behind it. It does not mean that either the idea or the instruments of economic progress have any cultural value for the mass of the people of a colony. This may not matter in the narrow economic sense. From the broader social point of view it is questionable if an advanced economic system could be maintained, after the initial spurt, and improbable that it would become the foundation of a social structure on a higher level of integration than the existing tribal communities, if the mass of the people never learn to feel that it matters for their well-being in the same way as their land or cattle or canoes do to-day. The alternative is for the vanguard of progress to be a limited class of rentiers and capitalists wedded to the new order by the profits and power they get out of it at the community's expense. It may be that the answer lies in a programme of "mass education" coupled with consciously directed political change. It will certainly take time—perhaps a decade, more probably several decades. And again it will not be accomplished painlessly.

The history of the Euro-american impact on colonial societies in different parts of the world confirms this opinion. It shows, also, the extraordinary vitality of non-European cultures. Nothing short of virtual extermination wipes out the whole of a people's culture.[1] In Africa one finds vigorous peoples seizing

---

[1] Professor M. J. Herskovits has shown, in many publications and in his book *The Myth of the Negro Past* that even the steamroller of slavery failed to crush the traditional cultural patterns and values of the New World negro populations out of existence. West African culture traits are very much alive among the negro populations of Brazil, British Honduras, the West Indies, etc. But owing to the scanty research (all the work of Ameri-

eagerly on everything offered by Euro-american contact; but the pulse of the indigenous cultures beats very strongly, not only in the hearts of the 98 per cent who are still living mainly according to the ways of their forefathers, but also in the hearts of the remaining 2 per cent. As a mere quantitative factor this must be reckoned with in any plans for a social transformation of colonial peoples in a short period. As a qualitative factor the tenacity with which non-European peoples cling to certain fundamental elements of their ancestors' cultural values is profoundly important.

The go-ahead reformer often finds this a source of concealed or open resistance to his *a priori* plans—as, for instance, matrilineal inheritance has been found to be in the Gold Coast Colony, and the reluctance of peasants to adopt land tenures or methods of cultivation believed to be conducive to higher output has been found to be everywhere. In this way the man on the spot, battling with the hour to hour tactical problems of translating policy into results, makes a discovery that those who make plans in terms of thousands of square miles and millions of people sometimes overlook. He learns that colonial peoples are not robots or children whom he can lead or direct wherever his logically perfect and, from our point of view, enlightened plans demand. He learns that they are not so much undifferentiated labour power to be turned on to this or that type of production at will. He finds that they do not unquestioningly accept his views of what is best for them, but often prefer to stick obstinately to their own "backward" habits of thought and action. He discovers that more and better sanitation, roads, hospitals, schools, houses, cash incomes do not by themselves make a better integrated and socially healthier community.

These ideas we have pictured our man-on-the-spot unlearning by experience are only too prevalent at present as a result of what is sometimes called the "welfare" approach to colonial

can anthropologists, incidentally) that has as yet been done in these areas, the influence of this fact on modern social problems cannot be assessed.

development. It sometimes strikes an anthropologist that this approach visualizes colonial man as consisting of a body that has to be adequately fed, clothed, housed, cleansed of disease and dirt, and turned on to maximum output, plus a blank cerebral cortex that can be stamped with any pattern of skills and knowledge we deem necessary by a long-enough exposure to schooling. The fact that colonial man also belongs—or used to belong—to an organized society with its own traditional cultural values, that he has habits of thought and goals of life of his own, is seldom considered relevant.

The conflict of values and standards in modern colonial societies goes back to the persistence of elements of the traditional culture and social organization side by side with new Euro-american ideas and values and forms of social relations. Is such conflict inevitable, and is it bound to be a drag on social progress? This question requires far more research in the study and in the field before an answer can be attempted. One reason for the occurrence of such conflicts of values does however deserve mention. It is the extraordinary shallowness of Euro-american culture in most colonies. The presence of the material equipment and administrative machinery of Euro-american civilization on a large scale, in a colony, and the participation of many members of colonial races in the technical management of this apparatus of civilization is apt to be misleading. In fact, those so engaged are extremely few in proportion to the total population of most colonies, and the apparatus itself has not been culturally assimilated. The majority of colonial populations can get along without it at a pinch.

The skills and knowledge associated with this new framework have no cultural roots in a colony. They have for the most part been proferred to and acquired by a chance selection of individuals in a spirit of utilitarian self-interest. In so far as there was a leading idea behind, for example, the educational system of most colonies, it was the idea that training individuals in Euro-american skills and knowledge would have a leavening influence on the whole society. In fact it does not work out that way. It creates a class of special skilled craftsmen for running the apparatus of civilization, who tend to stand outside their native social order both in terms of economic function and in terms of personal goals. This is true to some, though to a lesser extent, even of the professional and clerical class.

It is a fallacy to think that a transformation leading to a higher level of social integration, and capable of directing the driving forces of society into constructive new channels, can be effected solely by equipping a backward society with the end-product apparatus and end-product skills of our civilization. Literacy, the machine, and chemo-therapy are useful tools for adding to human welfare. They would, however, soon cease to exist if it were not for the extensive and historically deep-rooted network of institutions and cultural values of which they are an outcome. Literacy can be an extremely valuable tool in a previously pre-literate society. It cannot become an instrument of social transformation without the institutional matrix which gives it life and meaning; and poets and publishers are as important in this matrix as schools and colleges. The level of professional and technical proficiency in any colony will not come up to ours until there are professional associations and journals and research institutes locally staffed. The quality of political thinking will not improve until there are universities teaching the social sciences and students investigating social and economic problems in every colony.

But again this is not purely a quantitative problem. A five-year plan of mass acculturation would not establish Western civilization as the sole accepted way of life in a previously "backward" territory. It would probably accelerate the process of social disintegration and aggravate the conflict of cultures; and it would require draconian measures of enforcement. It is the question of cultural values again. Unless there is what J. S. Furnivall has called a "social demand" for (in other words, a general sense that the common ends of the society are being served by) the new material and social and intellectual equipment, it may merely increase aggregate physical prosperity at the cost of a deterioration in the quality of social life.

The central problem of colonial development, from an anthropologist's point of view, is that of changing the social system as a whole. It is, to begin with, the problem of integrating clusters of small-scale primitive societies held together in mechanical juxtaposition by the firm scaffolding of European rule into large-scale organic structures. This is essentially a political question. Whether or not the required changes can be planned or even regulated is an open question, in the present stage of sociological theory and with the present paucity of factual information about the social and political organizations of colonial peoples. It is certain, however, that the kind of colonial societies that will eventually emerge will be greatly influenced by the conception of what they should be like at present held by those responsible for colonial policy. The "wealth and welfare" policy, indispensable as it is, is no answer to this problem; for maximizing productivity and material welfare is merely a means to political ends. It can end up in fascism as easily as in democracy.

Closely connected with this problem and equally vital is the problem of investing the apparatus of Euro-american civilization with cultural value for the mass of colonial peoples, of creating social demand for it. Without this the maximization of wealth and welfare might as easily lead to a deterioration in the quality of social life among colonial peoples as to its improvement. To supplant head hunting by class war and witchcraft by quack doctors might be a loss rather than a gain.

There is so little scientific knowledge on this subject that it can only be discussed hypothetically. It is conceivable, for example, that a quicker solution will be found for this problem in settler colonies than in non-settler colonies. For in the former the European element regard the colony as their home. They live, and do not merely teach white civilization. They even fight and oppress for it. But the iron laws of economics bind them to the natives and the natives to them in an indissoluble interdependence. As their economy expands and their social structure becomes more complex these same laws compel them to admit the native to an ever-increasing share in their much-prized civilization. Colour-bar legislation, like racialist myths, is perhaps a symptom of the vain resistance to this inevitable process. And on the native side, there is perhaps something in the theory that what a class or a race or a nation has won with great sacrifice is the more precious and the more creatively used for that reason. Some such solution seems to have been achieved in New Zealand.[1] But it is worth pointing out that the Maori renaissance drew its strength from two sources. One was the persistence of certain foci and basic forms of social integration among them; the other was their whole-hearted acceptance of Euro-american cultural values.

On the other hand, it is possible that a gradual absorption and amalgamation of Euro-american technique and knowledge with the most vital elements of indigenous culture and forms of social organization in non-settler colonies will produce a more vigorous hybrid civilization. Such a process would be more likely to tap dynamic impulses inherent in the native social structures than in colonies where the indigenous inhabitants are not free to experiment. Thus the essentially democratic basis of political organization in many African societies[2] may prove to be a factor of immense value in the political evolution of the African colonies.

We can be certain of one thing, and that is that many surprises await us in the colonies. If, as anthropologists believe, many things are inevitable in human affairs, there is unquestionably also a wide margin of indeterminacy. There can never be final solutions to human problems. Every solution creates new problems. So there can only be an everlasting process of adjustment and re-adjustment as knowledge advances and social evolution goes on. In Africa, as no doubt in other "backward"

[1] Cf. Raymond Firth, *Primitive Economics of the New Zealand Maori*, and W. K. Hancock, *Survey of British Commonwealth Affairs*, II, 2.
[2] Cf. M. Fortes and E. E. Evans-Pritchard, *African Political Systems*.

parts, it is the historical role of the white man to propose, initiate, even impose, new social forms, economic relations and cultural values. But in the end the kinds of social structure and the quality of social life that will emerge will be determined by the colonial peoples themselves. And whether they like it or not, their own cultural traditions will play a great part in this.

Colonies and World Order
ANONYMOUS

In this contracting world of ever more rapid means of communication and of ever more extensive instruments of destruction the dependence of all forms of human progress on a sound international order is evident. Only if a third world catastrophe can be prevented and peaceful work and cultural relations adopted among the nations is it possible to build up societies in which man can develop his potentialities in freedom from fear and want. A realization of this is a natural accompaniment of the present breakdown in international relations. It echoes the thoughts of 1918 and 1919. On the other hand, few now have any illusions that a new and safe world order will be born of idealism alone. We are far from the optimism of the early League of Nations period. In other words, our wisdom is, as always, greater than that of our fathers.

But is it enough? A realism which is compounded of acceptance of the need for international security and hesitation in seeking ways of winning this security, leads many, when examining concrete problems of human advance, to dismiss the international aspects of their particular problems in an uneasy parenthesis. A sound world order is assumed so that particular contributions to the wealth and happiness of mankind can be constructed on the assumption that somehow or other further war will be prevented. It would be more realistic to focus each concrete reform not within a complete picture which so far has not been drawn, but within the setting of the requirements of world order. As things are, however, in the present fevers of war and doubt, the eyes of many leaders become afflicted with short sight when they look outside the existing walls of their own communities and of their own problems.

Among two groups, both of which may be constructive forces, the linking of colonial and international issues is apt to affect the eyesight. Leaders of the colonial peoples, particularly when obtaining concessions from an imperial authority, have little desire to gaze beyond the good relationship they hope for between their country and its rulers, through to a brave new world where relations will be manifold instead of dual. Even a newly independent country may for a generation see the world order as merely a new stage for a dialogue on its own Irish question. At the other extreme, a blind imperialist may like to feel that he alone shall decide what should be done with what he believes is his own; and others with a fine ideal of Commonwealth unity may deprecate international focussing which may lead to the neglect of valuable cultural ties within an empire of goodwill.

These are natural feelings. Any international policy which frustrates local progress or which destroys a healthy community of partnership deserves suspicion. Colonial peoples will not profit by a transition from national to international imperialism. They will not rejoice to be the guinea pigs of new international experiments. When they look back and see how colonies were regarded during the early expansion of Europe, the scrambles for Africa and the Pacific, and the decade of appeasement, they may conclude that any international policy affecting them will be to their prejudice.

Such a conclusion would be as useful as if a man denied himself food owing to the perils of indigestion. The problem of national communities, whose development is controlled by alien forces in the direction of which the community has no sufficient say, is a colonial question; it is and always has been an international question as well. The directing State has certain strategic and certain economic advantages, its position arouses jealousies or excites contempt; its most liberal programmes, together with the aspirations of its colonial peoples, may be checked by doubts as to what effects any changes may have on the balance of world forces. At the present time the colonial question has threatened to divide the American and British peoples. It diminished confidence between Britain and the Dominions. It is claimed by Chinese statesmen to be of interest to them. It is of importance in the reconstruction of Europe. It raises for the conscientious American queries as to the world system he may have to guarantee. It raises for Britain similar queries as to the rightness of colonial rule in all empires, for to them the same rules or absence of rules of responsibility must apply as are accepted by the British Empire. It is a concrete issue of the war, since enemy colonial territories have been conquered and since allied colonies have to be liberated by the international coalition of the United Nations.

Nevertheless, it is not to be concluded from this that international colonial policy should demand sacrifices from the colonial peoples without other return than a safer world order. On the contrary, whatever importance may rightly be attached to co-operation for peace between the Great Powers, there will be an international danger in approaching the treatment of colonies from the standpoint of the sole interests of those Great Powers. Even though old forms of exploitation are rejected and provision made for the promotion of welfare and development, resentment at tutelage may be the chief result, and colonial discontent will sharpen any international clash of interest. A first consideration in international policy should be not merely regard for the welfare of colonial peoples, but an effective will to obtain an effective association in the establishment of welfare on the part of the peoples concerned. Unless a place is reserved for the colonial peoples in the application of any international policy affecting them, even benevolent measures will appear alien and be resented or received with indifference, while failures will germinate plague-spots of discontent infecting the colours, races and nationalities that should collaborate. For these reasons, although in some colonies as in some States it may be necessary for some citizens to accept world security measures which restrict their full privileges, the international treatment of colonies must fundamentally assume that what is best for colonial peoples is best for world order.

It is a sign of this spirit that makes of significance recent attempts to find a new philosophical guide for, or justification of, colonial government. They cannot be dismissed as hypocritical or as merely theoretical. If they could lead to a common direction sign for colonial and international policies, it would be difficult for either to diverge from the common road.

There is a wide measure of verbal agreement that the main purpose of colonial government is the advancement of the welfare of colonial peoples, subject to the needs of the outside world. It is, however, doubtful whether without substantial modifications this doctrine of trusteeship is any longer capable of pointing to rules of practical policy or of exciting public enthusiasm. The British Government has long claimed that it is applicable to the whole of the colonial empire. General Smuts has examined trusteeship as the keynote of Native policy within the Union of South Africa. M. Pierlot, the Belgian Prime Minister, speaks in much the same language of the Congo. Taking African territories alone, the differences in practical policies of land, labour, education and economic and social programmes in general are great as between Kenya, Uganda, Tanganyika, the Union and the Belgian Congo. Trusteeship implies a kind of moral attitude. It is not a sufficient practical guide to modern administrative problems. It is open to divergent interpretations. Its use is resented by the more educated people in some of the colonies.

In amplification of the principle of trusteeship, the British position has been represented by Lord Hailey as meaning that the State in the colonies, as at home, would be not merely an agency for maintaining justice and equal rights, or for preventing abuse, but the most active agency for promoting social welfare and improving the general standard of living. To this end, his philosophy may be summarized as implying that: (1) the relations between colonies and colonial powers should be restated, not as those of trustees and wards, but as those of senior and junior partners; (2) in the colonies the modern State should accept the obligations incumbent on it in regard to the improvement of the social services and standards of living in its own domestic backward areas; (3) the objective of self-government should be pursued by the more rapid development of fully powered local institutions and the fuller participation of the people in their own administrative services; (4) existing institutions should be extended in order to assist the evolution of forms of self-government best suited to the traditions and circumstances of the people; and (5) the whole civilized world should endeavour to bring the economic conditions of populations producing raw materials more nearly to the level of those of industrialized countries.

The conception of partnership, which has been echoed by Government speakers in Great Britain, has its critics. It is thought that it implies an exclusive dominance of the colonial power which may be unfavourable to the rapid development of colonial self-government and of international collaboration. In the U.S.A. it has been interpreted as opposed to the international principle of trusteeship. Yet "trusteeship" is also out of date as indicative of the relations between the Netherlands European Kingdom and other Netherlands territories. The Government has declared its intention of calling a post-war conference between the Netherlands territories "directed towards a Commonwealth in which the Netherlands, Indonesia, Surinam and Curaçao will participate, with complete self-reliance and freedom of conduct for each part regarding its internal affairs, but with readiness to render mutual assistance." In the face of these difficulties, the phrase "equal status" has been coined and has been endorsed by the British Labour Party. It may well be thought that it kills the implication of seniority and inferiority which partnership permits. Its adoption would require a positive policy of equal association between all peoples. Its danger is that it may seem to promise more than it can perform.

However, without attaching overwhelming importance to mere philosophy, it would be psychologically useful to find a new phrase, which would indicate a world purpose and serve as a yardstick of separate colonial policies. To these ends, the following is suggested:

"Colonies shall be administered on the principle that they form a sacred trust of civilization; this implies that the authorities responsible for their administration shall direct their policy towards the rapid association of the peoples concerned as partners of the metropolitan countries; as such they will be entitled to participate in imperial, regional and world organization with equal status to that of independent communities of comparable importance."

If a principle of this nature were followed as a guide to international colonial policy, it would be found that various practical measures in application of it can be taken. These would contribute favourably to a better world order and to the progress and reforms arising out of the situations in the various colonies.

To what extent would the "liberation" of colonies be of this nature? This is a question which is usually put as concerning exclusively the relations between the colony and the colonial power. If there were no possibility of any future world war it might well be so. In present conditions, however, the warning is necessary that, though the liberation of caged birds into a jungle saves bird-seed, it does not contribute to the peace of the jungle or the welfare of the birds. The liberation of white South Africa in 1909 strengthened the British Empire as well as white South Africa, but it can now be doubted whether any comparable liberation which favoured one race would be tolerated. The liberation by the United States of the Philippine Islands provided for respect for the independence and territorial and administrative integrity of the islands. A more constructive policy of co-operation between the two countries than mere respect for independence will be required after the liberation of the islands from the Japanese. It is not sufficient to expect that a world organization or the great Powers will immediately safeguard world security. Indeed, in the light of the failure of the powers, particularly the Great Powers, to work the League experiment, and in the absence of any comparable planning for peace it is unrealistic to hope for any more than the gradual taming of the jungle. Any liberation which means self-determination without security, and which adds another small State to the international scene, will only encourage a new international scramble.

Yet liberation, complete self-government, Dominion status, or any similar constitutional objective has its proper place in colonial policies which take account of international realities. The present colonial political system has not proved an adequate safeguard for the weak. It causes friction among the strong. It fails to enlist the joint strength of the less strong. For this reason alone the rapid development of democratic and responsible government in the colonies is the correct international, as it is the correct colonial, policy. Such responsible government, it may be suggested, would be furthered by a system of time-tables of economic, social and political advances, leading to the final stage in which the self-governing colony would work out with the protecting power and powers the mutual contributions which could be made to security. The first conclusion is therefore that there are a number of colonies which are so advanced that their political development through negotiation with the colonial power is internationally advisable and does not require other international measures than those applicable to self-governing countries.

Certainly for these colonies on the ladder to self-government, the intervention of an international administrative authority would be harmful. Many people have gone further and condemn all forms of direct international control. It must be asked, however, what practical measures can be taken in the case of Italian and Japanese colonies when by the Atlantic Charter the solemn promise has been made that we seek no territorial aggrandizement. The only solution which will not provoke charges of ill faith is that of international administration. The choice will rest between open internationalism and an unhappy prolongation of inter-allied military control. In the first case there can be a single administration free from conflicts of loyalty with a set programme of political, economic and social advance, the fulfilment of which is subject to public scrutiny. In the second case, each officer will owe his first allegiance to his own country, purposeful policy will be frustrated by differing national conceptions, and the people will grow restive as they recover from the wounds of war, so that the greater the material success of such administration the sooner will come its psychological failure.

International administration is charged with inefficiency—and, queerly enough, this charge most frequently comes from those who resent criticisms of inter-allied military control. The Anglo-French Condominium of the New Hebrides is held up as an awful example. The truth is that we have no proper experience of international administration. The New Hebrides is subject to a series of checks and balances between French and British, designed not for the welfare of the people, but to prevent any effective development by French or British. The Anglo-Egyptian Sudan is administered by Great Britain. Tangiers is a cockpit of European rivalry. Yet it is noteworthy that Shanghai, where the international municipal council was at first hardly more than a confusion of conflicting commercial interests, developed some measure of community loyalty, and in circumstances of great difficulty came to evolve a social policy of growing value and appeal to the Chinese.

Thus, at the two ends of the ladder of colonial development, self-government for some and international administration for very few will serve the interests of international order. For colonies between these two classes the principle of international supervision as distinct from international administration needs examination. Many suggestions have been made for the extension of the mandates system, or, in other words, for a system of national administration subject to international supervision. Like the Mandates Commission, the new body should be international and independent; its members should not be restricted to nationals of colonial powers; they should be freed of responsibility to their own governments; they should include experts from the chief international functional organizations. Unlike the Mandates Commission, it would have powers of direct inspection, it would have a programme-planning, international secretariat, and it would be empowered in co-operation with the administrative authorities to negotiate loans and foster colonial development.

The reservation already made must be repeated. Any such system will not work in the case of all colonies. In particular, colonies with real claims to self-government will not wish for new complications in their negotiations for political rights. An unfamiliar, somewhat impersonal, international agency may be judged or misjudged in advanced territories as a new means of political frustration. Countries such as the Philippines, Cyprus, Ceylon, Java, Barbados, Jamaica, Puerto Rico and most other dependencies in the Caribbean are not suitable for mandatory treatment. Much of West Africa, British and French, Uganda, and other areas where indigenous influence is strong need no such new experiment, but rather the acceleration of the movement towards self-government. The chief uses of any new system, like the chief successes of the Mandates system, will be found in respect of primitive territories or of countries which cannot come under unrestricted national control unless international jealousies are to be created.

Whether the immediate political status of colonies should be that of self-governing communities, of international wards or of national wards, their economic and social needs will be similar to those of many independent states, and will vary in different parts of the world. Recognizing this, the British Government has accepted the principle of regional collaboration in colonial areas. General Smuts has spoken in its favour. Regionalism is, indeed, now the fashionable gospel. But it has yet to be written. Apostles of regional organisation range from those who wish for nothing more than advisory technical collaboration between the colonial services of a region and those who see the regional organization acting as the agency of a strong international authority and as the machinery for increasing democratic self-determination.

The regional treatment of common problems has already a large place in international order. The political divisions between neighbouring countries, their differences in laws and perhaps in languages and cultures, their conflicting national, and perhaps their conflicting imperial, loyalties put out of court any form of federalism. At the same time they may have close common interests in problems of health, transport, migration, economic and social policy. Their grouping for purposes of defence may be essential to meet the long-range offensive power of modern war. It may be easier for the Great Powers to accept concrete commitments for regions of obvious importance to them than to apply indiscriminately the principle that peace is indivisible. Regional organization may be a useful, even essential, instrument of international collaboration and of local betterment. If it is to serve these ends, however, in colonial regions and in regions where colonies and States have common interests, it must be inspired by a common purpose. It must be directed towards the association of the peoples in the control of their own affairs. It must be subject to public scrutiny. Its services must be based on a regional loyalty. Otherwise, for regionalism can be read spheres of influence shared on a condominium basis between the Great Powers.

Regional collaboration between colonies and other powers will be mainly on a functional basis. It will be concerned with specific problems of economic and social policy. Wider functional collaboration is also required. In this field the International Labour Organization has an important part to play. It is the one piece of the pre-war Geneva machinery which has been accepted by the U.S.A., and not inconsistently supported by Great Britain. It is the avowed intention of the British Government to use it as the chief agency of international social reconstruction. The system of conventions is the most evolved form of international law. Its employer and worker representation has given it a vitality so often lacking in inter-governmental co-operation. Its contribution to the improvement of labour laws in the colonies is considerable. Its weaknesses are glaring

—the absence of the U.S.S.R., the destruction of the European trade union movement, its exclusion from questions of economic policy, and the zeal with which the Great Powers have pigeon-holed it for possible future use. It is, however, an essential piece of international functional machinery. Without it, it will be impossible to tackle the vast task of the complementary improvement of national standards of living and to prevent bigger and better wars resulting from bigger and better opportunities for the sweating of labour.

In the colonies present poverty and the spreading of industrial revolution call for energetic measures of social reform and the subordination of economic to social policy. Imperial and local action will require international co-ordination since colonial political boundaries rarely coincide with the boundaries of welfare problems, and since the imperial closed estate is an impossible sentiment. The desideratum of co-ordination on grounds of social policy is reinforced by considerations of diplomatic policy. On the subject of colonies a division of feeling between the Haves and the Have-nots and between the American and British (which is not the same thing) appears insurmountable. If the colonial powers could accept internationally agreed programmes of colonial betterment the psychological dilemma of collaboration with non-colonial powers would tend to be sublimated. Put more concretely, the American people cannot be expected to contribute usefully to a system which rightly or wrongly they dislike. They may respond, however, to growing markets of growing prosperity resulting from international agreements directed towards the abolition of colonial want.

This implies an international economic policy of tropical development. It also implies an international social policy which will define the objectives of tropical development in terms of human welfare. The instruments of world economic policy are as yet experimental and incomplete. But an instrument of world social policy exists in the International Labour Organization. This organization through its established machinery should define the principle of labour policy which should govern the administration of colonies. It should bring within its machinery the representatives of those colonial peoples to whom in the progress towards self-government control over their internal social policy has been granted.

A question which has to be asked is whether these various devices to give practical effect to the principle of colonial responsibility should be co-ordinated in a single diplomatic document. The case for a statement of the principles of colonial rule has been cogently argued by the Anti-Slavery and Aborigines Protection Society.[1] Ultimately action along these lines through a special colonial conference or a colonial conference held in conjunction with the final peace conference is inevitable. It is not possible to go on everlastingly saying that the security and welfare of the world is the concern of all powers, but that there are peoples unable to stand by themselves who are the exclusive concern of single powers. At the present stage, however, a single convention must either be very general or attempt to deal with all the complex problems of colonial life from conditions in an advanced colony to those in the most primitive. A general text might have tremendous moral force, if it could be made both sufficiently idealistic to capture public imagination and sufficiently concrete to escape the reproach that it is a repetition of unfulfilled promises of the past. Something might be done in this direction; in view of suspicions as to the limited validity of the Atlantic Charter, something needs to be done. It should, however, be recognized that an early convention will be general, and that a comprehensive agreement can only have a chance of success if all the issues of colonial policy have been previously properly explored.

Our general conclusion is that on the international plane there should be unity of colonial policy, but that there should not be a strait jacket for all colonial peoples. The unity should result from something like the general principle which has already

[1] *An International Colonial Convention*, Anti-Slavery and Aborigines Protection Society, London, May 1943.

been suggested. International policy will emerge not as a succession of compromises in the interests of the Great Powers, but as constructive policies based on the concrete problems of the colonial peoples. The difference in programmes of international help will for their part also result from the differing colonial situations. This means that no one device such as an international mandatory system or code of rules will be suitable.

Instead, a number of measures need to be taken. Of these the most important are:

1. The enumeration of the colonies to which effective self-government is immediately guaranteed, accompanied, of course, by honest steps to secure this aim.
2. A similar determination of colonies so rapidly approaching self-government that no new international intervention would be of value.
3. The determination of the ex-enemy colonies to be administered internationally, and of the non-self-governing territories to be administered nationally under a mandatory system.
4. The development of regional organizations as agents of self-government and of international assistance.
5. The definition of principles of economic and social policy in colonies and the association of self-governing colonies in international agencies of economic and social policy.
6. The co-ordination of these measures in a world agreement which might be taken in two stages, the first in preparation for other measures, and the second in endorsement of those measures.

The whole of this policy must be dominated by respect for the wishes of colonial peoples and by a determination to associate them in the responsibilities which they will have to assume when they attain equality of partnership. In the present world, small nations, even if theoretically independent, are not strong enough to command full respect for their freedom. Any international and any colonial policy which fails to develop this strength will not succeed. But therefore for international and for imperial reasons, the measures taken must be conceived not merely for the protection of colonial peoples, but also for the development of their own means of self-protection.

How a Political Society Functions
The Story of the Fabian Colonial Bureau
by RITA HINDEN

The Democratic Background

In a highly organized democratic society, such as Britain, there are always ways of making oneself heard. Any group or society, which knows what it wants and has a point of view to offer, can capture at least a section of public opinion and bring its views to the attention of the authorities with an insistence not altogether to be ignored. Public opinion and Parliament, reinforcing and working through each other, are the powerful guardians of democratic rights and the levellers of injustice. Every citizen is free to make his approach to either, and his success will depend on his skill in putting over a case, the public response he can muster, the weight with which he is backed, and the strength of the opposition.

How can the appeal to public opinion and Parliament be made? Public opinion may be reached through the written or the spoken word. With a free Press there is no end (except in wartime under paper restrictions) to the pamphlets which may be printed, to the books which publishers may be pressed to accept, and somewhere inside the wide range of the British Press—or at least in its correspondence columns—a place will always be found for the expression of a reasonable, or even an unreasonable, point of view. Then there is the approach to the public through demonstrations, through meetings, through the numerous conferences in which some sections of the people delight, discussion groups, gatherings of all sorts. And though the public in its widest sense may have no opinion at all on very many specialized or complicated subjects, there are always groups of individuals and political organizations who will stand firmly on the rights and wrongs of even the most abstruse issues.

This broad, and not always easy, approach to public opinion, can to some extent be short-circuited by a more specific and direct approach to Parliament. Question time in the House of Commons is one of the most precious and important manifestations of British freedom. For an hour every day before the parliamentary business commences, Members may put their questions to the Ministers and demand an answer on any matter within the whole sphere of government. If a group of Members of Parliament feel sufficiently strongly on a subject (and what they feel is largely influenced by what public opinion in their constituencies feels), they can press their questions week in and week out, and it will need a stubborn Minister to refuse them all satisfaction. There are other channels within the procedure of the House for venting grievances or expatiating on particular problems. The Adjournment of the House may be moved by a private member on any day, which gives him an opportunity for talking for half an hour on the particular bee then buzzing in his bonnet, and the Minister or his deputy must be there to reply. There are certain opportunities—such as the Debate on the King's Speech, when almost any matter may be discussed; or Supply days when the Estimates for the different Departments are voted. Public opinion has a further outlet in the House of Lords. Procedure here has not been confined to the strait jacket which the weight of Government business imposes on the House of Commons, and it is possible for members to put down motions for debate at almost any time and to command the ear of the House for almost as many hours as desired.

Public Opinion and the Colonies

It was with this democratic background in mind that the Fabian Colonial Bureau started work at the end of 1940. Its experiences have by no means been special to itself, but they do sum up in a compact and vivid form the way in which a point of view can be effectively expressed, and even in some degree be translated into action. They afford an excellent example of how a political society can function within a democracy.

British public opinion on colonial affairs has been notoriously sluggish. This is deplorable because the authority for governing the Empire lies with the Colonial Office, which is directly responsible to the British Parliament, in turn directly responsible to the British electorate. With an indifferent electorate most M.P.s have not felt stimulated to enquire into the intricacies of colonial administration. There have always been a few stalwarts in Parliament, and a number of specialist organizations who have watched the interests of dependent peoples. But with some exceptions there was little coherence or organized drive in this work. There were all too few bodies who really understood and followed events in the different Colonies, who bothered to create personal contacts with the Colonies, and were able to talk with regular authority; and the people in the Colonies who were suffering from a sense of grievance rarely knew to whom to turn to champion their claims.

The Fabian Tradition

When the Fabian Society decided to establish a special department to deal with colonial affairs, its first action was to invite those colonial experts who were sympathetic with the Labour viewpoint to join a committee to advise on the work, and act as a link between the Bureau and outside opinion. Mr. Creech Jones, who for some years had been one of the very few Members of Parliament to take a detailed and lively interest in colonial affairs, agreed to act as Chairman, and provide the liaison between the Bureau and Parliament. From the start the Bureau determined to work within the Fabian tradition, which has always commenced with research. There are too many organizations in all spheres of public life, clamouring for action, denouncing, appealing to public conscience, and too few who base their appeals and denunciations on solid knowledge and a painstaking collection of the facts. The Fabian Society is admirably, almost uniquely, placed for a combination of research and political action. It has not the resources of a university which might tempt it to pursue research for research's sake. Circumstances compel it, therefore, to concentrate chiefly on applied research, or—it might be called—*ad hoc* research. At the same time, as an affiliated society, with a long record of loyalty to the Labour Party, it has unique opportunities for meeting and working freely and amicably with Labour Members of Parliament and the Labour movement in general. It is clear, therefore, that the Fabian Society can act as a direct channel for transmitting the results of its members' research work to the key people of the Labour movement.

Collecting Information

The Colonial Bureau started with the absolute minimum of staff. Far-reaching research was out of the question to begin with, but it was possible to go right ahead with the collection of regular information regarding current events in the Colonies, and the creation of direct contacts with progressive organizations inside the Colonies themselves. This alone was a heavy task—there are, after all, more than fifty British Colonies in the Empire. Colonial newspapers were ordered, read regularly, and, with the aid of volunteers, cut and filed. It very soon became clear what were the main problems agitating the people of the different Colonies at that particular moment. With the help of the Chairman and other interested Members of Parliament these problems could be raised in the House or brought to the direct attention of the Secretary of State in correspondence. It took longer to establish personal contacts with colonial peoples and to gain their confidence. There is a long heritage of suspicion to be worn down, and it would be rash to claim that, even after three years' unremitting work, success in this direction is anything like complete. But, gradually, as it was shown that the Bureau, and the increasing number of Members of Parliament who collaborated in its work, were able to ventilate the grievances of colonial peoples, and sometimes to secure redress, confidence grew and correspondence from all parts of the Empire began to trickle in.

Research and Political Action

But the Bureau could not be content to act merely as a channel for information on individual grievances. Most of these grievances were merely symptoms of deep-lying injustices and imperfections. Certain subjects demanded more careful study, and groups composed of some of the members of the Advisory Committee and some outside specialists, were set up to undertake detailed inquiries into special aspects of colonial administration. The first subject which forced itself on the attention of the Bureau was the inadequacy of trade union and other labour protection laws in the Colonies. A Committee was appointed on which a number of experienced trade unionists were invited to serve, and a careful study was made of every colonial trade union law. The weaknesses in industrial legislation in the Colonies soon came to light and the Committee did not need many meetings before it agreed that an approach to the Colonial Office must be made for an improvement in the legislation. A series of papers on industrial legislation were prepared, criticizing the existing laws and putting forward proposals for their amendment; suggesting, too, that British trade unionists might be sent out to the Colonies to help put colonial trade unionism on its feet. These papers were presented to the Colonial Office, which then met a delegation from the Bureau and spent many hours in detailed discussion of the Bureau's proposals. It is not too extravagant to claim that the enormous improvement in industrial legislation which has taken place throughout the colonial empire in the last few years owes something to this work done by the Bureau and to the perpetual questions raised on the subject in Parliament.[1]

The successful work of the Labour Committee has been followed by other similar investigations. Just a few examples. The question of mineral concessions in the Colonies and the distribution of the profits of mines is fundamental in any planning for colonial prosperity. One member of the Bureau's Advisory Committee volunteered to collect the relevant information.

[1] See *Labour Supervision in the Colonial Empire*, 1943. Col. 185. This Government White Paper makes special reference to the suggestions put forward by the Bureau.

This was discussed at length by the Committee which then put forward detailed criticisms and proposals, now under active consideration inside the Colonial Office. The future of Kenya is another vexed problem. It was reported that the settlers there were pressing for renewed settlement schemes, with public assistance, after the war. Again, a member of the Bureau volunteered to collect all the relevant information, and to prepare a full record of the history and achievements of white settlement in Kenya. On the basis of this information a line of policy was discussed and hammered out by the Bureau Committee. The problem of Kenya was then debated, both in the House of Commons on the Adjournment and in a full debate in the House of Lords. The Bureau followed this up by the publication of a pamphlet on the subject. Another example—constant complaints were being heard about the composition and working of the Colonial Services. It was a difficult subject on which to express an opinion without a thorough knowledge of the facts. A Committee of the Bureau undertook to consider the structure of the Colonial Office and the Colonial Services, and made a detailed study of how the Colonial Services are recruited and trained, where their weaknesses lie, and how far they offer opportunities for the colonial peoples themselves. Out of this study there arose a host of recommendations for the improvement of the services. The results of the investigation, which involved hard and lengthy committee work, were published in a booklet, *Downing Street and the Colonies*, and brought to the attention of the Colonial Office.

A final—but certainly not the least important—example, is the work of the Co-operative Committee of the Bureau. It has often been claimed that co-operation has a vital part to play in solving the problems of colonial poverty, and the Bureau was asked to undertake an investigation into the subject. A number of persons with specialist knowledge of this work (notably Mr. C. F. Strickland) were approached for advice, and they willingly prepared papers setting forth their own views and experience. A Committee, representative of the British and

International Co-operative Movement, was then called together to consider these papers. A young British co-operator volunteered to draft them into a report. Enormous interest has gathered round this work. The Colonial Secretary was informed of its preparation by the Chairman of the Bureau in the course of a colonial debate. At the time of writing, the report, which embodies the views and labour of quite a host of experienced co-operators, and puts forward a number of detailed and practical proposals for encouraging co-operation in the Colonies, is just complete and ready for presentation to the Colonial Office. The report has also suggested how the British Co-operative Movement can help in developing the young colonial movement and this part of its proposals has already received the willing endorsement of important sections of the British movement.[1]

Appeals from the Colonies

Simultaneously with the development of this more fundamental research, and the constructive thinking to which it has given rise, the Bureau has had to cope with the day-to-day problems which have been coming to its notice in increasing volume and urgency. A cable would suddenly arrive—for example, from Jamaica—saying "Five trade unionists detained. Two trade unions banned. Please help." Or, say, from the Gambia, "Mass protest meeting against new Press regulations. Please make representations Colonial Office." Or, friends in Mauritius would wire, "May Day demonstrations prohibited." Then would come letters pointing to the evils of forced labour in Kenya or Nigeria; telling of the infringement of civil liberties in Jamaica; asking for modifications to the new constitutional proposals in various of the West Indies; telling of rising costs of living without corresponding rises in wages; pointing to the failure to introduce rationing and the shortage of essential supplies; painting a picture of unrest among workers or of colour-bar incidents.

[1] *Co-operation in the Colonies* (George Allen & Unwin Ltd.).

Here are a few extracts chosen at random. From a correspondent in the heart of Africa:

> "Sir,—I have not time to mention so many matters, but I ask assistance if you it possible. We have been sandbagged, held down, held up, etc., as evidence herewith copy attached. I have been walked upon, sat upon, but also I have no helper. Hard laws are always created to hinder our chance and movements. I have seen againsted doz times the peoples who are fighting for the truth, freedom and peace for their country and for the rights of all peoples. The Associations here in the Colonies are disliked.
>
> Full assistance required."

Numerous documents are attached to bear out these cryptic allegations.

From Uganda come requests to help the Africans to a fairer share of the cotton trade. They write:

> "Here is one of our problems. Cotton is grown by natives only. Cotton ginning and lint is only in hands of Europeans and Asiatics, capitalists, we are left helpless. The local Government helps non-native capitalists to get the profit of our labour. We grow cotton ourselves, but the local government encourages syndicates and pools of non-Africans to take the profit instead of encouraging us. We grow cotton, while non-natives get profit. The money left in hands are for taxes only. The growers have made so many times their complaints to the Government, have nothing done on it."

From the West Indies come other complaints. In British Guiana two Italian doctors, well-beloved by the poorer part of the population, were interned because of their nationality. To help securing their release letters were sent to the Bureau.

> "I am enclosing copies of a Petition and two resolutions which explain themselves. These documents, together with

7,018 signatures of the petitioners, were presented to His Excellency the Governor, with an application that this matter should be forwarded to His Majesty's Secretary of State. In the name of humanity I appeal to you to do all you can for these doctors immediately—if you get their release for Christmas, a time of peace and goodwill, it will be a magnificent gesture by the Labour Party."

From a West African Colony comes this letter:

"The Secretary of the African Civil Service Association has asked me to recommend to him any organization in England which would help this association to secure the rights and privileges for which the Association has petitioned the Secretary of State for the Colonies. I could think of no other Society than the Fabian Colonial Bureau. You will receive pamphlets containing the complaints of the Association, and I am sure the Bureau will do all it can to secure readers thereto."

From Mauritius come complaints about:

"... the chaotic state of the Colony's food supply, the callous attitude of the responsible authorities towards the working classes.... In view of the dictatorial attitude of the local government, its utter failure to even give a semblance of Democracy to its administration, we have to grin and wait for the end of the war, when it will be possible for us to demand a Revision of our obsolete Constitution, which is the cause of all our ills. Just think about a population of 420,000 inhabitants where only 10,000 have a right to vote."

Sometimes individuals, perhaps from remote localities, write in a different strain.

"I have read through some of your research pamphlets and I was greatly impressed by the facts and opinions expressed in them. I have the ideals of a Socialist and I want to be one. So I think it fit to be in a society where I shall have access to books, pamphlets, etc., of the great Socialists. I hope this will pave the way towards my ambition."

All these letters and cables—and now after three years the trickle has become a stream—demand action. Very often effective action can be taken and results obtained. The Colonial Office —indeed, any Government Department—cannot refuse to respond to informed representations. When the Jamaican trade unionists were detained and their unions banned, there were no less than five parliamentary questions on the Order Paper almost immediately. Barely a couple of weeks had passed before these oppressive orders had been rescinded. There is little doubt that forced labour has been kept within its narrow limits and is now likely to dwindle to nothing, because of the many protests which were made against it in Britain. (The Chairman of the Bureau moved the Adjournment of the House on the subject.) The Italian doctors in British Guiana are now back at work. There are a dozen and one cases which may be cited where representations to the authorities have been satisfactorily met and the grievances of individuals allayed.

Building Up Support

But in all this work the Bureau has been conscious that for real strength it must broaden its base. It was not good enough to have a handful of enthusiasts working in London without the backing and interest of a wider public. It decided to offer membership facilities to anyone interested. In return for a small annual subscription members would receive all the publications of the Bureau, reports on its activities, and opportunities to attend Conferences and meetings. It was not easy to build up the first nucleus of supporters, but it can now be said, after three years' work, that there has grown up a steady membership of close on a thousand, and nearly double that number of subscribers to the Bureau's journal—*Empire*. The journal became possible through the generosity of one of the members of the Advisory Committee. It is still a small affair and appears only once in two months. But it has already been invaluable as a contact between the Bureau, its membership, and the outside world, and month by month its circulation grows. Attempts have also been made to reach directly to the public by a series of conferences. Two week-end conferences have been held in Oxford, two or three day-Conferences in London, and in 1943 two provincial Conferences were held in Leeds and Sheffield with the aid of the local Fabian Societies. The provincial conferences were attended by delegates from the local Labour Parties, trade unions, co-operative guilds, Common Wealth Groups, W.E.A.s, etc., and have proved of the first importance in creating interest in colonial affairs and spreading the knowledge of the Bureau's work.

Not only inside Britain, but in the Colonies themselves, the Bureau's base is being widened, and a two-way traffic of communication is being created. From the Colonies, friends and organizations send their cables and letters and also their newspapers and reports. From the office in London the publications of the Bureau are sent out. Not only are there very many individual subscribers now in the Colonies (both among Europeans of all classes and among Africans) but there are groups, organizations, bookshops, which order the Bureau's publications by the dozen (in some territories by the hundred) and resell them locally. In Nigeria a branch of the Fabian Society has been started and the Fabian Bookshop in London groans at times under the weight of its orders for literature. The orders are not all for the publications of the Colonial Bureau, but for the general literature of the Society as well and indeed, for books of all kinds. Recently, large orders for publications have arrived from so far afield as Uganda. There is barely a Colony which publications of the Bureau do not reach, and with which there has not been built up a regular interchange.

Conclusion

It is not easy for one who has lived intensively in this work for three years to stand dispassionately aside and see it in perspective. A fairer picture might have been given if someone other than the deeply-immersed Secretary of the Bureau had been asked to write this article. It seems to me, though, to be no exaggeration to say that the Bureau has more than fulfilled the original purpose with which it set out—"to act as a clearing house for information, and to interest the public, the Press and Parliament in colonial affairs." From all over Britain there now come demands to the Bureau for speakers, for bibliographies, for information, for literature. From all over the Empire each week brings in a heavy post. The publications of the Bureau have all met with an eager demand—most of them have already had to be reprinted. More and more do visitors from the Colonies (both European and Colonial) make a point of calling in on the Bureau on their arrival in London to exchange news and views. In both Houses of Parliament, and in the more serious organs of the British Press, there is always an opportunity for the knowledge and research collected by the Bureau to find a public platform. Finally, a direct and friendly relationship has been created with the Colonial Office itself, which has shown itself prepared to give the most full and courteous consideration to every one of the Bureau's representations—though "consideration" may not, of course, mean action.

All this considerable success is due to a very few factors. The Bureau has worked within the democratic constitutional framework of this country, utilizing every avenue and opportunity which democracy offers. It has been able to command respect because of the stress it laid on the accuracy of its statements, its willingness to engage in painstaking research and its persevering collection of information. It has had a valuable point of view to put over and has not flagged in so doing. And finally, it has had the good fortune to find altruistic and loyal collaborators who were prepared to champion the work inside Parliament and out, to give unstintingly of their special knowledge and time, and to expect no return other than the spread of colonial liberty in its widest sense. Of course this is not the method for effecting revolutions. But it *is* a method—the method of "eternal vigilance"—whereby the rights and freedoms of colonial peoples may be safeguarded, and opportunities assured them for shaping their own future in the way that they themselves desire.

(Reprinted from the *Fabian Quarterly*, April 1944.)

For Product Safety Concerns and Information please contact our EU representative GPSR@taylorandfrancis.com
Taylor & Francis Verlag GmbH, Kaufingerstraße 24, 80331 München, Germany

www.ingramcontent.com/pod-product-compliance
Lightning Source LLC
Chambersburg PA
CBHW061439300426
44114CB00014B/1748